Education of Minorities and Peace Education in Pluralistic Societies

Education of Minorities and Peace Education in Pluralistic Societies

EDITED BY
YAACOV IRAM

ASSISTANT EDITOR
HILLEL WAHRMAN

PRAEGER

Westport, Connecticut
London

Library of Congress Cataloging-in-Publication Data

Education of minorities and peace education in pluralistic societies / edited by Yaacov Iram : assistant editor, Hillel Wahrman.
    p. cm.
   Includes bibliographical references and index.
   ISBN 0–275–97821–4 (alk. paper)
    1. Minorities—Education—Cross-cultural studies. 2. Peace—Study and teaching—Cross-cultural studies. 3. Pluralism (Social sciences)—Cross-cultural studies. 4. Multicultural education—Cross-cultural studies. I. Iram, Yaacov. II. Wahrman, Hillel.
   LC3719.E375   2003
   303.6'6—dc21   2002029871

British Library Cataloguing in Publication Data is available.

Library of Congress Catalog Card Number: 2002029871
ISBN: 0–275–97821–4

First published in 2003

Praeger Publishers, 88 Post Road West, Westport, CT 06881
An imprint of Greenwood Publishing Group, Inc.
www.praeger.com

Printed in the United States of America

The paper used in this book complies with the Permanent Paper Standard issued by the National Information Standards Organization (Z39.48–1984).

10 9 8 7 6 5 4 3 2 1

This volume is an initiative of the UNESCO/
Burg Chair in Education for Human Values Tolerance
and Peace, Bar-Ilan University, Israel.

Contents

Introduction

YAACOV IRAM

This book provides an international perspective on two major and inter-related issues—minorities and peace—and the relationship between them and education. It is assumed that minorities' rights extend beyond the basic rights of life and liberty to include cultural, economic, social, political, and educational equality. Education is not only a human right but might be viewed as encompassing, sanctioning, and guaranteeing all other rights. Education should be charged with the responsibility of informing people of their other responsibilities and their rights. It should impart awareness of rights and oppose their denial whether by oppressive laws or inappropriate traditions. Thus, indeed, the various chapters in this book present a dual perspective of education about minorities and the rights of minorities with regard to education. These two perspectives propose that without respecting the dignity and rights of minorities, whether indigenous peoples or immigrants, no meaningful peaceful coexistence within societies and between societies or nation–states is possible. Intolerance, xenophobia, violence, and terrorism increase in times of economic recession, denial of rights, and exclusion of minority groups by denying equality of educational and economic opportunities, legal rights, and cultural recognition. This in turn causes the rise of political groups that are driven by a combination of racism and xenophobia and that are prevalent in many European and other countries. The United Nations and UNESCO (United Nations Educational, Scientific, and Cultural Organization) proclaimed the year 2001 as the United Nations Year of Dialogue among Civilizations (Resolution 53/22 of November 4, 1998, of the General Assembly of the United Nations). The Report of the director general of UNESCO stated:

The faster pace and huge volume of global interaction has prompted a greater awareness of cultural diversity. While it has given wider scope to the expression of such diversity, it has also permitted the representation of differences such as hierarchy, domination and conflict. Difference is often used as an excuse for intolerance, hatred and the annihilation of others. Yet the very same differences, in the framework of political equality, human rights and responsibility for others, can—and often do—offer the opportunity to explore new horizons and to enrich our lives. (UNESCO, 2001)

The present volume consists of two parts. Part I outlines the theoretical and conceptual contours of minority education and peace education. Part II presents country case studies in which the authors outline and analyze to what extent countries around the world address or neglect to address these issues. The chapters provide various research and analytical approaches (from political science, sociology, anthropology, economy, and education) to highlight multidisciplinary and multidimensional understanding of the issues at hand.

The book is addressed to educators, policymakers, and advanced students in education, sociology, political science, public policy, and conflict resolution.

A tentative conclusion that might be drawn from this volume in general, and from each country case study in particular, is that education of minorities and peace education are neither neutral nor separate from historical precedents and political circumstances. Another lesson that can be drawn is that no education system alone can create a just and equal society and that education by itself is not enough to achieve peace. Nevertheless, educational efforts assisted by other institutional commitments and actions are essential in order to create an atmosphere of justice, mutual recognition, and acceptance as preconditions for peaceful coexistence within groups and between groups.

As borders become more open and boundaries between groups and states more flexible, a multitude of immigrants will continue to flow between countries, thus increasing the presence of minorities. The alternative that all countries face is either to receive this phenomenon as a blessing or turn to exclusion and xenophobia. Lester Pearson (1955) warned almost 50 years ago that humanity is moving into

an age when different civilizations will have to learn to live side by side in peaceful interchange, learning from each other, studying each other's history and ideals, art and culture, mutually enriching each other's lives. The alternative in this overcrowded little world is misunderstanding, tension, clash and catastrophe. (83–84)

Pearson's warning is valid for most of the countries that on the threshold of the twenty-first century are diverse in almost every aspect we can think of.

Part I of the book focuses on the theoretical and conceptual framework of minority education (Chapters 1–3) and peace education (Chapters 4–5). In Chapter 1, Yaacov Iram outlines the international perspective for evaluating education of minorities. As a result of worldwide migration, wars, and other geopolitical conflicts and treaties, many modern nation–states consist of a mix of people of various ethnic, cultural, linguistic, and religious backgrounds. Indeed, there are very few countries that are monolithic or monocultural in origin. The pursuit of nations and ethnic groups for cultural or national identity and uniformity is often in difficult balance with the need for intergroup coexistence, as far as internal relations and external affairs are concerned. The existence of minorities will grow in most countries of the world because of both sociopolitical upheaval and economic crisis, which are expected to result in growing waves of migration. It is therefore the task of educators to alleviate the problem of minorities through multicultural education. The role of multicultural education is to promote awareness, then tolerance, and finally acceptance of ethnic, cultural, religious, and linguistic diversity within a given society. The promise of such an education is the enrichment of pluralism within societies. The prospects for fulfilling such a promise are real, but they depend to a large extent on education to strengthen mutual understanding, tolerance, acceptance, and cooperation between individuals, groups, and societies. This is the only alternative to further the advancement of societies and individuals toward contentment and self-fulfillment.

In Chapter 2, drawing on the work of Nancy Fraser (1995, 1997), a professor of political and social science at the New School in New York, Gita Steiner-Khamsi highlights the distinction between social redistribution and cultural recognition of minorities and presents in more depth a related interpretive framework that generated heated debates among scholars of multicultural education in the 1990s: universalism versus particularism in minority education. The chapter explores the debates that triggered a discursive shift from multiculturalism to antiracism and reflects on its impact on issues of identity formation. The author suggests to decenter or deemphasize ethnicity, nationality, or religion and instead proposes to explore conflict resolution approaches that are more contextual and relational and less essentializing, ethnicizing, and polarizing.

In Chapter 3, Martin Carnoy discusses the complex problem that faces multicultural societies such as the United States and Israel: how to integrate groups from highly varied cultures into a civil society with well-defined behavioral norms, a common language, and a clear conception of political rights and obligations without coercing these groups to give up their own sense of cultural identity. This chapter argues that the nature of the problem is changing. Major transformations in the world economy and the power situation of the nation–state, changes in the types of community networks individuals develop in the context of these changes, and changes in women's relationship to the family are altering the political construction of multiculturalism. He concludes that these changes might lead to a shift away from the growing trend toward a tolerant multiculturalism characteristic of the late-modern liberal democratic welfare state to be replaced at one level by a global-individual identity rooted in market values and at another level by ethnocentric or religious groups with global ties but locally situated and antithetical to liberal values.

In Chapter 4, Chadwick Alger asserts that the bedrock of peace education is attainment of belief in the possibility of attaining peace everywhere, a belief that is facilitated by the capacity to perceive widespread peace in the world today and awareness that we have learned a great deal about building peace in this century, through both practical experience and research in a number of relevant disciplines. The challenge for peace educators is to enable students to acquire knowledge about the growing array of peace tools that apply political, economic, social, and cultural factors in long-term peace building. Diplomacy, balance of power, arms control, economic development, ecological balance, humanitarian intervention, and peace education are just an example of the 24 peace tools identified by Alger. A class exercise is described that challenges students to select the most appropriate peace tools in developing a long-term strategy to cope with an exceedingly disruptive conflict. Students begin applying their peace strategy 30 years in the past, toward the end of attaining a vision of a situation that is more peaceful today than actually exists. This exercise gives students a deeper knowledge of peace tools and insight into the difficulties encountered in applying them.

In Chapter 5, Lennart Vriens elaborates the idea that peace education has to be developed as a modest concept on the basis of a broad concept of learning. The modest concept means that peace education cannot make peace, nor is it able to guarantee that people become peace loving. But it can offer an important contribution to the development of a "culture of peace," which justifies and supports policies aimed at attaining peace. Peace can be understood from several points of view: It can be interpreted in terms of values, norms, knowledge, and skills, which are to be specified in different cultural and current contexts. Fundamental peace values like trust, respect for life, solidarity, and nonviolence are affective and have their roots in the very early days of every human's life. These roots are a necessary basis for human learning, which is not only a cognitive but, first of all, an affective activity. This idea of a broad learning process as a necessary condition for peace education is illustrated by a short description of three peace education projects.

In Part II of the book various case studies are presented. In Chapter

6, Martin Carnoy points out that investment in education has been very large in the United States over the past 50 years, and particularly since the 1960s, the U.S. federal government has developed a number of education programs designed to help minorities and the poor "catch up" academically to higher social class children. At the same time, the government has implemented affirmative action programs in labor markets to break down discrimination. He examines in this chapter the impact of such programs on the education and income of three important minority groups in the United States: blacks, Latinos, and Asian Americans. The groups differ radically from each other in terms of these impacts, and the chapter analyzes why that might be the case.

In Chapter 7, Leslie Limage argues that the influence of social science policy–oriented research on definition, and hence some form of measurement of equality and equity, has shifted with the expansion of education over the past 50 years. A clearly different set of assumptions about the role of schooling underlies a certain idea of equality of condition. Another set of criteria is generated by assumptions concerning equality of opportunity. Public policy for education as a human right can be located in both. Public policy directed at poverty alleviation—or as more widely discussed in Europe in recent years, the elimination of social exclusion—can also be analyzed with both notions of equality. Models for ensuring some measure of equality and equity through schooling are shifting as political conflict and economic hardship are more structural than ever. In this discussion, primarily Anglo-Saxon models and ideologies about equality in or through education are set alongside the French republican model based on another approach. The situation for minorities in France is the main focus of this chapter.

In Chapter 8, Leslie Francis traces the complex relationship between minority religious interests and the public funding of schools in England and Wales from the creation of the Royal Lancasterian Society in 1808 to the 1944 Education Act. He traces the implications of the 1944 Education Act, which recognized the place of Anglican, Roman Catholic, and Jewish schools within the state-funded sector, and of subsequent legislation. He analyzes three crucial challenges that have undermined the stability of the religious provision of the 1944 Education Act. These changes are discussed in terms of a specific strand of educational philosophy that challenged the conceptual link between education and religion, the problems of social integration within a multicultural and religiously plural society, and the promotion of equal educational opportunities. He examines the way in which the main stakeholders within the church school system have presented their educational policy. Finally, Francis identifies three crucial ways in which religious groups have responded to the changing interface between education and religion in England and Wales during the past two decades.

The establishment of the Palestinian National Authority in 1993 gave the Palestinian people the opportunity for the first time in history to control their own educational system. In Chapter 9, Aziz Haidar examines how the Palestinian curriculum deals with the very existence of minorities in the Palestinian society and how minorities are presented, on the normative level, in the philosophy and policy of education and in textbooks. His study reveals that on the normative level the education system is pluralistically oriented: Pluralism includes the right of minorities to establish and maintain their own institutions and to develop their culture, language, religious traditions, and customs. On the level of policy, he found that the system is not a secular one: The emphasis on Islamic content is salient, and the curriculum plan ignores the fact that Palestinian society is composed of different religious and cultural groups. This trend is very clear in the National Education textbooks for public schools. In all units devoted to the study of society, values and morals, traditions, or institutions, the examples and prototypes are taken from Islamic history and instruction. Nevertheless, Christian communities maintain their own educational institutions. This marks a voluntary separation that the state (Palestinian Authority) allows within its education system, and thus two textbooks of Christian religion (for grades 1 and 6) were also recently written for this sector.

One of the major conflicts in Israeli society focuses on the Jewish-Arab axis. Israeli Jews and Arabs are wary of each other, and latent hostility permeates the atmosphere between the two societal groups and is directly related to the Israeli-Arab conflict. As time passes, the gap between the two population groups grows wider, and the two sectors have become increasingly more polarized. The two following chapters focus on education relating to the Arab Bedouin population in Israel. In Chapter 10, Yaacov Katz and Yaacov Yablon discuss the promotion of intergroup attitudes in Israel through Internet technology. An Information and Communication Technology (ICT) project was especially designed to lower the level of conflict between Jewish and Bedouin Arab high school students. In the project the societal values of understanding, equality, tolerance, and peace were intensely promoted through the medium of three different complementary educational strategies. Students participated in workshops conducted by experts trained in the art of mediation and bridge building, interacted intensively through e-mail and an Internet-based chatroom, and participated in two face-to-face daylong meetings. All three strategies were specially designed to complementarily promote understanding, equality, tolerance, and peace between Jewish and Bedouin Arab students. The results of the project indicate that intensive Internet communication based on chatroom and e-mail, bolstered by face-to-face contact and participation in workshops, significantly promotes intergroup understanding and cooperation. The technology used in the project provided the Jewish and Bedouin Arab participants with additional incentive and motivation to interact, thereby laying a solid foundation for positive intergroup attitudinal change.

In Chapter 11, Rivka Glaubman and Yaacov Katz discuss the Bedouin community in the Israeli Negev. The authors claim that the Bedouin population dispersed throughout the southern Negev region of Israel suffers from chronic social, economic, and most especially, educational disadvantage and neglect. Bedouin schools, run by the Israel Ministry of Education through the Negev Bedouin Authority, have inferior physical facilities, less-qualified teaching and auxiliary personnel, a significantly lower matriculation rate, a severely higher dropout rate, and much less parental involvement in the education of their children than comparable Jewish and Arab schools in Israel. The present study, which investigated the specific issues and the detailed aspects of the Negev Bedouin education system, pinpointed the areas where significant intervention by the Ministry of Education is necessary in order to significantly improve the system and, based on the research findings, compiled a list of vital recommendations to be implemented in order to combat the existing disadvantages and neglect.

In Chapter 12, Majid Al-Haj analyzes the Jewish-Arab relations and the education system in Israel from the perspective of "controlled multiculturalism." This chapter deals with possibilities and challenges for the development of multicultural education in Israel. More specifically, it analyzes majority-minority relations in the wider society and their reflection in the education system. The analysis shows that the education system in Israel has evolved vis-à-vis a number of contradictions that derive from the state's ethnonational structure and weak civil culture. As a result, there is a great disparity between the social structure, which is broadly multicultural, and the education system, which has been designed to be a mechanism of control rather than a catalyst for multiculturalism. This system is a means to instill an asymmetric structure of dual values, one for the majority and the other for the minority. This situation might well be designated controlled multiculturalism.

In Chapter 13, Hillel Wahrman identifies the silencing of conflicts as a peace education strategy in Israeli civics textbooks. Promoting attitudes of peace and tolerance among young adults can generate two opposing educational strategies: The first excludes controversial issues from the curriculum, minimizing exposure to society's divisions and fractions. The second exposes public debate, encouraging a balanced view and deliberative attitudes. Research literature reflects the tendency in Western civics textbooks to avoid issues invoking bitter public dispute by employing the first, more passive educational strategy. This chapter illustrates how Israeli civic textbooks tend to do the same, choosing a low-profile presentation of the Israeli "Jewish-democratic" debate. Four categories are suggested as an analytical framework for demonstrating the presentation of the concept of "Jewish state" in Israeli civics textbooks: centrality, meaning, relevancy, and value judgment. Israeli civic textbooks appear to downgrade the debate in all four. Wahrman argues that this choice of strategy is disputable. Issues don't disappear, and coexistence depends on continued dialogue between conflicting groups. For this, it is necessary to study the full spectrum of political concepts and ideas existing in society. Thus, the advantage of the second educational strategy for peace education is examined.

In Chapter 14, Walter Ackerman deals with the various ways in which Jewish education has reflected the minority status of Jews. This chapter treats structured forms of Jewish education, examines a broad curricular statement, cites examples of the price of acculturation, and addresses patterns of justification for voluntary Jewish schooling or other forms of education.

The United Nations declared the year 2000 as "The Year for the Culture of Peace" and the years 2001–2010 as the "International Decade for a Culture of Peace and Non-Violence for the Children of the World." A "culture of peace" implies more than a passive and quiescent state due to an absence of war and violence. To attain a culture of peace, one must actively strive toward positive values that enable different cultures and nations to coexist harmoniously. These values are based on helping the underprivileged, sharing knowledge, and fostering tolerance between peoples. Tolerance, which leads to the establishment of a pluralistic society, requires an understanding of both the shared and unique aspects of different peoples and cultures.

We live in an age saturated with advances in information technology and telecommunications. In this turbulent era of change, people rediscover the need for regional identity as well as the need for values. Stable values provide security in a continually changing world. The dignity of the individual represents a basic value, which serves as a stepping-stone to other values: freedom of speech, freedom from suffering, and tolerance, which is a prerequisite to attaining an enduring peace. Education plays a paramount role in imparting the values of tolerance, multiculturalism, and peace to the next generation. Through tolerance, one can strive to transcend religious and political boundaries and bridge cultural and ethnic differences. Tolerance and pluralism require both knowledge of what people share in common and understanding of their differences. Without this awareness, there can be no multicultural education. It is hoped that the authors of this volume have succeeded in imparting both awareness and understanding of the importance of these values.

Preliminary versions of most of the chapters were presented at two international conferences: *Education as a Bridge to Peace* and *Education of Ethnic Minorities in Pluralistic Societies*, sponsored by the Josef Burg Chair in Education for Human Values, Tolerance and Peace—UNESCO Chair. The editor wishes to express gratitude to the authors for revising, extending, and updating their original lectures for this volume.

Special thanks are also due to the secretary of the Chair, Tzila Pollak.

The editor acknowledges the invaluable contribution made by Hillel Wahrman. His skills and advice helped to transform the authors' submissions into this complete volume.

REFERENCES

Fraser, N. (1995). From Redistribution to Recognition? Dilemmas of Justice in a "Post-Socialist" Age. *New Left Review* 212: 68–93.

Fraser, N. (1997). *Justice Interrupts: Critical Reflections on the "Postsocialist" Condition*. New York: Routledge.

Pearson, L. (1955). *Democracy in World Politics*. Princeton, NJ: Princeton University Press.

UNESCO. (2001). *Framework for Action*. Document 161 EX/INF 14, May 21.

PART I

Theory and Concepts

CHAPTER 1

Education of Minorities:
Problems, Promises, and Prospects—
An International Perspective

YAACOV IRAM

When David Livingstone's work in Africa became known, a missionary society wrote to him and asked, "Have you found a good road to where you are?" The letter indicated that if he had found a "good road," the missionary society was prepared to send some men to help with his work. Livingstone's answer was clear and to the point: "If you have men who will come only over a good road, I don't need your help. I want men who will come if there is no road." The purpose of this chapter is to delineate the problems, to point out the promises and importance, and to assess the prospects of education of ethnic minorities in pluralistic democracies. In many respects we are expected to do groundbreaking work since there are no "good roads" that were already paved and that could lead us to reach our goal of educating minorities. In other cases, where roads exist, we should improve them and make them more accessible.

PROBLEMS IN EDUCATION OF MINORITIES

Minority groups can be defined in various ways by region—by ethnic background, by language use, by socioeconomic status, by religion, by gender, by educational attainment, by lifestyle, and more. These diverse definitional bases are not all of equal political importance, if we defuse political importance as measured by "the extent of conflict in society regarding who exercises power over whom" (Thomas, 1986: 399). Furthermore, the political importance (and power status) of a particular minority group varies from one society to another and from one time to another within the same society.

＿e education of ethnic minorities is closely related to issues such as ＿ıtural diversity and equality of educational opportunity. As the problems of ethnicity and migration continue to provoke conflicts at home and to become global in scope, involving people of many different backgrounds, it becomes incumbent upon us, educationists, to find "good roads" and upon educators, teachers, to better prepare young people with the knowledge, perspectives, willingness, and skills that will enable them to be willing to live with and become more effective in collaborating with people different from themselves. Such an education is referred to in negative terms, such as *antibias education* and *antiracist education* (Taylor and Bagley, 1995), or by titles with positive connotations, such as *multicultural education, intercultural education*, and *international/transnational/global education*. Unfortunately, most of these ideas and programs have not been implemented in most schools or where implemented were not done so successfully. However, if we want to live in societies that encourage the participation of, and welcome the perspectives, histories, and contributions of, all its members, if we wish to create ultimately a society that rejects oppression, discrimination, xenophobia, and racism, we must double and triple our efforts at all levels and structures of education, from kindergarten to university, to promote and implement existing programs and to continue new and more effective means.

Most nations today are pluralistic and multicultural societies, and most have a majority and one or more minority groups, depending on the definition of minority. For the purposes of this chapter, minority status does not necessarily imply numerical inferiority. It refers rather to "the quality of power relations between groups": Thus, a population is defined as a minority "if it occupies some form of subordinate power position in relation to another population in the same society" (Ogbu, 1983: 169). According to this definition, many groups may rightly claim the status of minority group, employing criteria such as their percentage in the total population or their share of power, prestige, or wealth.

As none of the prevalent typologies or classifications of minority groups (Mitter, 1999; Ogbu, 1978: 21–25, 1983: 169–172) fit social diversity in its totality, it will be more useful to apply, with some modifications, a conceptual framework that deals with modes of interaction between dominant or majority groups and subordinate or minority groups in pluralistic societies (Smolicz, 1985: 245–267). Three modes of majority-minority interaction can be used to analyze intergroup relations in any given society; they are assimilation, multiculturalism, and separatism. *Assimilation* implies the adoption by the minority group of the language, traditions, mores, and values of the host society (in case of immigrants) or of the dominant group (usually the majority), up to the point of abandoning its original language and culture. *Separatism* is the rejection by one or both sides of any moves toward desegregation or integration, thus adopting a position of mutual exclusion whether it is indifferent side-by-side existence or, worse, conflictual existence and no cultural transactions whatsoever. *Multiculturalism* implies adjustment of all groups, minority and majority alike, and resorting to intentional coexistence out of a willingness to make mutual adjustment and acceptance (Bhatnager, 1981; Iram, 1987).

Low academic achievement of ethnic minority children (in many countries, it is synonymous with newly arrived immigrants) is related to issues such as (1) racism in teachers and in the school system; (2) cultural bias in the curriculum and educational materials (e.g., denigrating certain groups, stereotyping); (3) lack of racial and cultural awareness in the training of teachers; (4) hiring and promotion problems in regard to ethnic minority teachers and administrators; and (5) wider cultural, racial, and socioeconomic problems (Male, 1986: 477).

The challenge and mission of educators is to prepare future teachers and reeducate in-service teachers with the knowledge and skills that will enable them to work effectively with students from a wide range of backgrounds. This knowledge and skill must be generated through research by educationists and transferred by teachers to students, most of whom will live most of their lives in highly interdependent intercultural or multicultural societies, whether in the United States, Israel, Russia, England, France, or Germany (Tulasiewicz and Adams, 1995), or in newly reestablished countries such as Bosnia-Herzegovina (Bosnians, Serbs, Croatians) or the independent republics of the former USSR. The task is to transform attitudes from monoculturalism to multiculturalism—namely, the process through which a person develops competence in as well as appreciation of and tolerance for several cultures (Johnson, 1977). In pluralistic societies, multiculturalism is imperative in order to be able to communicate with, understand, and participate in a cultural context other than one's own within the same sociopolitical framework. Schools must be the major focus of efforts to teach multiculturalism in the spheres of language, culture, and intergroup relations (Masemann and Iram, 1987).

In some cases, multicultural education might lead to *intercultural education*, namely, "an attempt to generate a cultural synthesis [and not just a coexistence]: the production of new cultural models grafted onto the existing base of national cultures which, while remaining in place, themselves become enriched as a result of the process" (Tulasiewicz and Adams, 1995: 265).

The task of equality or equity provision in the education of ethnic minorities toward multiculturalism is not an easy task in light of what we know about the ways in which people learn about cultures other than their own, about the reluctance of governments to act decisively both in legislation and provisions, and finally, about the implementation of declared policies. Nevertheless, we are obliged to fulfill this task, given the time, place, and circumstance in which we now live. An education that takes place in the twenty-first century cannot ignore such vital, crucial, and moral issues.

PROMISES IN EDUCATION OF MINORITIES

The issue of minority education is, of course, part of the larger question of how various minority groups are to be treated and whether they are to have access to mainstream society, meaning structural (versus cultural) integration, and access to and participation in economy and polity while retaining their group identity regardless of whether that identity is based on religion, race, color, or language. The following remarks are based in part on a special issue of *Education and Urban Society* (August 1986, Vol. 4, No. 4), that was devoted to the analysis of "Policy Issues in the Education of Minorities: A Worldwide View." The countries chosen for analysis were Australia, Canada, England, West Germany, India, Israel (written by the author of this chapter), Japan, and Malaysia. These countries were selected because they represented factors such as race, color, caste, religion, nationality, immigrant status, and worldview (traditional versus modernism).

Countries differ in the extent to which their national governments, courts, civil rights groups, and teachers' unions play a role in minority education. They differ also in the means they employ to cope with issues such as busing, quotas, multicultural education, and racial balancing of pupils and teachers. It is both reassuring and discouraging that most of the countries examined in this special issue of the journal, and to some extent all countries, continue to struggle with questions relating to the education of minorities. This suggests that the slowness in solving problems of the education of minorities is due not only to ineptness but to the basic difficulties inherent in the problem of minorities as well as the kind of education organized for majority members of society. We might be discouraged because racism, unfairness, discrimination, and lack of equal educational opportunity for minorities continue to exist in many countries; and in some countries, such as the former Yugoslavia, educational inequities have increased (Daun et al., 2001). Many societies, it seems, are increasingly subject to multinational migration whether the migration of ethnic workers or refugees. This modern migration across geopolitical borders and cultural boundaries in pursuit of economic needs and political interests is motivated by expectations of individuals and groups that their cultural identity as well as their political and economic equality will be guaranteed. It does not accept the superiority of dominant cultures nor the insult nor the rejection that accompanies dominance. Cultural equality, let alone socioeconomic equity, must be legislated in order to ensure multiculturalism. However, de facto, let alone de jure, multiculturalism alone does not assure the promotion of unity and harmony. It can be integrative or divisive, depending on how it is conceptualized and legislated.

Multiculturalism is premised on respect for individuals and cultural diversity. This respect does not require that each culture become equally acceptable to each and every individual but that we respect each culture equally, that we value the rich mosaic of individual and cultural difference, the rainbow nature of a society within our national boundaries and beyond them. It requires that we recognize the right to unique identity for both individuals and groups and that we guarantee the freedom of cultural development, economic equality, political participation, and educational opportunities.

The experience of human migration and resettlement shows that respect for cultural differences is not achieved by the willingness to tolerate the customs, beliefs, languages, and social structures of other cultures at a distance or from a position of dominance. Distance and dominance restrict the obligation to understand and appreciate others and to treat them equally.

To really understand cultures other than our own requires thoughtful, systematic inquiry into the similarities and differences of meaning, organization, and practice of our own and of other ethnocultural groups. And as a result, it requires acceptance and assurance of cultural and political rights, both of individuals and of groups.

A liberal society can be distinguished by the way it treats its multiple cultures (minorities), assuring individual rights to dignity, ethnicity, free speech, and due process—without discrimination based on race, national origin, color, ethnicity, language, religion, or gender. These are the characteristics of *authentic identity* that protect both individuals and cultural groups from the assimilative tendencies of dominant cultures (Appiah and Gates, 1995).

Multicultural education implies multilingual teaching whenever demanded. Multilingual competency enables cross-cultural dialogue. Such a dialogue requires, always, cultural sensitivization, namely, sensitizing ourselves to the point of recognizing the substance of others' beliefs, claims, habits, practices, and needs. This is not a process of relativizing one's owns cultural beliefs, identity, and perceptions; rather, it allows for a dialogue of recognition, intercultural understanding, and equality of participation.

PROSPECTS

Based on previous comparative studies on Canada and Israel by Masemann and Iram (1987) and on France and Poland (Mitter, 1999), I would like to offer the following conclusions regarding the prospects for future policy development as it pertains to the education of minorities.

First, it seems that constitutional provisions are not necessarily a guarantee of equality or equity, particularly when there is disparity in status among ethnocultural and linguistic groups and even more so when groups occupy dominate and subordinate statuses within a national framework—for example, English-speaking versus French-speaking Canadians (Ghosh, 1995; McAndrew, 1994; McNeill, 1995); Jews and Arabs in Israel (Al-Haj, 1998; Iram and Schmida, 1998; Rouhana, 1997); Muslims in France (Groux, 2002; Limage, 2000), in Greece (Kassotakis and Roussakis, 1999), or in England (Ashraf, 1988; Halstead 1993); and Poland and its minority groups of Ukrainians, Belo Russians, Lithuanians, and Germans (Mitter, 1999; Tomiak, 1991). All these countries have constitutional or legislative provisions for education of minorities and declared policies on multiculturalism. Nevertheless, these do not ensure cultural, linguistic, economic, and sometimes even religious and political equal status (Council of Europe, 1994; OECD, 1989).

Second, it is difficult to measure or assess the success of multicultural development or, in a wider perspective, respect for human rights. That is because the outcomes of tolerance and intercultural understanding are evanescent and may actually be threatened if cultural retention rather than cultural sharing is the outcome of programs for cultural development or if political events such as warfare consistently present a negative picture of intergroup relations (Iram, 2001). This was proven during the strife of cessation of republics from the former Soviet Union and the status of minorities within the newly independent states that emerged (Glenn, 1995; Mitter, 1997). Similar conclusions can be drawn from the tragic strife over the demise of Yugoslavia (Daun et al., 2001) and from the continued conflict in the Middle East that also negatively affects the relationship between Jews and Arabs in Israel (Al-Haj, 1998; Iram, 2002).

Third, multicultural development may be difficult to foster by government decree if its foundations are not already laid in the history and social structure of a country (Torney-Purta, Schwille, and Amadeo, 1999).

Fourth, official language policy is an important part of multicultural development, and the educational framework of such policies demonstrates the degree of commitment to linguistic and cultural equality. Thus, for example, the Canadian Constitution and the Charter of Rights and Freedoms "enshrine group and individual rights to education in one or both of the official languages" (Masemann and Iram, 1987: 116). The existence of an official multiculturalism policy and a Multiculturalism Sector in the Department of the Secretary of State in Canada are tangible evidence of Canada's commitment to multiculturalism.

Fifth, the political realities of overt hostility to, or subordination of, groups may far outweigh the harmonious wishes of policymakers or educators. The case of Israel proves that in spite of declared policies and numerous programs to cope with problems of multiculturalism, none have been resolved satisfactorily thus far. Since these problems are of a political, social, and cultural nature, they cannot be solved by the education system alone without active support and involvement of other social institutions and without positive changes in the geopolitical sphere (Iram, 2002; Masemann and Iram, 1987).

Similarly, experiments of creating mixed schools for children of Catholic and Protestant backgrounds were introduced by the Education (Northern Ireland) Act of 1978 "to facilitate the establishment in Northern Ireland of schools likely to be attended by pupils of different religious affiliations or cultural traditions." But, for a variety of reasons, mainly the civic disturbances and terrorist outbreaks, the pupil population so far affected by this experiment was less than 5 percent in 2000 (Sutherland, 2001: 257). Curricular reforms since 1989 focused on the cross-curricular theme "Education for Mutual Understanding" (Northern Ireland Curriculum Council, 1989) have stressed "the need to know about and understand the interdependence of the different religious and cultural communities within Northern Ireland and the consequences of their integration and segregation" (Smith and Robinson, 1992: 16). Sutherland (2001) concludes: "Even if such efforts have so far been unsuccessful in affecting the whole of [Ireland's] society, it has to be recognized that they have at least created pockets of goodwill and mutual understanding important for the lives of individuals if not yet for all the population" (260).

Sixth, there have been significant steps made nationally and internationally in multicultural programming and ideas in the educational systems of many countries, but on the vast scale of things, these programs are only the beginning and have to be updated and expanded to confront changing circumstances or tensions that emerge too frequently.

And finally, there is a clear need in countries to assess demographic trends and to plan for a future in which the rights of minorities and multiculturalism development are safeguarded. This need becomes urgent in light of increased migration resulting from of geopolitical changes that cause frequent movements of peoples of various cultural, linguistic, and religious backgrounds across boundaries notably in Europe and in the United States (Shapiro and Alker, 1996). As a result, it is now more than ever before hard to define nation–states in ways that presuppose cultural, linguistic, or religious homogeneity (Winther-Jensen, 1996). The educational complex implications of migration and the formation of minorities have been manifested in international studies (Glenn and de Jong, 1996; Gurr, 1993; Torney-Purta, Schwille, and Amadeo, 1999).

The years ahead will demonstrate how well various policies such as providing economic justice, strengthening cultural unity, and maintaining peace among the ethnic groups will prevail. Providing equal (and not favored) educational and economic opportunities to all will indeed promote economic and educational parity among ethnic groups and provide the cultural diversity and peaceful social coexistence so much desired.

I would like to conclude with a few words of caution, or rather realism, quoting American author and critic Henry Louis Mencken (1880–1956). His words might add some perspective to the current situation and future challenges we presently face: "For every complicated problem there is an answer that is short, simple, and *wrong*." There are indeed no short and simple answers to the problem of education of minorities. We must take—and in many instances, even construct—the long and hard road of working to transform the manner in which we conceive the education of minorities in heterogeneous societies and the education of immigrants in particular.

Andre Gide said:

> Everything has been said before,
> But, since nobody listens,
> We have to keep going back and begin again.

Indeed there is a wealth of information on recent migration trends and a vast accumulation of know-how on the proper ways to educate immigrant children. It is incumbent upon all of us to listen, learn, and put this knowledge into practice.

REFERENCES

Al-Haj, M. (1998). Arab Education: Development versus Control. In Y. Iram and M. Schmida, *The Educational System of Israel* (pp. 91–110). Westport, CT: Greenwood Press.

Appiah, K., and Gates, H.L. (Eds.). (1995). *Identities*. Chicago: University of Chicago Press.

Ashraf, S.A. (1988). Education of Muslim Children in the U.K.: Some Aspects. *Muslim Education Quarterly* 5(3).

Bhatnager, J. (Ed.). (1981). *Educating Immigrants*. London: Croom Helm.

Council of Europe. (1994). European Education Research Workshop on Minority Education, Bautzen (Saxony).

Daun, H., Ivic, I., Popachic, D., Kolouh-Westin, L., Pecikan, A., and Carrim, N. (2001). *Education and Democracy—Curricula and Student Attitudes in Four Countries: Bosnia-Herzegovina, Yugoslavia, Mozambique and South Africa*. Paper presented at the 45th annual meeting of the Comparative and International Education Society, Washington, DC.

Ghosh, R. (1995). New Perspectives on Multiculturalism in Education. *McGill Journal of Education* 30(3): 231–238.

Glenn, C.L. (1995). *Educational Freedom in Eastern Europe*. Washington, DC: Cato Institute.

Glenn, C.L., and de Jong, E.J. (1996). *Educating Immigrant Children: Schools and Language Minorities in Twelve Nations*. New York: Garland Publishing.

Groux, D. (2002). *Equality Paradigms in French Education: Impact on Integration and Diversity*. Paper presented at the 46th annual conference of the Comparative and International Education Society, University of Central Florida, Orlando.

Gurr, T.R. (1993). *Minorities at Risk—A Global View of Ethnopolitical Conflicts*. Washington, DC: United States Institute of Peace Press.

Halstead, M. (1993). Educating Muslim Minorities: Some Western European Approaches. In W. Tulasiewicz and C.Y. To (Eds.), *World Religions and Educational Practice* (pp. 161–176). New York: Cassel.

Iram, Y. (1987). Changing Patterns of Immigrant Absorption in Israel: Educational Implications. *Canadian and International Education* 16(2): 55–72.

Iram, Y. (2001). Education for Democracy in Pluralistic Societies: The Case of Israel. In L.J. Limage (Ed.), *Democratizing Education and Educating Democratic Citizens: International and Historical Perspectives* (pp. 213–226). New York: Routledge Falmer.

Iram, Y. (2002). *Education for Coexistence and Peace—The Israeli Palestinian Case*. Paper presented at the 46th annual conference of the Comparative and International Education Society, University of Central Florida, Orlando.

Iram, Y., and Schmida, M. (1998). *The Educational System of Israel*. Westport, CT: Greenwood Press.

Johnson, N.B. (1977). On the Relationship of Anthropology to Multicultural Teaching and Learning. *Journal of Teacher Education* 28(3): 10–15.

Kassotakis, M., and Roussakis, Y. (1999). Some Aspects of Minority Education in Greece. In A.-V. Rigas (Ed.), *Education of Ethnic Minorities: Unity and Diversity*. Proceedings of the 12th International Congress of the World Association for Educational Research (pp. 99–112). Athens: Ellinika Grammata.

Limage, L.J. (2000). Islamic Identity and Education: The Case of France. *Comparative Education* 36(1): 73–94.

Limage, L.J. (Ed.). (2001). *Democratizing Education and Educating Democratic Citizens: International and Historical Perspectives*. New York: Routledge Falmer.

Male, G.A. (1986). Policy Issues in the Education of Minorities—England. *Education and Urban Society* 18(4): 477–486.

Masemann, V., and Iram, Y. (1987). The Right to Education for Multicultural Development: Canada and Israel. In N.B. Tarrow (Ed.), *Human Rights and Education* (pp. 101–119). Oxford: Pergamon Press.

McAndrew, M. (1994). Ethnicity, Multiculturalism and Multicultural Education in Canada. In R. Ghosh and D. Ray (Eds.), *Social Change and Education* (3rd ed.). Toronto: Harcourt.

McNeill, J.L. (1995). Multicultural Education in Canada in Global Context. In Y. Iram (Ed.), *The Role and Place of the Humanities in Education for the World of the 21st Century.* Proceedings of the 11th International Congress of the World Association for Educational Research (pp. 111–124). Ramat Gan: Bar-Ilan University and WAER.

Mitter, W. (1994). *Basic Issues Concerning Education of Minorities* (doc. DESC/Rech, 1994/53). Strasbourg: Council of Europe.

Mitter, W. (1997). Diversity and Convergent Trends in Multicultural Education in Russia and Its Neighbouring Countries. In K. Watson, C. Modgil, and S. Modgil (Eds.), *Educational Dilemmas: Debate and Diversity* (pp. 221–228). London: Cassel.

Mitter, W. (1999). Nation–States in Transformation in the Mirror of Socio-political and Educational Trends. In A.-V. Rigas (Ed.), *Education of Ethnic Minorities: Unity and Diversity.* Proceedings of the 12th Congress of the World Association for Educational Research (pp. 10–20). Athens: Ellinika Grammata.

Northern Ireland Curriculum Council. (1989). *Cross Curricular Themes.* Belfast: NICC, Stranmillis College.

Northern Ireland Department of Education. (1990). *Education for Mutual Understanding.* Belfast: Education and Training Inspectorate, DENI.

OECD. (1989). *One School: Many Cultures.* Paris: CERI.

Ogbu, J.U. (1978). *Minority Education and Caste.* New York: Academic Press.

Ogbu, J.U. (1983). Minority Status in Plural Societies. *Comparative Education Review* 27(3): 168–190.

Rouhana, N.N. (1997). *Palestinian Citizens in an Ethnic Jewish State: Identities in Conflict.* New Haven, CT: Yale University Press.

Shapiro, M., and Alker, H. (Eds.). (1996). *Challenging Boundaries: Global Flows, Territorial Identities.* Minneapolis: University of Minnesota Press.

Smith, A., and Robinson, A. (1992). *Education for Mutual Understanding: Perceptions and Policy.* Coleraine, Northern Ireland: University of Ulster.

Smolicz, J.J. (1985). Multiculturalism and an Overarching Framework of Value: Education Responses to Assimilation, Interaction and Separatism in Ethnically Plural Societies. *Bildung und Erziehung* (Suppl. 2): 245–267.

Sutherland, M.B. (2001). Education for Citizenship in the United Kingdom— Caught or Taught? In L.J. Limage (Ed.), *Democratizing Education and Educating Democratic Citizens: International and Historical Perspectives* (pp. 245– 266). New York: Routledge Falmer.

Taylor, M.J., and Bagley, C.A. (1995). Multicultural Antiracist Education. In Y. Iram (Ed.), *The Role and Place of the Humanities in Education for the World of the 21st Century.* Proceedings of the 11th International Congress of the World Association for Educational Research (pp. 251–262). Ramat Gan: Bar-Ilan University and WAER.

Thomas, R.M. (1986). Policy Issues in the Education of Minorities—Malaysia. *Education and Urban Society* 18(4): 399–411.

Tomiak, J. (Ed.). (1991). *Schooling, Educational Policy and Ethnic Identity.* New York: New York University Press.

Torney-Purta, J., Schwille, J., and Amadeo, J.A. (Eds.). (1999). *Civic Education across Countries: Twenty-four National Case Studies from the IEA Civic Education Project.* Delft, Netherlands: Ecuron Publishers.

Tulasiewicz, W., and Adams, T. (1995). Multicultural Classrooms and Intercultural Education in the European Community. In Y. Iram (Ed.), *The Role and Place of the Humanities in Education for the World of the 21st Century.* Proceedings of the 11th International Congress of the World Association for Educational Research (pp. 263–270). Ramat Gan: Bar-Ilan University and WAER.

Winther-Jensen, T. (Ed.). (1996). *Challenges to European Education: Cultural Values, National Identities and Global Responsibilities.* Frankfurt am Main: Peter Lang.

CHAPTER 2

Cultural Recognition or Social Redistribution: Predicaments of Minority Education

GITA STEINER-KHAMSI

According to Nancy Fraser, the struggles of minorities can be divided into two different forms of struggles: one aims at the recognition of minority languages and cultures, and another seeks to redistribute economic and political resources in ways that reverse institutionalized forms of exclusion (Fraser, 1997).

Drawing on Fraser's work, I will first highlight her differentiation between *social redistribution* and *cultural recognition* and reflect on its implication for education. Second, I will present in more depth a related theoretical framework that has generated heated debates among scholars of multicultural education theory in the 1990s: universalism versus particularism. I illustrate this debate by discussing the discursive shift from multiculturalism to antiracism from a comparative perspective. Third, I will draw attention to anthropological and social psychological studies on identity and difference and examine the relational nature of identity formation. It is in this section that I suggest to apply a conflict resolution approach for interethnic conflicts. My conclusions might seem somewhat radical for countries such as Israel that are bipolar (Israeli-Arab) and caught in a protracted social conflict. I suggest to decenter or deemphasize ethnicity, nationality, or religion and instead propose to explore conflict resolution approaches that are more contextual and relational and less essentializing, ethnicizing, and polarizing. My argument is driven by the concern to have to respond to the basic dilemma of minority education: How can we pursue a policy strategy that aims at social redistribution without losing sight of cultural differences? And how can we promote cultural recognition without creating segregated schooling?

SOCIAL REDISTRIBUTION VERSUS CULTURAL RECOGNITION

Fraser, a political philosopher, identifies the struggle for cultural recognition as the dominant form of political struggle in the twentieth century. I would not go as far as Fraser, who views the struggle for cultural recognition as typical for the newly emerging "postsocialist struggles" in which group identity supplants class interest as the chief medium of political mobilization. Instead, I see the struggles of minorities to have their language, religion, and ethnicity publicly acknowledged as a recurrent theme in ethnic and race relations. In education, in particular, questions such as whose language, whose history, and whose knowledge should be taught in schools are by no means new. These questions have been major concerns of politicians, policy analysts, researchers, and educators in different parts of the world and at different periods of history. They have constituted pressing issues for countries of immigration as well as for multireligious, multilingual, multinational, or multicultural societies.

Nevertheless, I agree with Fraser's general assessment that in many countries class struggle, which aimed at a redistribution of economic resources, has been displaced by struggles for cultural recognition of minorities. For a long time, political tensions in regions of interethnic conflict such as the Middle East, Northern Ireland, or Cyprus were used as prototypical examples for such a shift. However, the politics of cultural recognition is manifested also in other countries. Countries of immigration such as the United States, Australia, Canada, and Great Britain, to name a few, have witnessed major ethnicity movements in the 1970s and 1980s. More recently, ethnicity has become a powerful, often destructive, force for political mobilization in postsocialist countries. In these central and eastern European countries, ethnicity and ethnonationalist movements have revived the nineteenth-century notion of nation–states as culturally homogeneous territories. Political scientist Claus Offe (1997) views the current ethnic revival in central and eastern Europe as a response to decades of imposed pan-Soviet identity, during which citizens in socialist nation–states were Russified and culturally alienated.

In all these three different political contexts—in regions of interethnic conflict, in multicultural societies, and in postsocialist countries—the struggle over religious, ethnic, and linguistic minority rights, and the responses to these struggles, have become the major source for social conflicts, some of which are settled peacefully, others by means of oppression, violence, and war. It is for these ongoing struggles for ethnicity that several scholars have concluded that in the late twentieth century class struggle has fused with—or others would even suggest have been replaced by—ethnic struggles. From this point of view, the battlefield has shifted from class to ethnic struggle, and as a consequence, social conflicts among different segments of a population are no longer carried out mainly *horizontally*—based on socioeconomic characteristics—but rather *vertically*—along ethnic, religious, and linguistic lines. There is considerable evidence for this geometrical shift from horizontal to vertical conflicts. In fact, the struggle over culture and, implicitly, the struggle over identity—manifested in social conflicts between immigrants, national minorities, ethnic minorities, and the majority—have come to constitute a major research topic.

Fraser (1997) describes redistribution and recognition as two distinct paradigms of justice, with different political remedies. The remedy for economic injustice is political—economic restructuring of some sort such as reorganizing the division of labor; redistributing income; revising citizen rights with regard to political rights, residential rights, welfare rights; and in education, in particular, improving access, outcome, and quality of education for all. In contrast, the remedy for cultural injustice is some sort of cultural or symbolic change that reflects a recognition and positively valorizing of cultural, linguistic, and religious diversity. For school systems this would mean mainstreaming cultural diversity in curricula, textbooks, and teaching so that knowledge, values, skills, and culture transmitted in schools become commonly shared by the various social groups in a society. This would imply a recognition and integration of various languages, religions, and cultures in one unified school system.

The situation becomes murky if we were to decide between a struggle for recognition and a struggle for redistribution. In education, both struggles are inextricably linked to each other. If we were to focus on a politics of recognition only, we would be left with segregated schooling as the best solution since each social group could effectively exert the right to implement its own language of instruction. For it is only under the condition of residential and education segregation that the relatively homogenous community can preserve its language, its religious and cultural practices, and impose its own worldview on curricula, textbooks, and teaching. Segregated schooling, however, is not only socially divisive; it also creates problems of inequality. In the history of education, we cannot find one single example of a "separate but equal" education policy that has benefited minorities. It did not work in the segregated South of the United States, nor in Apartheid South Africa, nor does it work in those regions of interethnic conflict where segregated schooling has been established. In all these regions, inequality arises as a result of unequal resources and quality in the different segregated school systems. Segregated schooling becomes a class barrier for minority students since it leads, more often than not, to a dead end with regard to further education, denying minorities access to higher education because it is in most places majority oriented. In most countries, segregated schooling ends with upper secondary schools, and minority students pursuing further education would need to switch to tertiary or higher education institutions offered by the majority.

Minorities' exclusion from higher education applies especially to regions without a "hinterland" and without a "shelter higher educational system" that absorb minority students from the neighboring country. For a long time, the Hungarian minority in Romania, for example, was able to complete schooling in a segregated school system. Upon completion of their studies, students were granted access to higher education in neighboring Hungary. There are many other examples of higher education systems that provide shelter to national minorities from adjacent regions such as Kazakh universities that attract Mongolians of Kazakh descent or Slovenian tertiary educational institutions enrolling Austrians of Slovenian descent. However, in recent years, the situation has changed drastically for minorities in multiethnic or multinational states, and major shifts have occurred. Because of the financial crises in postsocialist countries, school systems in these regions have ceased to absorb national minorities from neighboring countries. As a consequence, segregated schooling functions nowadays very much like a glass ceiling for minorities.

The other strategy, focusing exclusively on a politics of redistribution, also falls short of alleviating injustice. A politics of redistribution treats students as individuals and tends to neglect their particular cultural rights and needs as members of a specific linguistic, ethnic, or religious group. Redistribution policies in education are often assimilationist since they tend to be insensitive to the fact that any notion of knowledge, values, or skills to which schools prescribe are embedded in a cultural context. Thus, a culture-blind or color-blind approach to equality unwillingly, or sometimes willingly, favors perspectives, abilities, and strengths of majority students. For minority students a politics of redistribution means that they can only succeed educationally if they assimilate. Therefore, an exclusive focus on redistribution does not solve problems of injustice and inequality since it undermines equal educational access and outcomes for minorities.

Given that neither of the two strategies—an educational politics of redistribution or an educational politics of recognition—is a remedy for injustice and discrimination, if pursued alone, we are left with no other choice than examining the implications of a double strategy. What would an education system look like if it reflects both redistribution and recognition? For education, in particular, the remedy of injustice would be the right to maintain one's language, religion, and culture without being denied access to social, political, and economic resources. This is clearly easier said than done, and in fact, educational policies in different countries seem to move back and forth between these two political strategies.

FROM MULTICULTURALISM TO ANTIRACISM TO CONFLICT RESOLUTION

This section will illustrate the dichotomy between redistribution and recognition, or between universalism and particularism, from a comparative perspective. At the same time, an attempt will be made to document how educational policies in countries of immigration are constantly undergoing changes, often switching back and forth between redistribution and recognition practices.

Multicultural educational policies in England and Wales, for example, came under serious attack in the mid-1980s (Steiner-Khamsi, 1990, 1992) for overemphasizing cultural differences and neglecting social inequality. Multiculturalists were suspected of pursuing solely a "Three-S-Approach," by which the habits of ethnic minorities—that is, how to cook a Samosa, tie a Sari, or play a Steelpan—are demonstrated to their white classmates. Consequently, the multicultural approach, at least initially, simply led to a celebration of ethnicity and cultural variety in the classroom.

From the perspectives of many community leaders, multiculturalists tended to preserve community cultures—often reduced to eating, dressing, and festival habits—as a means to enrich the entire society. Their line of argumentation can be summarized as follows: The culturalist focus of multicultural education has diverted from the struggle for equal opportunities in education. Racism was not considered at an institutional level. Rather, injustice and discrimination were reduced to a matter of intolerance, manifested by prejudiced individuals. By restricting racism to the inappropriate behavior of a handful of ignorant individuals, injustices on institutional and structural levels remained to be addressed. Moreover, the multicultural approach suited the New Right's interest in justifying inequalities between ethnic groups by pointing out cultural differences. Multicultural education helped, unwillingly, to establish hierarchies between ethnic groups by distinguishing between immigrant groups that are—based on language, religion, and cultural practices—culturally close (e.g., Christian Greek Cypriotes) and those that appeared culturally alien (e.g., Muslim Pakistanis).

In contrast, the antiracist approach in education grew out of the black struggle in the United Kingdom. In the 1980s, the Labour Party–oriented local education authorities adopted an antiracist approach as the new education policy replacing the multicultural one. The antiracist movement backed up the minorities in claiming their right for equal provision and opportunity in education, health services, housing, and law. Most of them, originally coming from former British colonies and overseas territories, could trace their claim back historically: "We are here, because you were there" (Gilroy, 1987) was a statement expressed by the two main immigrant groups from countries of the Indian subcontinent and from the Caribbean.

Rather than emphasizing cultural differences and demanding tolerance, antiracists in Great Britain turned their attention to forms of exclusion and called for the enforcement of universal rights. They averted the emphasis on ethnic minorities, initially intended to serve as a means to appeal for tolerance toward minority cultures and languages, and instead focused on racism in schools and on its various manifestations, for example, in textbooks or in the employment practices for teaching staff. Instead of enforcing interethnic and interracial harmony, antiracist training programs center on notions of conflict, power, exploitation, and structural discrimination (Gaine, 1988) and in some more psychologically oriented programs also on (white) guilt (see Sivanandan, 1985; Steiner-Khamsi, 1992).

Also, whereas multiculturalists emphasized difference and particularism, antiracists stressed human rights and universalism. The multicultural strategy is closely related to a politics of recognition, whereas the antiracist movement targeted a politics of redistribution. Hence, the shift from multicultural education to antiracism in the mid-1980s reflects a shift from a struggle for recognition to one for redistribution.

A few years later, however, the distinction between multicultural education and antiracist education became increasingly blurred. Stuart Hall and other scholars focusing on discrimination, exclusion, and institutional racism (Donald and Rattansi 1993; Hall, 1993; McCarthy and Crichlow, 1993) acknowledged the importance of ethnicity for political mobilization against racism. Stuart Hall's "new ethnicities" (1993: 252), however, differ considerably from earlier folklorizing and exoticizing versions of multiculturalism. He suggests to "decouple" (257) ethnicity from its equivalence with nationalism, imperialism, racism, and the state and instead frame ethnicity in terms of identity. The antiracist movement and the critical debates on ethnicity forced British multiculturalists to move beyond a shallow multiculturalism that had characterized many of the earlier multicultural education policies in Great Britain and in other countries of immigration. In retrospect, multicultural education in the United Kingdom has greatly benefited from the antiracist movement of the 1980s.

In the last few years, both multicultural education and antiracist education have been criticized for promoting polarization. They have been attacked for perpetuating a binary perspective on intergroup relations by artificially dividing individuals into whites and blacks, majority and ethnic minorities, and natives and immigrants and, on a broader level, distinguishing between periphery and core, between sending and receiving countries of immigration, or as Stuart Hall has put it, between the "West" and the "rest" (Hall, 1992).

Today, research and practice of multicultural education and antiracist education concepts are facing major challenges: The research has to come to grips with the more recent debates in the social sciences and in philosophy that are relevant to the field. In light of the debates on redistribution/recognition, universalism/particularism, and also essentialism and difference, researchers need to come out against criticism of having pursued an essentialist and simplistic notion of race and ethnicity. Practitioners, in turn, need to prove that they have truly surmounted traditional approaches, which had previously amounted to nothing more than celebrating diversity and promoting a "harmonious empty pluralism" (Mohanty, 1994: 146).

Having witnessed from up close the different phases of minority education policies in countries of immigration since the 1970s—assimilation, multiculturalism, and antiracism—I applaud the anticulturalist turn that the antiracist movement has managed to evoke. The focus on structural inequality, institutional racism, and legal discrimination constitutes an important first step toward a politics of redistribution. I am suggesting to critically examine politically naive struggles for cultural recognition that ignore that these struggles "occur in a world of tremendous material inequality" (Fraser, 1995: 74) in education, income and property ownership, access to paid work, and health care. Preserving language, culture, and religion cannot be a means to an end, especially if it is at the cost of being treated unequally. Having said this, I propose to move beyond a politics of recognition because justice today requires both redistribution and recognition.

Along with Fraser, I suggest therefore to develop an approach that only identifies and defends those versions of a politics of recognition that can be coherently combined with demands for equality. In this new approach, any form of cultural recognition that leads to segregation and exclusion needs to be rejected on the grounds that it diminishes the pressure to distribute economic, political, and social resources equally. In educational practice this means abandoning ethnicity as the main frame of reference for minority education. For ethnicity functions as a boundary marker that prevents intergroup communication, negotiations, and conflict resolution. Another way of presenting this approach is by highlighting its relational dimension. Unlike the culturalist concepts of assimilation and multiculturalism that tended to focus on minorities, and the antiracism concept that targeted the majority, the conflict resolution approach examines both, that is, focuses on intergroup relations. I will illustrate the applications of the conflict resolution approach for interethnic work with adolescents, which I choose to call intergroup youth-work.

OPPOSITIONAL AND RELATIONAL IDENTITIES

A useful concept that suggests to deemphasize ethnicity and to turn our attention to intergroup relations has been formulated by John Ogbu (1987, 1991, 1995). Ogbu, a social anthropologist, presents a series of interesting comparative and ethnographic studies of intergroup relations in which he introduces the concept of "oppositional identity." He uses the concept to explain why academic achievements of one ethnic group vary considerably depending on the national setting. He shows that minorities are performing academically better in countries where they have the status of an immigrant minority than in countries where they are involuntary minorities. Ogbu refers to the fact that West Indian children are the least successful in Britain, where they are seen as citizens of a former colony. On the other hand, they are academically most successful in the United States, where they are one immigrant group among others. In Canada, where they are identified as part of the Commonwealth, they score in the academic middle ranges.

Ogbu identified a series of survival strategies that children of involuntary minorities develop to resist assimilation to values that are associated with whites. To survive socially among their peers, they choose to develop an oppositional cultural frame of reference and identity, which can become detrimental when it comes to school learning. Referring to his ethnographic study in Stockton, California, he writes:

It follows that involuntary minority students who adopt attitudes conducive to school success are often accused by their peers of acting like their enemy, i.e., like their "oppressors." Among U.S. blacks, such students may be accused of acting white or acting like Uncle Toms. They are accused of being disloyal to the group and to the cause of the group, and they risk being isolated from their peers. (Ogbu, 1991: 27)

For several reasons, Ogbu's work seems relevant for intergroup youth-work: First, he studies in depth how adolescents actively reproduce a cultural frame of reference and an identity that helps them to survive in a racialized society. Then his research perspective reflects the relational nature of identity formation processes. He shows that in a racialized society adolescents constantly use ethnicity and "race" as identity markers. Moreover, he depicts the severe limitation of adult interventions, potentially a cause for reinforcing oppositional identity, and he points out, instead, the strong peer influence.

Ogbu's work and studies of other authors reviewed so far suggest that antiracist and intergroup youth-workers should deemphasize and deessentialize ethnic and race relations and instead develop innovative ways that allow adolescents to drop ethnicity and "race" as the main cultural frame of reference. This approach differs fundamentally from a "color-blind" perspective or from other apolitical approaches, since it acknowledges the fact that ethnicity, nationality, and race are powerful markers that are used to legitimate inequity.

FROM INTERGROUP TO INTERPERSONAL CONFLICTS

We now need to turn our attention to the key question that addresses every form of intergroup approach: What makes us believe that framing a conflict in terms of interpersonal conflicts is more effective than dealing with these conflicts as ethnic and racial intergroup conflicts?

Evaluation research studies dealing with intergroup conflict resolution programs suggest that the long-term outcome or the efficacy of programs that focus especially and exclusively on ethnicity and "race" are indeed minimal. I would like to refer to a well-known Swiss study carried out by Peter Casparis (1992: 39–52). Casparis evaluated the short-term and long-term effects of a program that aimed at improving intergroup relations by addressing ethnic and racial tensions explicitly. The group on which he focused his study consisted of white and black Swiss adolescents, young immigrants, and two white Swiss adolescents who identified themselves as "Skins." The two Skins had had previous brushes with the law for trespassing a Brazilian party and for engaging in racist, violent, and vandalist actions. The organizers of the event dismissed their charges under the condition that the two Skins participate in a multiethnic and multiracial group that discusses ethnic and racial conflicts. Two researches participated in the sessions as participant observers. They documented that the two Skins engaged actively in sharing their views and experiences on race relations, and they seemed to come to grips with their past racist actions. Moreover, over the course of the 10 sessions, the two Skins developed close friendships with other members of the group across lines of ethnicity and race. However, the program did not succeed in having any long-term or generalization effects. During the program the Skins started to frame the immigrants and blacks of the group they were becoming friendly with as "special cases" and as "atypical" for immigrants and blacks in general.

DIFFERENCE AND IDENTITY

Recognizing the basic assumption that identity is always based on the perception of individual difference, and moreover recognizing findings in developmental psychology that suggest that the search for sexual, professional, and political identities is a key theme during the phase of adolescence, the question antiracist youth-workers need to come to grips with is the following: Do we want to offer, or reinforce, cultural and racial categories for the identity formation process during adolescence?

There is a striking inconsistency in how adults react to the identity choices of adolescents. Adults tend to take the slightest manifestations of ethnic and racial identity among youth very seriously and expect them to last for the entire life span, whereas other manifestations of identity choices, such as sexual, professional, and political preferences, are generally viewed as transitory. At stake here is the question, For what purposes do adults see ethnic and racial self-representations of adolescents as unmalleable?

At this point, we cannot present definitive explanations and answers to this question. One of the plausible answers, however, relates to ethnic and race relations as a societal concern. It is a commonly held belief that ethnic and racial identity contribute more than any other form of self-representation to social cohesion or social disruption in society. It is interesting to note here that sociologists and educators in Germany have only turned their attention to white or German identity after Reunification, when Germany was hit by an outburst of increased racism, neofascism, and anti-Semitism. In the early 1990s, several authors suggested viewing the outburst of racism in the context of the overall national identity crisis in Germany. According to these authors (Heitmeyer et al., 1992; see also criticism by Leiprecht, 1993), adolescents from former East Germany were especially bound to be afflicted by a major identity crisis. Adolescents from former East Germany were believed to be the ones who experienced more than any other German group the economic and social disadvantages of Reunification. They were the ones who were seen as second-class Germans, suffering from the modernization process (German *Modernitätsverlierer*) and losing their jobs as a result of Reunification. Their racism toward immigrants and asylum seekers was interpreted as a demonstration of newly awakened Germanness, that is, as an attempt to cut non-Germans off from rights and resources in order to demonstrate that everything in the reunified German territory belongs rightfully and exclusively to Germans. These studies suggest that this act of exclusion by male German adolescents, often very brutal and violent, is closely linked to their urge to reconstitute a sense of ethnic identity as Germans. Being racist and acting exclusive allowed them to regain a sense of collective identity and helped them to constitute a functional ingroup with common values (machismo, German supremacy, etc.). I find these studies worth reflecting on, since they draw on a relational concept of identity formation, in which exclusionary actions are viewed as a means to generate a sense of social identity, belongingness, or inclusion. From a comparative perspective, however, this body of research dealing with the cohesive effects of exclusion as a basis for explaining racism (German *identitätsstiftende Wirkung von Ausgrenzung*) is fundamentally flawed. It disregards the racial formation of Germany and other countries, where ethnicity, nationality, and race permeate every social interaction. In addition, they neglect the fact that ethnicity, nationality, and race had already been in place as divisive lines before Reunification and hence could readily be activated as markers of exclusion and inclusion.

PROTRACTED SOCIAL CONFLICTS IN BIPOLAR SOCIETIES

Examining ethnicity as a marker for exclusion and inclusion, that is, for constituting out-groups and in-groups, has a well-established tradition in social psychological research. In this body of research, special attention has been given to social conflicts in bipolar societies, in which the population is divided into two camps, into Germans and non-Germans, to use the example mentioned above, into whites and blacks (United States), Jews and Arabs (Israel), or Protestants and Catholics (Northern Ireland). Depending on the political context, bipolarity is formed along lines of ethnicity, race, or religion. It is important to note here that not all societies are bipolar with regard to race and ethnic relations. Many Central and Latin American countries, for example, are multipolar since individuals in these countries categorize each other and themselves in ways that reflect a highly differentiated class and race spectrum (Degler, 1986). In fact, there is an interesting new body of transnationalism research emerging that examines the tensions that arise for individuals who move from a multipolar society to a bipolar society, or the other way around. Basch, Glick Schiller, and Szanton Blanc (1994), for example, examined the dynamics of racial identity for Caribbean immigrants in New York City. Moving from Caribbean societies that are characterized by a multipolar race construction to a country that is bipolar, they resent being categorized as either whites or blacks.

In the Middle East, bipolarity constitutes a major conflict. In fact, it is an issue so complex in nature that there seems to be little agreement as to how to label and explain the conflict. Nevertheless, whether bipolarity is framed in terms of the "Israeli-Arab conflict," the "Israeli-Palestinian conflict," the conflict between "Jews and Muslims," or the conflict between "Jews and Arabs," and whether the causes for the conflict are attributed to nationality, religion, or ethnicity, there is agreement about the bipolar and deep-rooted nature of the social conflict in the Middle East. Azar (1990) coined the term "protracted social conflict" to denote intense intergroup conflicts that appear intractable and irresolvable. Examples of such conflicts include those in the Middle East, Northern Ireland, and Cyprus. Fisher, a social psychologist, describes protracted social conflicts as follows: "A continuing state of tension is heightened by episodes of escalation often involving violence, which is typically terminated by mutual exhaustion and/or some form of peacekeeping" (1989: 4).

Both social psychologists (Bar-Tal, 1990; Bunker, Benedict et al., 1995; Deutsch, 1985; Fisher, 1989) and political scientists (see Azar, 1990) acknowledge that traditional approaches to conflict management prove ineffective, because the underlying issues do not seem to get resolved.

CONCLUSION

In this chapter I have attempted to situate the basic dilemma of minority education—social distribution without neglecting cultural differences, cultural recognition without promoting segregated schooling—in the context of the Middle East, characterized by its bipolarity and protracted conflict. My preliminary analysis leads me to conclude that deemphasizing bipolar differences is an important step for a pedagogy of justice that is based on recognition and redistribution.

I have explained elsewhere in more depth why we should move away from educational approaches that tend to see each student or each youth as a representative of a specific nation, race, ethnicity, or religion and why it is more effective to decenter ethnicity or to deemphasize ethnicity (Steiner-Khamsi, 1992; Steiner-Khamsi and Spreen, 1996) in multicultural settings. The three reasons can be summarized as follows:

First, contrary to common belief held among multiculturalists and antiracist youth-workers, there is not too little, but rather too much—awareness among youth with regard to cultural diversity, "race," and ethnic relations.

Second, multicultural and antiracist youth-work that focuses merely on minorities is prey to neglect the relational nature of identity formations and hence is oblivious to inclusionary and exclusionary processes that account for ethnic and racial intergroup tensions.

And finally, there are serious constraints to adults teaching adolescents ethical and social issues, and it seems that we would be better off finding innovative strategies so that adolescents can learn from each other how to improve their intergroup relations (Steiner-Khamsi and Spreen, 1996).

I have also attempted to explore the usefulness of an interpersonal conflict resolution approach for bipolar societies, situating my argument on research in different disciplines. My first argument—the need to decenter or deemphasize ethnicity—is based on theoretical debates in social philosophy (redistribution/recognition) and in multicultural education theory (universalism/particularism). The second argument—the need to focus on interactions and interethnic contexts—has been built on anthropological studies of intergroup relations (Ogbu). Finally, the third argument—the need to engage in a conflict resolution approach—has been drawn from social psychological research. Since the focus in this section was on educational work with adolescents, reference was made to studies that demonstrate the limits of adults teaching specific values such as tolerance for difference or respect for diversity to adolescents in ways that are effective. Instead, a more effective educational approach would contain a strong peer leadership component where students learn from each other rather than from adults.

REFERENCES

Azar, E.E. (1990). *The Management of Protracted Social Conflict: Theory and Cases.* Aldershot, UK: Gower.

Bar-Tal, D. (1990). *Group Beliefs: A Conception for Analyzing Group Structure, Processes, and Behavior.* New York: Springer.

Basch, L., Glick Schiller, N., and Szanton Blanc, C. (1994). *Nations Unbound: Transnational Projects, Postcolonial Predicaments, and Deterritorialized Nation-States.* Langhorne, PA: Gordon and Breach.

Bunker, B., Benedict, R., Jeffrey, Z., et al. (1995). *Conflict, Cooperation, and Justice: Essays Inspired by the Work of Morton Deutsch.* San Francisco: Jossey-Bass.

Casparis, P. (1992). *Eidgenössische Jugendkommission: Bericht der eidgenössischen Jugendkommission.* Bern: EDMZ.

Degler, C.N. (1986). *Neither Black Nor White: Slavery and Race Relations in Brazil and the United States.* Madison: University of Wisconsin Press.

Deutsch, M. (1985). *Distributive Justice: A Social Psychological Perspective.* New Haven, CT: Yale University Press.

Donald, J., and Rattansi, A. (1993). *"Race," Culture and Difference.* London: Sage.

Fisher, R.J. (1989). *The Social Psychology of Intergroup and International Conflict Resolution.* New York: Springer.

Fraser, N. (1995). From Redistribution to Recognition? Dilemmas of Justice in a "Post-Socialist" Age. *New Left Review* 212: 68–93.

Fraser, N. (1997). *Justice Interruptus: Critical Reflections on the "Postsocialist" Condition.* New York: Routledge.

Gaine, C. (1988). *No Problem Here: A Practical Approach to Education and "Race" in White Schools.* London: Hutchinson.

Gilroy, P. (1987). *There Ain't No Black in the Union Jack: The Cultural Politics of Race and Nation.* London: Hutchinson.

Hall, S. (1992). The West and the Rest. In S. Hall and B. Gieben (Eds.), *Formations of Modernity* (pp. 275–331). Cambridge: Polity Press.

Hall, S. (1993). New Ethnicities. In J. Donald and A. Rattansi (Eds.), *"Race," Culture and Difference* (pp. 252–259). London: Sage.

Heitmeyer, W., et al. (1992). *Die Bielefelder Rechtsextremismus-Studie—Erste Langzeituntersuchung zur politischen Sozialisation männlicher Jugendlicher* Weinheim: Juventus.

Leiprecht, R. (1993). Das Modell unmittelbar und/oder direkte Konkurrenz: Erklärung von Rechtsextremismus oder Rechtfertigungsangebot? *Informationsdienst zur Ausländerarbeit* (1–2): 115–120.

McCarthy, C., and Crichlow, W. (Eds.). (1993). *Race, Identity and Representation in Education*. New York: Routledge.

Mohanty, C.T. (1994). On Race and Voice: Challenges for Liberal Education in the 1990s. In H.A. Giroux and P. McLaren (Eds.), *Between Borders: Pedagogy and the Politics of Cultural Studies* (pp. 145–166). New York: Routledge.

Offe, C. (1997). *Varieties of Transition: The East European and East German Experience*. Cambridge, MA: MIT Press.

Ogbu, J. (1987). Variability in Minority School Performance: A Problem in Search of an Explanation. *Anthropology and Education Quarterly* 18(2): 312–334.

Ogbu, J. (1991). Immigrant and Involuntary Minorities in Comparative Perspectives. In M. Gibson and J. Ogbu (Eds.), *Minority Status and Schooling* (pp. 3–33). New York: Garland.

Ogbu, J. (1995). Understanding Cultural Diversity and Learning. In J.A. Banks and C.A. McGee Banks (Eds.), *Handbook of Multicultural Education* (pp. 582–593). New York: Macmillan.

Sivanandan, A. (1985). RAT and the Degradation of Black Struggle. *Race and Class* 26(4): 1–34.

Steiner-Khamsi, G. (1990). Community Languages and Anti-Racist Education: The Open Battlefield. *Educational Studies* 16(1): 33–47.

Steiner-Khamsi, G. (1992). *Multikulturelle Bildungspolitik in der Postmoderne*. Opladen: Leske und Budrich.

Steiner-Khamsi, G., and Spreen, C. (1996). Oppositional and Relational Identity: A Comparative Perspective. In W. Lorenz and A. Aluffi-Pentini (Eds.), *Anti-Racist Work with Young People* (pp. 26–46). London: Russell.

CHAPTER 3

Multiculturalism and Civic Education in a Globalizing Economy

MARTIN CARNOY

The subject is of great importance and also highly charged politically. Multicultural societies such as the United States and Israel face a major and complex problem: how to integrate groups from highly varied cultures into a civil society with well-defined behavioral norms, a common language, and a clear conception of political rights and obligations, without coercing these groups to give up their own sense of cultural identity. The nature of the problem is changing. Major transformations in the world economy and the power situation of the nation–state, changes in the types of community networks individuals develop in the context of these changes, and changes in women's relationship to the family are altering the political construction of multiculturalism. This, in turn, changes the discussion of civic education.

The primary issue is obvious: We as democratic, liberal societies base our legal/political systems on a set of rights and obligations that allows individuals to do what they want as long as they do not violate the rights of others, Yet modern nation–states also require their members to undergo certain rites of passage in order to induct them into the national community. This includes learning the common language, adopting the social norms, and internalizing the historical symbols and beliefs that define nationality. In modern nation–states, one major institution developed to carry out the socialization process, especially of youth, is the school. There are others. For many years in the United States and still today in Israel, compulsory military service has played a major role in socializing young people into a national culture. Since membership in the national community is voluntary, most individuals are not only willing to pass through these induction institutions but want to do it.

The question, then, is not whether induction but how and on what terms. In a democratic society, schooling and even the military are sites of political struggle. Carnoy and Levin (1985) argued that historically political control of schools was important to different groups in society precisely because schools were supposed to prepare youth for economic and social success. Besides, schools as a public institution had and have vast resources to hire people and to buy goods and services. In a multicultural democratic society where all youth have to go to school, what and how they are taught in school, or alternatively, what kind of school they attend, can be subject to considerable conflict. The degree of conflict depends on how the various cultural groups feel about the state-defined socialization process. Some groups don't agree with the civic education provided because they dispute the society's cultural norms. Other groups may *want* their children to be fully incorporated into civil society as defined by the schools but believe that state-provided education systemically fails to do this, either because it is inadequate or because it discriminates.

In many instances, these disputes lead to multicultural educational approaches that provide not only civic education but also cognitive skills in ways that recognize and even nourish differences in cultural styles and cultural norms. Why would groups that dominate nation–state politics give in to such local autonomy and control? The answer to this question lies in the complex relationship of the nation–state to the social interests, cultures, regions, and nationalities that compose the state. In what sociologist Anthony Giddens (1991) calls *late modernity*, national elites have been increasingly willing to allow minority groups who feel excluded from national identity to build pride in their excluded identity through ethnicity-centered programs in public schools. This has worked largely because of the growing legitimacy and resources of the modern industrial welfare nation–state, often posed against the power bases of local communities.

GLOBALIZATION AND WORK

With globalization, all this changes. Let's start with the workplace. Increased competition in the context of a globalized economy and an information/communication revolution has had a major effect on the workplace in the advanced postindustrial societies. Employers in these societies are in the process of constructing "flexible production" based on an ideal of "flexible work," where labor contracts are tailored to specific firm needs in space and time. The restructuring of firms and organizations, facilitated by new technology and stimulated by global competition, is indeed ushering in a fundamental transformation of work: the disaggregation of labor in the labor process. We are witnessing the reversal of the historical trend of salarization of work and socialization of production that was the dominant feature of the industrial era. Instead, the new social and economic organization based on information technologies aims at decentralizing management, individualizing work, and customizing markets, thereby fragmenting labor and segmenting societies. At the same time, new information technologies facilitate the decentralization of work tasks and their coordination in an interactive network of communication in real time, be it between continents or between floors of the same building. The emergence of lean production methods goes hand in hand with widespread business practices of subcontracting, outsourcing, offshoring, consulting, and accordingly, downsizing and customizing. Part-time jobs, temporary work, flexible working time, and self-employment are on the rise in all countries. The overall trend points clearly toward a total transformation of work arrangements in advanced societies.

The individualization of work and the disaggregation of labor are processes that affect the entire fabric of our societies. This is because of the centrality of work for social life, and because of the tight connection between work, family, community, and the state in our social organization. The transformation of the work process shatters the institution of the welfare state, on which the social contract of our societies has been based for the last half century. How can flexible work and flexible employment possibly coexist with rigid entitlements based on the notion of "permanent jobs"? The individualization of work and the shrinkage of the public safety net stress the main institutions/social forms that help people in the transition periods of their lives, families, and communities as they try to adapt to the new requirements of work life. But communities based on shared work practices, such as labor unions and working-class cultures, are fading away. Unions increasingly become political institutions rather than representatives of workplace organizations. Several waves of accelerated urbanization, suburbanization, and territorial sprawl have also by and large undermined the material base of neighborhood sociability, while new forms of electronic communication are still too limited and too elitist to allow for the widespread emergence of new, virtual communities.

As for the family, the massive incorporation of women into the labor force and the welcome cultural drive for equal rights of individuals within the family have also weakened its supportive potential just when it is most needed during the difficult transition period toward new forms of work and personal life. I am not going to go into detail about this transformation here, but its driving force is women's rejection of an identity assigned to them by the patriarchal modern nation–state and the search for a new identity through wage work and a new network of personal, nonfamily relations. This redefinition of women's culture by women has a profound effect on the construction of families and also on men's identities. It also affects the notion of ethnic identities, fracturing patriarchal constructions of ethnicity for some individuals and reinforcing them for others.

GLOBALIZATION AND NATIONALITY

The important features of an individual's national identity are that it represents a real, not virtual, community and that it bonds him or her ethically to others in the national community differently than to human beings in general or to family members or to others in the same ethnic group. Individuals "belonging" to that community don't know others in the community personally. Yet, they *feel* that they share a lot in common with them, enough to fight collectively for their rights when threatened, to respond similarly to historical symbols, and to be comfortable with them when in an alien environment, such as in another country. The bond to others who speak the same language, live in the same territory, socialized in the same school system, and were raised in the same legal and political institutions is surprisingly strong even when ethnicities of origin differ substantially. That said, those of the same nationality may have strong feelings of conflict with each other. Class, ethnicity, religion, and race are all potential sources of separation within the same nation. If nationality represents a real community, "national" institutions must reduce these feelings of conflict or risk delegitimation and disintegration. At the same time, they must recognize that individuals living within the same nation can and do have multiple identities.

There are many good reasons why economic globalization (and the internal disintegration of the Soviet system) is having a profound effect on the nation–state and nationality as it evolved in the industrial capitalist countries after World War II. Does globalization mean the gradual disappearance of the nation–state and national identity or, more likely, a different role for the state and a "new" conception of nationality? The answer is not simple, but I argue that nation–states do play and will continue to play an important role in a global environment no longer influenced by big power military competition. They will be needed particularly to develop and sustain bonds between people of different interests and capacities, bonds that sustain continued economic and social development.

The most obvious arguments for the decline of the nation–state lie in the current compression of time and space on a global scale.

As markets for goods and services, including cultural products such as films, television programs, and books, become increasingly global, consumers who can afford, or believe that eventually they will be able to get, these products identify less with a particular local or national way of life and more with a global conception of living. As people are more mobile, the strangeness of people in other nations seems less foreign. Political philosopher David Miller puts it this way: "Insofar as out belief that we share a distinct national identity depends on a certain degree of ignorance about how people are actually leading their lives in other places, it is eroded by direct contact with those cultures" (Miller, 1995: 156).

As financial capital circulates globally, it has an increasing stake in nation–state behavior that conforms to international "economic rules." This stake has real political power. The health of national economies depends on such financial flows. Further, multinational corporations are an increasingly dominant force in defining a nation's capacity to export (and produce) and invest in production locations worldwide. So nation–state economic behavior is increasingly proscribed by the international financial "community's" conception of how states should organize their national economies[1] and by multinational corporations' fiscal needs in deciding where to locate production.

And as competition increases on a global scale, states tend to enter increasingly into supranational economic associations. The most obvious case is the European Union (EU), whose origins were partially economic but also an outgrowth of the nationalist wars that devastated Europe in the first half of the century and the military threat of the Soviet Union. The EU's voluntary march down the road to a supranationalist government of economic policy diminishes the power of European nation–states and tends to reduce national identity.

All this suggests that national states are losing power and that as they lose power, national identity and the national "community" decline. Thus, globalization and the economic power of the nation–state are in direct contradiction, producing, on the one hand, supranational organizations through which state elites seek, in Manuel Castells's words, "to carve out, collectively, some level of sovereignty from the new global disorder, and then distribute the benefits among its members, under endlessly negotiated rules" (Castells, 1997: 267) and, on the other hand, the resurgence of local identities and the communities built around them. Simply put, globalization contributes forcefully to the decline in *economic capacity* of the nation–state to develop and nourish national identity and to the decline of its *political legitimacy* as representing the varied interests of the diverse groups living within the national boundaries.

At the least, globalization forces states to focus more on acting as economic growth promoter for their national economies than as protectors of the national identity or a nationalist project. The "project" of the nation–state tends to become limited mainly to promoting economic growth and much less to promoting "equal treatment" among various ethnic groups living within national boundaries. The state shifts power to local and regional governments and is less able to equalize the interests of various identities represented in the nation–state. It pushes the problems of ethnic conflict to the local level and limits its responsibility to developing the economic environment in which *individuals* can increase their material well-being and form more extensive social networks.

GLOBALIZATION AND MULTICULTURALISM

The multiculturalism that we know, defined primarily by the modern nation–state, work system, and family structure that created particular social class, ethnic, and gender networks and identities, is being transformed. With the individualization of workers and their separation from "permanent" jobs, the search for identity *is* intensified. In that sense, multiculturalism should become a more important feature of most societies. But the counter to this potential trend is that for many the market and its notions of merit, material reward, and local and global networks based on professional (market) interests are increasingly the new source of identity. Nationality increasingly becomes linked with "market power." This is one new "global" concept of identity that has important national elements and that gives new meaning to the state. In that sense, multiculturalism declines in favor of an individually centered "global" identity.

But the market does not work well as a source of identity for everyone. Markets also increase material differences among individuals, so that even if the market creates a sense of community among those who share the same professional networks, it also continuously destroys communities, isolating individuals until they are able to find new networks.

In this context, the alternative for many is to search for other, non-market identities, and these identities also are becoming more global. Religious identity is certainly one of these new global movements. Fundamentalism is on the rise worldwide. Religious fundamentalism rejects the market as authority, and although fundamentalist groups have targeted the nation–state as a power base, there is an inherent contradiction between religious fundamentalism and a territorially defined nation. But the same contradiction does not exist when it comes to local communities or to globalized movements for religious identity.

Regionalism and even more localized ethnic movements are on the rise as sources of identity. Ethnicity may be highly localized, or it may have more global features (Hispanicity, for example, although not global, is hemispheric). These movements reject national territorial definitions, although they often play off national symbols to define themselves.

The main point is that with globalization the nation–state will decline as the point of reference for how the search for identity plays out. This trend may be the source of major social conflict. If everyone finds their identities in market culture, perhaps mixed with a dose of religious morality (this is the neoconservative construction of the new utopia), accepting market valuations of their self-worth, then social conflict would be minimal. It might also be minimal if economic growth in the national territory is rapid and most individuals find themselves materially better off. This seems to be true in the United States today even if the income distribution continues to become more unequal. But there is no reason that this will always be the case, particularly if economic growth slows down. Men and women do not live by bread alone. The recent Asian economic crisis is a good example of what might be in store for other nation–states that base their national identities on growth. As local identities proliferate and some localities/ethnicities feel excluded from the high end of the market, the absence of a nation–state capable of reincorporating them does not bode well for social stability.

WHITHER CIVIC EDUCATION?

Civic education is also a product of the nation–state. In centralized systems, civic education is a means to instill ever-changing versions of the symbols and interpretations of *national* identity, including changing definitions of citizenship. In France, the conception of the "Republic" and the meaning of the French "nation" are central to forming nationality in French children and youth and to defining French culture. The enormous emphasis on the *French* language, literature, art, food, and political history is central to civic education as defined by the Ministry of Education. This has been even more emphasized as France continues down the road to European union and is assaulted by films and music from the United States.

Even in a highly decentralized education system such as that of the United States, civic education developed as part of spreading conceptions of nationality. True, there were local variations of nationality, such as in the South, but these were eventually contested at the national level. Even multiculturalism issues in civic education were traditionally fought out at the federal or state (such as California) level: bilingual education, funds for women's athletics, and textbook adoptions (where textbooks portray women and various ethnic groups differently).

One of the main themes of civic education in liberal democratic nation–states, such as France or the United States, particularly in the recent late-modern phase, has been tolerance for the beliefs of other citizens in "private" spheres of life that do not affect citizenship rights and obligations. Thus, the flowering of multicultural education in the United States and northern Europe, particularly Scandinavia and Holland. Why not allow parents from varied ethnic groups to have the option of a public education that includes a home language, a broader version of national history that includes their point of view, and so forth? Yet the binding part of civic education was always that these groups accepted the political rights and obligations and the same tolerance for others fundamental to liberal constructs of social relations. Of course, one major problem for multicultural education under this liberal limitation is whether emphasizing separate identities and cultural norms can include teaching cultural norms that distinctly limit choice for the youth being socialized. For example, many cultures have distinct limitations on women's choices. Should these be part of children's civic education in a liberal democratic society's publicly financed schools? At the same time, feminist groups have successfully brought to the table the issue of the limits that women have traditionally faced in *so-called* democratic liberal societies. Shouldn't civic education present a feminist critique of even recent, highly male-centered civic education and how it portrays rights and obligations? If the democratic nation–state and its public education system stand for anything historically, it is the continual tendency to expand the notion of critical capacity in its citizens and their understanding of their rights, obligations, and choices available to them. This includes the right to seek identities they feel comfortable with and certainly tolerance and intellectual inclusion of others' beliefs.[2] Multiculturalism and multicultural education in public schooling ideologically centered in the nation–state have been shaped by this tendency.

But now, with globalization and the push to decentralize educational decisions from the nation–state to localities and from localities to schools, in both the highly centralized education systems and in the decentralized ones, civic education decisions are spreading out to regions, states, and municipalities, even schools themselves. The most extreme version of decentralization, much under discussion in the United States, moves to extend public funding to religious private schools through voucher plans and to charter schools formed by groups of teachers and parents. As long as communities share the same notion of nationality, of the rights and obligations both explicit and implicit of a liberal, tolerant, democratic society, and of that society's rights and obligations vis-à-vis noncitizens, civic education controlled at the regional, local, or school level may be more effective in reflecting local needs. Many have put more faith in local control in the past because national governments have a habit of being repressive or bureaucratic and incompetent to localities and localities allegedly better reflect local needs—except, of course, when localities are repressive, only reflect the local needs of some and not others, or are less competent than centralized bureaucracies. Such was certainly the case of the American South until the 1970s, and change required massive federal intervention.

What should we expect as multicultural civic education gradually loses its centralized locus in steadily weakening nation–states and heads into the multicultural community? What should we expect for civic education as globalization pushes people out of traditional ethnic identities into globalized/individualized market identities? Two competing trends develop. On the one hand, we should see those well incorporated into the global-individual market identity become relatively indifferent to civic education and pushing for emphasis on economics education, computer skills, English training (in non-English-speaking communities), and so forth. On the other, we should see strengthened countermovements for cultural identity, especially among those groups not well incorporated into the global economy and among regions and localities that suffer rather than profit from globalization. But where there is conflict over which cultural identity local communities should develop in their civic education, majorities may not tolerate minorities, depending on the nature of the civic culture in each community. This may lead to severe splits in communities.

In highly developed civil societies with deeply seated notions of tolerance, such as the Netherlands, we would expect that these conflicts can be successfully played out at the local level. Indeed, increasingly localized control of multicultural civic education over the past 10 years seems to have led to a more "successful" version of multicultural education that still fits well within the overall framework of Dutch "liberalism" and democracy. The capacity to develop and implement such successful projects will vary from community to community, but that variance in capacity also exists under centralized versions of multicultural education.

In the United States, the situation is less clear. For example, California's white population (which represents 50 percent of the population but 80 percent of the voters) and part of its ethnic populations have voted in the past decade to restrict social services to illegal immigrants (legislation since deemed unconstitutional), to eliminate affirmative action in public sector institutions, and to make bilingual education illegal, replacing it with one year of English immersion programs for limited-English proficiency students but otherwise English-only classrooms. Other states are following suit in such antiminority legislation. So "local" solutions to multicultural education may well be to eliminate it in societies where much of the "majority" also feels unincluded in global success or threatened by globalization. Minorities may therefore have increased interest in "breaking off" into privately run schools that they control and might get public funding for, exempted from laws that govern publicly run schools.

What does this produce? Under the worst of circumstances, it could mean the shift away from the growing trend toward a tolerant multiculturalism characteristic of the late-modern liberal democratic welfare state. This would be replaced by, at one level, a global-individual identity rooted in market values and individualized sense of worth, based largely on material gain and professional and personal networks organized around knowledge and information. At another level, it could be replaced by ethnocentric or religious groups with global ties but locally situated, antithetical to liberal values, highly insider/outsider oriented, and in conflict with the values of other groups. In the best of circumstances, local communities will come up with more effective versions of multicultural education than would nation–states, reflecting local needs but also adhering to inclusive notions of civil rights and tolerance of differences. But these best of circumstances still require an arbiter, and that arbiter, for the foreseeable future, is the political and legal structure developed in the nation–state or an entity (such as a region) that can duplicate a democratic nation–state, creating the same kind of loyalties and bonds among members that produce economic and social development.

So multiculturalism is in a new phase, and civic education is shifting more and more to localities, but the democratic nation–state is still crucial to the economic and social project, in terms of the political institutions the nation–state produced in the past and the new institutions it will create to sustain future development. The nation–state is also crucial to sustaining civic education and to defining multiculturalism in a way that sustains the choices people have in building their (multiple) identities and shapes the meaning of pluralism.

But the fact that the nation–state remains at the locus of the multicultural project does not guarantee that it will use its continued influence effectively in redefining multiculturalism. Democracies are hardly infallible. Those that have lasted longest have been able to find a common ground between private expression and collective needs among highly diverse interests. In the new global environment, this task will become increasingly difficult as these interests may diverge even further under the conflicting forces of economic competition, increasing economic inequality, greater individual isolation, and the global religious movements that limit rather than expand individual choice.

NOTES

1. Fred L. Block, *The Vampire State and Other Myths and Fallacies about the U.S. Economy* (New York: New Press, 1996), n. 14. Block has called this the "dictatorship of international financial markets." Quoted in Evans (1997): 67.

2. See Reich (1998) for a discussion of the contradiction for liberal democracies in not providing the opportunity to seek ethnic or religious identity and the contradiction for particular subcultures in a liberal democracy in not providing opportunities to youth to "reject" their parents' ethnic or religious identity. Reich argues for a more global, incorporative view of multiculturalism that expands choice and tolerance.

REFERENCES

Carnoy, M., and Levin, H.M. (1985). *Schooling and Work in the Democratic State.* Stanford, CA: Stanford University Press.

Castells, M. (1997). *The Power of Identity.* London: Blackwell.

Evans, P. (1997). Eclipse of the State? *World Politics* 50 (October): 62–87.

Giddens, A. (1991). *Modernity and Self-Identity: Self and Society in the Late Modern Age.* Cambridge: Polity Press.

Miller, D. (1995). *On Nationality.* Oxford: Oxford University Press.

Reich, R. (1998). *Liberalism, Multiculturalism, and Education.* Unpublished Ph.D. dissertation, School of Education, Stanford University.

CHAPTER 4

What Should Be the Foundations of Peace Education?

CHADWICK F. ALGER

We all approach peace education out of our own personal experience. If we are to empower our students to understand and cope with threats to peace across national and cultural borders, we must understand the challenges encountered by our colleagues in other nations and cultures and how they are coping with these challenges.

I have chosen as my title "The Foundations of Peace Education" because I want to present my conclusions about what I believe must be included in any peace curriculum. I am not saying that the elements that I shall present must be included in all peace courses. Nor must they be presented in the order in which I shall present them. Each peace course must be shaped in response to the needs of specific students who are living in specific social contexts. In our courses, we must begin dialogue with our students that is responsive to the circumstances that they are encountering in their daily lives. On the other hand, what I am saying is that students will not be fully prepared to work for peace unless at some point they encounter all of the elements that I will present.

PEACE IS POSSIBLE

First, I fervently believe that the bedrock of peace education is (1) attainment of belief in the possibility of peace everywhere! Each of us faces the challenge to this belief in different kinds of ways. As a political scientist specializing in international relations, I confront it continually because many in the mainstream of international relations scholarship tend to assume that war is inevitable. This is largely because political and diplomatic history tends to be a history of wars and to treat peace as those intervals between wars. In my own teaching, I prefer not to begin by strongly declaring my belief in the widespread possibility for peace. Rather, I believe that it inevitably develops out of a peace curriculum that offers three more fundamentals: (2) placing threats to peace in a comprehensive historical context, (3) careful usage of key concepts, such as peace, violence, and power, and (4) broad exposure to what we have learned in our pursuit of peace. In addition, I believe that it is very useful to offer students an opportunity to put into practice what they are learning by (5) developing their own peace strategies in a specific case of disruptive conflict and (6) comparing their strategies with those employed by fellow students working on other cases. This chapter will focus on these additional five points.

HISTORICAL CONTEXT

In acquiring the necessary historical context for approaching challenges to peace, we must ask three basic questions: (1) Where are we now? (2) Where are we coming from? (3) Where should we be heading? They are in response to Elise Boulding's plea that we should approach peace in the context of a 200-year present (E. Boulding, 1988: 3–15). Too often those immersed in a disruptive conflict are so totally immersed in their present sea of troubles that they have a very narrow comprehension of the present, are largely ignorant of where they are coming from, and have very limited vision of where they are headed.

The first question—Where are we now?—is very important because it challenges us to acquire a *comprehensive* view of the present. We are all aware that most media define news as "bad news." Thus, peace educators must help students to understand that they must search beyond the daily press, TV, and radio news in order to acquire full understanding of the present and thereby to obtain the ability to perceive potential for building preferred futures. Ada Aharoni has offered a poignant example:

We worked very hard preparing the "20 Years to the Bridge Symposium: Jewish and Arab/Palestinian Women for Peace in the Middle East." We . . . invited all the major media to cover it, so as to spread the climate and hope of peace to the wide public that are so fearful and discouraged nowadays, in both the Jewish and Arab/Palestinian sectors. However, no media came! The next day, one Palestinian was killed in Abu Tor, and one Israeli soldier was attacked near Jerusalem—all the media reported minutely and repeatedly on both incidents. 230 Jewish and Arab/ Palestinian women have an intensive Symposium with open, constructive discussions on how to pave the "Peace in the Middle East," and it is not considered "news," whereas when 1 or 2 men are killed or attacked it is major news! (Aharoni, 1998)

The second question—Where are we coming from?—challenges us to realize that we have a tendency to perceive the past through eyes focused on present conflicts thereby selecting items that illuminate the roots of present conflicts rather than those that draw attention to past events that reveal potential for peace building in the present. Thus many in Yugoslavia have quickly forgotten that peaceful communities in the past, composed of cooperating Serbs, Croats, and Bosnians, can offer foundations for future peace. From a much broader perspective, Kenneth Boulding has reminded us that historians have devoted a disproportionate amount of research and writing to war: "Therefore, in the interest of human survival, there is a desperate need to develop images of the relevant past . . . what might be called the 'other side' of history, in which peace is seen essentially as the norm and war is seen as an interruption in the long process of the development of knowledge and skill, especially in the management of conflict" (K. Boulding, 1989a: 463–464).

The third question—Where should we be heading?—presents most students with an almost insuperable challenge. Certainly the pursuit of peace requires a vision of a peaceful world. Nevertheless, although students are quick to respond when asked to describe elements of peacelessness in the present, most find it overwhelmingly difficult—virtually impossible—to offer a vision of a peaceful future. This is intertwined with their inability to believe in the possibility of peace. Hopefully students will begin to be liberated from this constraint by elements of the peace education curriculum that follow.

BASIC CONCEPTS

Careless use of concepts contributes much to confusion and failure in efforts to overcome extremely disruptive conflict. The relevant concepts are numerous, but here we shall illustrate this point with four very key concepts: peace, conflict, violence, and power. First, it is absolutely necessary to carefully explore the broad array of meanings of *peace*. Charles Chatfield has laid the foundations with three components: "a sense of juridical order associated with the Latin word pax; a sense of ethical social relationships conveyed by the Greek word eirene; and a sense of well-being that flows from spiritual wholeness, conveyed by the Hebrew shalom" (Chatfield, 1986: 11).

In more recent peace studies terminology, we begin with a dichotomy. There is "negative peace," or the absence of physical violence; and there is "positive peace," or the existence of economic and social justice. These abstractions, extended by examination of a number of dimensions of each, then prepare us for understanding why some people define peace as eliminating weapons of mass destruction and others define peace as conditions in which there is adequate food, clothing, shelter, and medical care. They help us to learn that people tend to define peace as removing that which injects the most severe fear, suffering, and pain into their daily life. Eventually understanding of the diversity of meanings of peace teaches us that the politics of building peace requires that those involved understand the definition of peace of their so-called enemies and begin building social structures that incorporate elements of more than one meaning of peace.

Second, we must carefully distinguish among different forms of *conflict*. Essential is the distinction between violent and nonviolent conflict. Although the difference is obvious, much confusion is caused by frequent tendencies to use *violence* and *conflict* as synonyms and then to propose strategies for "preventing conflict." Once, during a vigorous debate in the UN General Assembly, a journalist sitting next to me declared: "There they go again, this is supposed to be the *United* Nations, but they are fighting again." He failed to understand the triumph that had been achieved by transforming that conflict from the battlefield to a parliamentary debate. Conflict is essential for peace building. It is employed in political campaigns, legislative debates, and diplomatic negotiations. Indeed, Galtung's manual *Conflict Transformation by Peaceful Means* declares that conflict is both a destroyer and creator, "as potentially dangerous both now and in the future because of the violence, but as a golden opportunity to create something new" (Galtung, 1997: 4).

Third, coping with confusion in the usage of the term *conflict* is inevitably intertwined with usage of the concepts *violence* and *nonviolence*. Many equate nonviolence with a kind of pacifism that avoids conflict and accepts the status quo, because they do not yet understand the role of nonviolent action in peace building. At the same time, in more affluent cultures there is resistance to employment of the term *structural violence* to identify human suffering and slow loss of life that is caused by economic and social structures. But the term is vitally useful in facilitating dialogue between those fearing quick death (direct violence) and those fearing slow death (structural violence). Of course, would-be peace builders confront puzzling challenges in applying these concepts. One puzzle is, How far can nonviolent action go without becoming structural violence? For example, some of those employing nonviolent action against abortion clinics in the United States can be perceived as perpetrating structural violence against those women who believe that personal choice is their right.

Fourth, it is vital that peace education examine the various dimensions of the concept *power*. There is a tendency to equate power with force, although, after careful thought, we all know differently. Here Kenneth Boulding is again extremely helpful in his volume *Three Faces of Power* (1989b). He summarizes a far-ranging examination of kinds of power into three dimensions: (1) threat power, the power to destroy, (2) economic power, the power to produce and exchange, and (3) integrative power, the power to create such relations as love, respect, friendship, and legitimacy. His analysis causes us to ponder how selective history, and enduring social structures created for coping with perceived external threats, encourage us to depend on threat power. At the same time, he makes us aware of how neglectful we have been in recognizing the integrative dimension of power in peace studies. Certainly the European Community is now dramatically illustrating the integrative dimension of power. It causes us to ask: Was the fear generated by two world wars necessary for the creation of the Community? Why was the integrative power illustrated by the Hague Conferences of 1899 and 1907 not more fully employed?

WHAT HAVE WE LEARNED? THE EMERGING TOOL CHEST

In peace education it is essential that we emphasize how much we have learned about peace building. Despite the fact that we still have much to learn, the basic problem is that most of the time we are not applying in practice what we already know. It is useful to present what we have learned in the context of the practice out of which it has emerged. This inevitably means that each of us will select that practice emerging out of those human activities that are the subject of our personal experiences, research, and teaching. In my teaching, I focus on peace learning that has emerged out of experiences in the United Nations and its predecessor, the League of Nations (Alger, 1996b, 1999).

My peace-building tool chest has ever more drawers, as a result of the impact of the same technological changes on relations between peoples. My most recent version has six drawers, with a total of 24 compartments (see Figure 4.1). I will present a very quick overview of these tools in the order of their historical emergence, indicating how each evolved out of experience with earlier ones (see Figure 4.2).

The first drawer, *nineteenth-Century*, has two tools. (1) *Diplomacy* is a significant human achievement that deserves much credit for the fact that most states have peaceful relations with most other states most of the time. The system of embassies that each country has in the capitals of many other countries has developed over many centuries. Formerly consisting primarily of career diplomats representing their Foreign Ministry, now many embassies include representatives of other government departments responsible for health, labor, education, trade, environment, and so forth.

Although we have emphasized that the interstate diplomatic system preserves the peace most of the time, nevertheless disputes do arise and create situations in which states fear aggression by others. In such cases

Figure 4.1
Peace Builder's Tool Chest

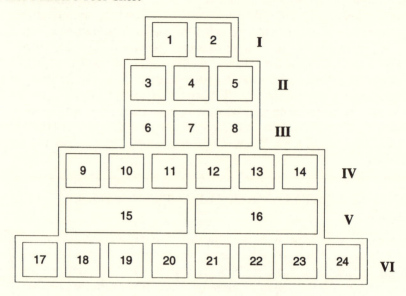

(2) *Balance of Power* may be used to deter aggression. In the sense in which we are using the term, employment of balance of power means that a state attempts to acquire sufficient military and related capacity to deter aggression or attempts to deter aggression by making alliances with other states. When balance of power is employed as a deterrent, it may help to deter aggression. On the other hand, reciprocal application of balance of power has frequently led to deadly arms races.

The second drawer, *League of Nations Covenant*, adds three more tools. (3) *Collective Security*, devised to overcome the weaknesses of balance of power as a deterrent to aggression, obligated all who were members of the League to "undertake to respect and preserve as against external aggression the territorial integrity and existing political independence of all Members of the League." Those who advocated collective security believed that the pledge of *all* to resist aggression by *any* member would be such an overwhelming deterrent that none would have reasonable ground for fearing aggression. But the obvious common sense of collective security in the abstract ignores the fact that *all* may not be able or willing to resist aggression by *any* other member.

(4) *Peaceful Settlement* was intended to prevent the outbreak of violence in those instances when routine diplomacy fails to do so. In cases where a dispute may "lead to a rupture" the Covenant required states to "submit the matter either to arbitration or judicial settlement or to inquiry by the [League] Council." In other words, members involved in a dispute

Figure 4.2
The Emergence of Peace Tools

	Nineteenth Century	1919 League of Nations Covenant	1945 UN Charter	1950–1989 UN Practice	1990– UN Practice	NGOs/Peoples Movements
NEGATIVE PEACE	Diplomacy (1) Balance of Power (2)	Collective Security (3) Peaceful Settlement (4) Disarmament/Arms Control (5)	Collective Security Peaceful Settlement Disarmament/Arms Control	Collective Security Peacekeeping (9) Peaceful Settlement Disarmament/Arms Control	Collective Security Peacekeeping Peaceful Settlement Disarmament/Arms Control Humanitarian Intervention (15) Preventive Diplomacy (16)	Track II Diplomacy (17) Conversion (18) Defensive Defense (19)
	I	II				
POSITIVE PEACE			Functionalism (6) Self-Determination (7) Human Rights (8)	Functionalism Self-Determination Human Rights Economic Development (10) Economic Equity (NIEO) (11) Communications Equity (12) Ecological Balance (13) Governance for the Commons (14)	Functionalism Self-Determination Human Rights Economic Development Economic Equity (NIEO) Communications Equity Ecological Balance Governance for the Commons	Nonviolence (20) Citizen Defense (21) Self-Reliance (22) Feminist Perspective (23) Peace Education (24)
			III	IV	V	VI

NGOs = Nongovernmental organizations; NIEO = New International Economic Order.

agree to involve certain "third parties" when they alone cannot control escalating hostility. In employing third parties, states are drawing on human experience in a variety of other contexts: labor-management disputes, disputes between buyers and sellers, marital disputes, and so on.

(5) *Disarmament/Arms Control* responded to those who believed that arms races had contributed to the outbreak of World War I and believed that elimination, or at least reduction, of arms would enhance chances for peace. This was an effort to codify disarmament and arms control proposals that had been advanced in earlier times. Although Covenant provisions for disarmament/arms control never fulfilled the aspirations of advocates, they did facilitate the negotiation of numerous arms control measures in the 1930s. These provided valuable experience, and also a great deal of skepticism, for those who would again face similar circumstances after World War II.

League experience with these three negative peace tools (stopping the violence) revealed a desperate need for positive peace tools (building peaceful social structures). Building on important League experience, the *UN Charter*, drawer three, provided three additional tools, in addition to continuation of the three tools in drawer two. (6) *Functionalism* encourages states to cooperate in solving common economic and social problems that might disrupt normal relationships and even lead to violence. Drafters of the Charter had in mind examples such as worldwide depression in the 1930s and the inability of states to collaborate in coping with this disaster. The depression led to strikes, extreme social unrest, and violence in many countries and significantly contributed to the development of totalitarian governments and aggression in some cases. Emphasis on economic and social cooperation in the Charter is signified by the creation of the Economic and Social Council (ECOSOC) alongside the Security Council (responsible for collective security), which had been the only council in the League. ECOSOC was created "with a view to the creation of conditions of stability and well-being which are necessary for peaceful and friendly relations among nations." Its mission includes the achievement of higher standards of living, full employment, solutions of international economic, social, health, and related problems, and international cultural and educational cooperation. At the same time, ECOSOC has the responsibility of coordinating the activities of some 30 agencies in the UN system with responsibility for health, labor, education, development, environment, population, trade, and a number of other global problems.

Following League of Nation practice, some colonies of defeated colonial powers became UN Trusteeships. But (7) *Self-Determination* was dramatically extended in the UN Charter by inclusion of Chapter XI, a "Declaration Regarding Non-Self-Governing Territories," which covered the many overseas colonies not under trusteeship. This Declaration asserts that those administrating colonies are obligated "to develop self-government . . . and to assist them in the progressive development of their free political institutions." Eventually, this Declaration provided the foundation for prodding the overseas colonial powers to begin relinquishing control of their colonies. This led to a strengthened Declaration by the General Assembly in 1960: "Declaration on the Granting of Independence to Colonial Countries and Peoples." Both the Trusteeship Council and the General Assembly played a very significant role in the largely peaceful dismantlement of overseas empires. In this respect, self-determination has proven to be a very useful peace tool. This remarkable transformation of the interstate system more than doubled the number of independent states and the number of UN members. Presently the world confronts a new generation of self-determination demands by peoples in multination states (as in Yugoslavia) and in multistate nations (e.g., the Kurds). Unfortunately, there has been as yet no effort to draw on past experience in developing multilateral institutions for coping with a new era of self-determination demands.

(8) *Human Rights* are mentioned seven times in the Charter, including the second sentence of the Preamble, which announces determination "to reaffirm faith in fundamental human rights, in the dignity and worth of the human person, in the equal rights of men and women and of nations large and small." As in the case of economic and social cooperation, the Charter states that human rights shall be promoted in order to "create conditions and well-being which are necessary for peaceful and friendly relations among nations." Building on the brief references to human rights in the Charter, the UN General Assembly soon produced the Universal Declaration on Human Rights in 1947, which is now widely accepted as part of international common law and has even been applied by domestic courts in a number of states. In order to strengthen the legal status of the Declaration, its principles were in 1966 put in treaty form by the General Assembly as the International Covenant on Civil and Political Rights and the International Covenant on Economic, Social and Cultural Rights. In addition, an array of more specialized treaties have been developed on genocide, racial discrimination, women's rights, children's rights, forced labor, cruel and inhumane punishment, rights of refugees, and other dimensions of human rights. All of these can be applied toward the end of preventing the creation of unacceptable conditions of human depravity that may lead to severe unrest and even violence.

The fourth drawer, *UN Practice (1950–1959)*, adds six tools. (9) *Peacekeeping* is not explicitly provided for by the UN Charter but was invented out of challenges confronted in the UN "laboratory." In its simplest form, it essentially involves a cease-fire, followed by creation of a demilitarized corridor on each side of a truce line. This neutral corridor is patrolled by a UN peacekeeping force, protected by the UN flag and small arms. The end of the Cold War has permitted rapid expansion of the number of peacekeeping forces, to Cambodia, the former Yugoslavia, the Iraq-Kuwait border, Somalia, and other places. In some instances, as in Somalia and the former Yugoslavia, UN forces have been employed without first acquiring a cease-fire and in situations where there is no clear authority that could grant permission for entry of the UN force. These efforts tend to be referred to as "peace enforcement," that is, limited use of arms toward the end of restoring peace. Whether "peace enforcement" will become a useful peace tool is still much in doubt because even limited use of violence toward the end of "restoring peace" may quickly escalate into widespread violence.

Prodded by the growing divide between the rich and the poor in the United Nations, three peace tools developed out of UN practice were largely a product of growing insight on the relevance of economic conditions and relationships for peace. (10) *Economic Development* became a growing policy concern both within the United Nations and outside. The basic idea was that the rich-poor gap could be diminished if the rich countries provided development aid to the poor countries so that they could "take off" and become developed. Many people would argue that both bilateral and multilateral economic development programs have often contributed to peace by diminishing poverty. But overall they did not diminish the rich-poor gap in the world. This led to a "Third World" charge that the international economic structure was preventing their development. Thus, they demanded (11) *International Economic Equity (NIEO)*, often referred to as a New International Economic Order. This included demands for stabilization of commodity prices, pegging the price of Third World commodities to those of manufactured products bought from industrialized countries, access to technology useful in development, and international regulation of multinational corporations. Failure of the Third World to obtain response to these demands contributed to frustration that led to demands for (12) *International Communications Equity*, or a New International Information and Communications Order. After World War II, "free flow of communication" had been emphasized as a prerequisite for peace. But in the 1970s Third World countries became increasingly concerned about the one-way international flow of news, radio and TV broadcasts, films, books, and magazines. Out of this dissatisfaction came demands for "free and balanced flow of communication" that were largely made in UNESCO (United Nation Educational, Scientific, and Cultural Organization) meetings. These demands too have acquired slight response, although the reliable mutual knowledge—across cultures and nations—that is encouraged by balanced flow could contribute to peace in all parts of the world.

The rapidly growing impact of new technologies on the environment and the commons (oceans, space, and Antarctica) has added new dimensions to peace. (13) *Ecological Balance* became a widely recognized problem in world relations as a result of the UN Environment Conference held in Stockholm in 1972. Whereas in 1972 very few tended to see ecological balance as a dimension of peace, this perspective is now widely shared. (14) *Governance for the Commons* has been most dramatically moved forward by the United Nations Law of the Sea Treaty, completed after 10 years of negotiations, which has established an International Sea Bed Authority with its own Assembly, Council, and Secretariat, as well as an International Tribunal for the Law of the Sea.

The fifth drawer, *UN Practice (1990–   )*, adds two more negative peace tools that have gained prominence after the Cold War as a result of growth in multilateral peace efforts. They could certainly be employed as positive peace tools, but they have tended to be employed in reaction to violence and threats of imminent violence, rather than in long-term peace building. (15) *Humanitarian Intervention* occurs within the borders of states without their explicit consent, responding to egregious violations of human rights and also to prevent escalation of a domestic dispute that could jeopardize the security of other states. (16) *Preventive Diplomacy* is defined by former Secretary General Boutros-Ghali as "action to prevent disputes from arising between parties, to prevent existing disputes from escalating into conflicts and to limit the spread of the latter when they occur." For Boutros-Ghali preventive diplomacy requires three elements: measures to create confidence, early warning based on information gathering, and informal or formal fact-finding. "It may also involve preventive deployment and, in some situations, demilitarized zones" (1995: 46–51).

The sixth drawer, *Nongovernmental Organizations (NGOs) and Peoples Movements*, reflects the increasing importance of NGOs and peoples movements, or what we increasingly refer to as "civil society" in peace building. Of course, these movements have from time to time been advocates of all peace tools, certainly including disarmament/arms control, human rights, and ecological balance. But we believe that they have been primarily instrumental in developing eight peace tools. The first, (17) *Track II Diplomacy*, addresses the limitations of diplomacy and peaceful settlement by recognizing that stalled negotiations, or those broken off by governmental representatives, may be revived by initiatives outside of government. Consisting at least in part of people outside of government, this approach offers a "second track" that sometimes may include alternative representatives of governments, often at a lower level.

The next four tools aim at limiting the development and deployment of arms. (18) *Conversion* from military to civilian production undercuts arguments that military production provides jobs—for factory workers, engineers, and researchers—by demonstrating that more jobs could be created by providing for housing, home appliances, and other domestic needs. (19) *Defensive Defense* argues for defense that employs weapons that are essentially defensive in nature such as short-range mechanized forces and interception aircraft, thereby attempting to halt the tendency to acquire bigger and bigger weapons with ever more distant reach. (20) *Nonviolence* is used by social movements in energetic pursuit of social change, while avoiding the use of arms and thereby diminishing the need for armed police and military forces employed for internal security. (21) *Citizen Defense* is closely related to nonviolence employed for social change, but this tool employs nonviolent techniques for national defense. It goes one step further than defensive defense by also eliminating defensive weapons. Citizen defense relies on the deterrence of large-scale, well-publicized organization and planning for massive refusal to cooperate with any invader and to deprive them of the basic needs and services required by an occupying army (Sharp, 1985).

The next two peace tools largely focus on creating economic and social aspects of a peaceful society from the grassroots. (22) *Self-Reliance* emerged as a peace tool in the context of dialogue focused primarily on the economic dimensions of peace that evolved from functionalism to economic development to international economic equity. It asserts that development should develop individual human beings, not things, and that this kind of development requires that people have the capacity to seek fulfillment through self-reliance, thereby avoiding dependency. (23) The *Feminist Perspective* is particularly useful in shedding light on the degree to which values associated with militarism and military organizations permeate societies and how that came to be. At the same time, the feminist perspective provides a vision of alternative kinds of societies, by questioning the inevitability of violence as a tool in the pursuit of peace and security. It illuminates the sources of the "violence habit" and offers visions of alternative ways for solving human problems (Reardon, 1990).

(24) *Peace Education* is the last tool to be presented because it comprises all that has gone before. Indeed, the successful employment of all that we have learned about peace building in the twentieth century is dependent on peace education. It makes possible the placing of peace issues on the agenda of the vast array of disciplines and professions that have something to contribute to the pursuit of peace. Peace education should also be placed more prominently on the agendas of the thousands of organizations in civil society that are increasingly involved in peace-building movements. To those of us involved in peace education in schools and universities, the entire sixth drawer (NGOs/Peoples Movements) is particularly relevant because it suggests opportunities for all of our students to participate in peace building and thereby to obtain

the unparalleled kind of learning that comes out of thoughtful practice (Alger, 1995, 1996a).

PUTTING THE PIECES TOGETHER: DEVELOPING PEACE STRATEGIES AND PEACE EDUCATION

After we have acquired the necessary broad historical context, have attained reasonably precise usage of concepts, and have a well-stocked tool chest, we are much more inclined to believe that peace is possible. At this point we are prepared to put all of the pieces together, that is, to apply what we have learned in an arena of intense peacelessness. Thus in a peace studies seminar, participants might be asked to choose one of the present widely reported cases as a laboratory—for example, Cameroon, Liberia, Yugoslavia, Colombia—so that there is likely to be much material readily available. Then turn back the clock 30 years. Thus, it is now 1973. We know what has happened in 2003, and it is the student's challenge to develop a peace strategy, in 5-year increments, that would have made 2003 more peaceful than it now is.

The first step in putting the pieces together into a peace-building strategy is to create what could be called an "attainable vision" of what might have been achieved by 2003. This challenging task requires a dialogue among (1) a vision of peace in 2003, (2) conditions in 1973, and (3) relevant earlier history. It is very important to emphasize that this effort to place the case being examined in historical context involves not only a search for the roots of present peacelessness. It also demands an effort to discover past dimensions of peace whose potential failed to be exploited and for insight on why this was so. The effort to construct an attainable vision inevitably requires an examination of how peace is defined in different sectors of involved societies. An attainable vision will be the product of a dialogue among these different definitions of peace, with a result that is responsive to all involved in a specific case of disruptive conflict.

Once an attainable vision has been developed, it is time to open up the tool chest. Of course, this assumes that students have already learned the nature of each tool and have some knowledge of how it has been employed in the past and of appropriate and inappropriate uses. Important here is to overcome the tendency of many people to approach a peace-building problem with a propensity to believe that their favorite tool will solve all problems Each tool must be selected only after careful analysis of the situation in which it is to be applied and after knowledge about when it might be useful and when it might make things worse. For example, sometimes balance of power (in military terms) can restrain aggressors. On the other hand, it can lead to arms races and thereby undermine efforts to achieve peace. Students could be urged to approach their tool box with an assumption that *all* tools are useful under some conditions and that *all* tools can occasionally make things worse. They are certainly not required to use all tools, but at the end of their paper, they are required to explain why any tool not employed was left out of their strategy.

Now that the tool box is open, we face the challenge of deciding what should be done first, that is, what will our peace strategy be for the 1973 to 1978 period? Should we begin to work for disarmament now? Or will this be easier later, after greater economic equity among the contending parties has been achieved? Will political conditions make it possible to begin moving now toward greater economic equity, or will it first be necessary to develop a people's movement dedicated to economic equity? Will this be possible before a people's movement is able to achieve greater civil and political rights that would make an economic equity movement possible? Given the fact that these economic and social changes could take a decade or more, should we simultaneously make at least modest efforts toward some form of arms control?

These few examples make it quite clear that deciding where to begin with a 30-year peace strategy is almost as difficult as developing an attainable vision. Nevertheless, as students are challenged to decide which tool should be used first, and which tools should be used in combination, they acquire a deeper understanding of each tool. And once the first stage strategy has been developed, it is somewhat easier to follow on with the other 5-year increments that lead up to 2003. On the other hand, both students and professor are continually challenged in assessing how long it will take for a specific tool to bring about desired changes. At the same time, there is an inevitable continuing dialogue between efforts to apply peace tools and growing knowledge about the actual state of affairs in 1973 and 2003, as well as between efforts to apply the tools and the definition of an attainable vision. This inevitable fluidity in historical facts, a future vision, and peace strategies offers students deeper understanding of the challenges faced by peace builders. But students face a deadline that is in some respects sterner than that confronted by "real" peace builders: Academic deadlines require that they bring their search to an end.

COMPARATIVE EVALUATION OF PEACE-BUILDING STRATEGIES

In the final meetings of the seminar, there are vitally important opportunities for comparison of the cases. First we ask: What were the root causes of disruptive conflict in each case? In discussion we attempt to make a list of which root causes were very significant and which of lesser significance. In those cases where similar root causes were identified, but different tools were employed, an opportunity is offered for comparative evaluation of different strategies. For example, in two cases where ethnic conflict was a root cause of intensive conflict, why was greater self-determination offered in one case but greater functional economic cooperation across ethnic divisions advocated in another case?

Second, based on a report from each student, we make a table indicating which tools were employed and in which stage of the peace strategy they were introduced. Here we are likely to find that some students tend to see stronger peoples movements with peace-building goals as essential in the first stage of peace building, whereas others place greater emphasis on existing political authorities. Discussion tends to illuminate whether the difference is a result of different conditions in the case being examined or a result of a student's assumptions about the value of people's movements that is independent of factors in the case being examined. This tends to provoke a useful challenge that requires that the person confident in the peace-building capacity of peoples movements justify his or her choice of this tool in this specific case.

CONCLUSION: THE CHALLENGES FOR PEACE EDUCATORS

We began by emphasizing that "the bedrock of peace education" is attainment of the belief that peace is possible everywhere, a belief that is facilitated by the capacity to perceive the widespread existence of peace in the world today. We then stressed the importance of approaching peace in a historical context that links present conditions to a preferred vision of the future and a relevant historical context that does not neglect past conditions of peace. Bringing to bear a broad historical context demonstrates that we have learned a great deal about building peace in this century, as exemplified by the growing array of peace tools that have emerged out of League of Nations and United Nations experience. Different peace educators could, of course, develop a somewhat different array of peace tools out of other contexts. Our choice is based largely on our belief in the value of presenting emerging peace tools as evidence of a historical learning process that is global in scope.

The challenge for peace educators is not only to enable students to acquire knowledge about the growing array of peace tools but also to facilitate the development of student competence in applying them. We concluded with a description of the strategy that we use in challenging students to acquire competence in employing available peace tools by developing a strategy for coping with an exceedingly disruptive conflict. Our 30-year peace-building exercise illuminates our belief that peace education must emphasize the importance of long-term peace building that illuminates the broad array of political, economic, social, and cultural factors that contribute to peace. At the same time, this broad approach reveals to students how all citizens, no matter what their profession or station in life, can play a role in peace building in their everyday life.

REFERENCES

Aharoni, A. (1998). Media and Peace Symposiums. *Internet Message to International Peace Research Association*, December 16. For this and other relevant citations see her home page at http://tx.technion.ac.il/~ada/home.html.

Alger, C. (1995). Building Peace: A Global Learning Process. In M.M. Merryfield and R.C. Remy (Eds.), *Teaching About International Conflict and Peace* (pp. 127–162). Albany: State University of New York Press.

Alger, C. (1996a). Adult Education for Peacebuilding: A Challenge to Peace Research and Peace Education. In R.J. Burns and R. Aspeslagh (Eds.), *Three Decades of Peace Education around the World: An Anthology* (pp. 263–272). New York: Garland.

Alger, C. (1996b), The Emerging Tool Chest for Peace Builders. *International Journal of Peace Studies* 1(2): 21–45.

Alger, C.F. (1999). The Expanding Tool Chest for Peacebuilders. In H.-W. Jeong (Ed.), *The New Agenda for Peace Research* (pp. 13–44). Aldershot, UK: Ashgate.

Boulding, E. (1988). *Building a Global Civil Culture: Education for an Interdependent World*. New York: Teacher's College Press.

Boulding, K. (1989a). A Proposal for a Research Program in the History of Peace. *Peace and Change* 14(4): 461–469.

Boulding, K. (1989b). *Three Faces of Power*. Newbury Park, CA: Sage, Publications.

Boutros-Ghali, B. (1995). *An Agenda for Peace* (2nd ed.). New York: United Nations Department of Public Information.

Chatfield, C. (1986). Concepts of Peace in History. *Peace and Change* 11(2): 11–21.

Galtung, J. (1996). *Peace by Peaceful Means: Peace and Conflict, Development and Civilization*. Thousand Oaks, CA: Sage Publications.

Galtung, J. (1997). *Conflict Transformation by Peaceful Means (the Transcend Method)*. Geneva: UN Disaster Management Training Programme.

Reardon, B. (1990). Feminist Concepts of Peace and Security. In P. Smoker, R. Davies, and B. Muske (Eds.), *A Reader in Peace Studies* (pp. 136–143). New York: Pergamon Press.

Sharp, G. (1985). *National Security through Civilian-Backed Defense*. Omaha, NE: Association for Transarmament Studies.

CHAPTER 5

Education for Peace: Concepts, Contexts, and Challenges

LENNART VRIENS

PEACE EDUCATION AS AN OPTIMISTIC IDEA

Peace education is based on the assumption that peace can be learned. If two centuries of extreme nationalism were able to teach the peoples of Europe to accept war as a strategy for political ends, it should also be possible to teach people alternative orientations. This idea arose at the time of the Enlightenment. The protagonists of this message of progress were convinced that education could contribute to a better future for all people on earth. They felt that if people were equipped with better insight into the real nature of old problems and were ready to use their knowledge to bring about a better and more peaceful world, they should be able to change a dark and violent world into a peaceful, enlightened, prosperous, and democratic world. This optimistic idea about the positive possibilities of education was one of the incentives for educational reform. Educational reformers like Leo Tolstoy, Ellen Key, Maria Montessori, Kees Boeke, and others stated that common education was responsible for human aggression and that their alternative ideas should be able to overcome this problem. The title of one of Montessori's most famous books, *Door het Kind naar een Nieuwe Wereld* (Through the Child toward a New World), illustrates this optimistic overestimation of the potential of education.

This view received much criticism. Practical educators indicated that it was impossible to exercise sufficient control over the various aspects of education and pointed out that it was absurd to think children could be programmed into peaceful people. Scientists who investigated human aggression and violence from other points of view were inclined to understand these phenomena as an inevitable part of human nature. Pedagogical theorists stressed the right of every child to choose his own position in life, including political responsibilities, and warned against the danger of indoctrination, which underlies these naive "mechanistic" theories of education. Furthermore, peace education was often criticized for its political notions. Especially in the 1980s, peace education was accused of pacifistic naivety, of overt or covert communism, and of being morally insane. And last but not least, the postmodern debate of the 1980s marked the end of the optimism of the Enlightenment as the basis for Western culture (Vriens, 1994, 1996).

As a consequence, most peace educators in our decade have a more modest notion of the possibilities to bring about peace by education. Peace education cannot make peace, nor is it able to guarantee that people become peace loving. But it can offer an important contribution to the development of a "culture of peace," which justifies and supports policies aimed at peace. This type of peace education has two major tasks. It should enable young people to form an opinion about peace issues by confronting them with information and arguments. Second, it should invite and challenge them to accept responsibility for the preservation of our world and the realization of a humane future.

A MODEST CONCEPT OF PEACE EDUCATION

Peace education resembles other forms of problem-oriented education, such as development education, environment education, and human rights education, in that it combines personal and political goals. This type of education requires careful justification. Peace education may be legitimized by pointing out its importance for the lives of our children. The personal goals of the learning process, that is, contributing to the development of attitudes and the acquisition of knowledge and skills, rather speak for themselves, but the "political" goals are not so self-evident. The latter have to be translated into pedagogical goals if they are to be justified in terms of the importance for the lives of children. Three questions should be answered. First, we should find out whether a specific peace issue manifests itself in the lives of children. If not, the second question is whether the peace issue can be incorporated in children's lives. And finally we must ask ourselves if this orientation is important for the development of the child.

But the importance of peace education for the lives of our children is not its only legitimation. Peace education may also change our culture of violence into a culture of peace and justice.

A consequence of this double goal is that peace education has both a personal and a structural dimension. The personal dimension includes providing people with knowledge and skills for the development of both their involvement in the peace problem and their acceptance of responsibilities in their individual circumstances. The structural level emphasizes the duty to criticize political systems, including their potential violence or their tendency to resort to violence, and to scrutinize the justifications politicians put forward and their responsibilities to change them. In this continuous process of "alternating between the person and the structures" (Vriens and Aspeslagh, 1985), peace education avoids the one-sidedness of pure individualism as well as that of a purely societal orientation.

This type of peace education is primarily legitimated as a form of education. Education is defined here as helping children to become adults, which means autonomous participants in social and cultural life. Peace education distinguishes itself from other educational themes by its explicit orientation on a nonviolent solution of conflict, the challenge of a humane future, and its articulation in terms of responsibilities. Just as common education is justified by the notion that it can help children to become responsible adults, peace education focuses on the notion that children can be taught to understand peace and will be able to integrate it as a challenge into their personal lives.

PEACE AS A MULTILEVEL AND MULTICULTURAL PROBLEM

The translation of peace into an educational task poses a number of problems. For one thing, we should realize that although *peace* is used freely in everyday language, it is a rather difficult concept to define. Peace is something like a container concept; it is used to describe conflicts on a global political level, or it is used in the description of problems in big and small groups, and it also refers to personal inner experiences. Most scientists doubt if all these conflicts have anything to do with each other. For instance, peace researchers stress that wars should not merely be viewed as an accumulation of small conflicts or aggressive acts. On the other hand, it is difficult to understand the structural idea of wars without taking the people into account who invent the strategies and make the decisions. It will also be clear that peace and war manifest themselves in different situations.

In the 1970s and the 1980s peace research, peace action, and to a certain extent, peace education were strongly influenced by the threat of nuclear war. As a result of the Second Cold War, every war was judged in terms of its consequences for the big conflict between the North Atlantic Treaty Organization (NATO) and the Warsaw Pact. Conflicts that were of little importance for the balance of power were forgotten or adopted by one of the two parties who tried to strengthen their position. Such an adoption by West or East seldom resolved conflicts; rather, it created new violence and sorrow for the local populations.

In our decade, after the fall of the Berlin Wall, we have to develop peace education in an ambiguous world situation. On the one hand, the world is split up by many bloody local conflicts, mostly within states, between often well-armed small groups whose members do not hesitate to recruit children and youngsters to fight for them. On the other hand, there is a tendency toward the so-called global village, in which global and regional international organizations like the United Nations Organization, the International Court of Justice, and the European Union become increasingly important. Although most nation–states are still rather reluctant to give up their political autonomy, the moral authority of these global organizations is growing stronger, which is justified by the 1948 Universal Declaration of Human Rights.

Without going into the specifics of the relations and dependencies between individual people, social institutions, and political structures, I think it can be helpful to realize that peace can be understood from several points of view. Peace can be interpreted in terms of values, norms, knowledge, and skills, which are to be specified in different cultural and current contexts. In the realm of knowledge and skills, there are a lot of differences between the microlevel of personal, social, and cultural life and the macrolevel of global problems and different cultures. In the realm of values and norms, I think that personal peace, peace in the group, and peace as a political issue are intimately connected, especially when we link up with the concept of positive peace. In this concept, peace is defined as more than the absence of war, which is a description in negative terms. Peace is looked upon as an accepted global order of legal and social justice, based on the acceptance of human rights and "democratic" values such as respect for life, tolerance, social justice, mutual trust, cooperation, and solidarity. These values are important not only for global relations but also for cultural autonomy and diversity in meso-situations and personal and social life at the microlevel.

PEACE EDUCATION IN VARIOUS CULTURAL CONTEXTS

Although peace education is based on the idea of peace for all people in the world, it has to be tuned to different situations. It has to be adapted to problems and conflicts connected to cultural and political backgrounds. This means that peace educators must have a dialectic attitude. They have to combine a global value orientation with local problem involvement in specific historical circumstances. I will give some examples to illustrate this idea from a general point of view. After World War II, in the 1950s peace education in the Netherlands manifested itself mainly as education for international understanding; during the 1960s, it focused on political problems of war and peace from different points of view; in the 1970s, the focus shifted to the teaching of conflict resolution and nonviolence; in the 1980s, it centered around education against nuclear armament and the Cold War; and finally in the 1990s, it primarily focused on teaching people to overcome prejudices, xenophobia, and violence. In this last period the theme of positive peace education was often linked with the commemoration of World War II, which was used to reflect on fundamental human rights, the nature of freedom and responsibility, and the promotion of friendship between people from different ethnic and cultural backgrounds in our own country. At this moment the problem of violence in the media and violent behavior of youngsters in the public domain receives quite a lot of attention. This is an intriguing problem, but there is only one peace education project that focuses explicitly on this topic (Deboutte, 1997).

In the Dutch situation, peace education deals with children who have had no real war experiences. Its main task is to help children to form an opinion about problems of war and peace and to become alert to opportunities to bring about a culture of peace and solidarity in our country, which in turn will contribute to a more peaceful world. But in countries involved in war or in countries where people are suffering from recent war trauma, peace education will have other priorities. It will take part in helping to overcome the damaging effects of violence on children. This is a necessary condition for finding a new positive outlook on life. Consequently, it has to deal with the restoration of normal child life, including education. It has to make space for the necessary mourning about what is lost, and it must inform about what really happened. It also has to help the youngsters to acquire new self-respect, and if possible, it must prepare for reconciliation. In such circumstances, peace education can be interpreted as a necessary "natural therapy" for the disturbance of basic life conditions and values. It will be clear that some traumatized children will need professional help.

In countries like Israel, societies not actually involved in a war but under permanent political tension, peace education could focus on contributing to overcoming enmity between the parties involved in the conflict and to the opportunities to live together in peace. It can offer an outlook on a humane future for all, a future in which conflicts can be seen as a shared challenge that can be resolved in a nonviolent way.

Finally, in developing countries, peace education will have to deal with problems of poverty, hunger, and other inhumane situations that can be characterized as structurally violent. Evidently, these problems cannot be isolated from other fundamental human rights such as the rights of women, the rights of the child, and the rights of cultural minorities, which are all too often violated.

This short and inevitably superficial overview of peace education in several cultural and political contexts illustrates that the various views on peace education will not always be compatible. Peace is a multilevel and multicultural phenomenon, and so is peace education. Yet it is important for peace educators to exchange views and to learn from each other's. If we share experiences, our efforts are more likely to contribute to a global peace culture in which the most important peace values and norms are shared and can be a challenge for every person to shape his own life.

PEACE EDUCATION: CONTENT AND FORM

The distinction between the realm of values and norms, on the one hand, and the realm of knowledge and skills, on the other, has consequences for the theory and practice of peace education in general. It offers opportunities for a better understanding of the content of peace education, of *what* should be learned and of its form, of *how things* should be learned.

With regard to the content of peace education, it is important to realize that the ability to judge peace issues can only be developed if knowledge and skills are structured and directed by values and norms. Peace is a normative concept, so peace knowledge is essentially value bound. Without values, peace is meaningless and cannot legitimate human action.

On the other hand, the so-called peace values of human rights and democracy, such as nonviolence, respect for life, tolerance, trust, solidarity, and cooperation, are empty words without knowledge of the problems at hand. We might be dealing with major global conflicts like wars or unjust trade structures, with political dilemmas like armament or development of a peaceful economy, or with social phenomena like group aggression, (religious) prejudices, or cultural violence, but it may also refer to a person's inner life, for example, peace spirituality or building up an attitude of nonviolence. Knowledge at all these levels can enhance people's capacities to understand what is really going on in the world and in their minds. It develops insight into the problems, it offers tools to think and to justify choices, it expands orientations and diversifies arguments, and it contributes to creativity. But values and norms must become part of a person's individual experience. Therefore, their knowledge must be confronted with the practice of daily life. By applying this knowledge to actual life, people develop skills and meet norms that regulate and limit their responsibilities.

The *form* of peace education is possibly even more important than its content. According to Johan Galtung (1973) the form of peace education has its own values and norms. The first message of all education—and peace education can hardly escape this law—is a message of structural violence that is defined as a one-sided form of communication, express-ing unequal relationships between student and teacher, teacher and sys-tem, and so on. Indirectly pupils are given to understand that they are inferior to the educator because they do not possess the same amount of knowledge and still have a lot to learn. This is a message of power and dependency that obstructs their emancipation and prevents them from becoming self-confident individuals. In societies with a variety of cul-tures and an educational system controlled by the dominant culture, the inequality is even worse. In his famous book *Pedagogy of the Oppressed*, Paulo Freire (1972) analyzed and illustrated the mechanisms of cultural imperialism in Western education in the so-called Third World.

I will not discuss these ideas in detail. Suffice it to say that Galtung and Freire opened our eyes to the violent potential of education. But I also want to stress that unequal division of power in the pedagogical relationship is not necessarily violent. Parents and teachers often use their power to help the child. Nevertheless, Galtung and Freire had a point when they argued that the form of (peace) education conveys a message apart from its content. In my opinion, this requires a broad concept of teaching and learning, which involves the integration of the development of values, norms, knowledge, and skills. I will develop this idea by confronting the teaching-learning process of peace education with the well-known classification of educational domains: the cognitive domain, the affective domain, and the domain of action (Bloom, 1956; Krathwohl, Bloom, and Masia, 1964).

THE AFFECTIVE AS BASIS, THE COGNITIVE AS REFLECTIVE SUPERSTRUCTURE, ACTION AS THE TEST

Peace education, like education in general, is primarily carried out in the affective domain. The reason for this is that peace is essentially a matter of values, and values originate in individual experience. Funda-mental peace values like trust, respect for life, solidarity, nonviolence, being open to other points of view, and creativity have their roots in the very early days of every human's life. They are experienced in an im-mediate, bodily confrontation with the world, before the acquisition of language. If a child misses this first basis, it will hardly be possible to compensate this lack by means of an explanation in language. How, for example, can we explain to a child the value of trusting other people if this child has never experienced that he can trust people and has never been trusted by others? How can we tell people that solidarity is better than egocentrism if other people never took care of them or helped them when help was needed? Or how can we teach children to be nonviolent when they live in a context in which violence is a fully accepted pattern of behavior for the powerful? The educator cannot change such conditions through rational argument; the only way he might be able to exercise influence is through personal contact, by getting in touch with the affective core of the other person.

Probably all human learning begins in the affective domain. The young child begins to build up his social world by imitation and identification. Imitation and identification are the most dominant mechanisms of the learning process that mediate human culture. Children get their first access to the world of other people by imitation of their parents' behavior and the behavior of other educators. Imitation strengthens the attention of the other person, and attention opens the way for the development of dialogue between a newborn person and those who have already found their way in the world. This creates, as Nossent (1995) shows, from the beginning a mutual adaptation of the child and the adult. Imitation is a precognitive and maybe an unconscious mechanism that manifests itself first in physical expression and results in bodily experiences. Successful imitation is a solid basis for identification, in which a child discovers values and norms as structural principles of life. In this implicit personal unconscious process of trying to be like the adults who show what is important in the world, the child develops his own orientations that he uses to interpret the world.

From this point of view, all human learning starts in the affective domain. The same can be said about motivation for learning. Creative learning and problem solving start with intuition; insights and solutions for problems are often elaborations of vague ideas, which are present before they can be formulated in cognitive terms. Frequently the solution is found even before we can clearly formulate the problem.

In this broad theory the cognitive domain is viewed as a kind of superstructure in the process of learning that has to be built on the affective basis. The cognitive domain is the result of human culture; learning is a cognitive activity. People are members of a culture who can and must be introduced to the meanings of that culture. This is done mainly through language. Although there is also structuring through environment and cultural practices, the cognitive domain is inherently structured by languages: People store their experiences in language, they discuss the meanings of a culture in language, and they reflect on the meanings of a culture by means of language. The languages in the cognitive domain offer different views on several aspects of culture and have their own grammars.

One of the most influential languages of the cognitive domain is the language of science. This language has shaped our Western culture thoroughly with its promise of progress, and it often pretends to be the only good instrument to understand the world. However, in our "postmodern" multicultural world, this claim seems no longer justified, not even in the realm of scientific discourse (Lyotard, 1983; Rorty, 1989). Besides, we have to realize that the cognitive domain includes more than scientific analysis and reflection. It contains professional languages, the languages of everyday life, of economy, of images, of stories, of poetry, of literature, of art. All these languages are connected with and colored by the affective domain.

The third important educational domain is that of human action. In this domain, a person develops the capacities and skills to contribute to our human culture and to its change. This action domain is the practical "test situation" for human attitudes and knowledge. It enables a person to realize the behavioral values and norms in the practice of his own daily life. This completes the learning process.

CONSEQUENCES

Our broad theory clearly shows that teaching and learning are not neutral processes. Moreover, every learning experience is bound up with a number of values, values that are not always recognized as such because they are quasi-naturally incorporated in environment, routines, rituals, and so on. One of the tasks of education is to make pupils and students aware of the value context of what is learned.

The assumption that learning processes are rooted in the affective basis leads to a number of conclusions and recommendations for pedagogical and educational practice. I shall discuss some recommendations for peace education. They are also relevant in other fields of education.

A first conclusion is that, especially in peace education, it is important to realize that the form of teaching and education processes must reflect their content. The process of teaching in itself conveys a message, and this message must be in accordance with the values that are to be transferred. It is often because of discrepancies between the two messages that educators are prevented from being successful. For example, telling children that aggressive behavior is not good will not be understood when this message is communicated in a very aggressive way or in a context in which aggression is a quite normal behavior. For pedagogical practice this means that parents and teachers must develop a reflective attitude on their own practice with the aim to build a real value-based pedagogical atmosphere. This situation enables the young person to learn values by living them and to accept them by imitation and identification.

A second conclusion is concerned with culture. Peace education has to be realized in specific time-bound and cultural contexts, which means that it always carries a number of unreflected cultural values and norms with it. Perhaps this partly explains why phenomena like racism, prejudices, xenophobia, and religious intolerance are so difficult to overcome. They have strong roots in the affective basis of human culture and behavior and are therefore particularly hard to change, let alone that it could be tackled by means of a rational strategy. Often people are hardly aware of this inconsistency.

A third conclusion is that a real pedagogical atmosphere requires the personal involvement of the educator. But this involvement must not prevent the youngster from deciding about his own position and developing his own identity. Involvement must also allow for distance so that the younger person can take responsibility for his own development. In his lessons the teacher has to be careful with the presentation of his own involvement. Of course, the pupil has the right to know the position of the teacher, but this position is only a guarantee for his learning processes and not the beginning of undebatable aims.

Fourth, since peace issues are always a mix of values, norms, and knowledge, teaching peace must be a complex process in which the pupil learns to distinguish between different kinds of arguments. If we discuss a peace problem, the process starts in the affective domain with the exploration of intuition. Cognitive knowledge is used to "objectify" the problem and to confront intuitive knowledge with other points of view. In this reflective process the pupil can be introduced into the different languages that can help understand the issue. In this process, he can discover the best language to attack the problems.

A fifth conclusion is that every motivation for learning is grounded in the affective domain. The child likes to learn something even before he "understands" it, or he is challenged only by sympathy for the educator or teacher who tells him that it is important to learn this. Only after this first motivation will reasonable argumentation become part of his motivation. For example: "It is not nice to learn, but it is important!" or "It is difficult to master this, but if you don't do it now, it will become more and more difficult!" Because a child is not only motivated by the responsible adults, it is important to look for intrinsic motivation. With regard to peace education this entails that one look for manifestations of a particular subject in the child's own domain and that these manifestations be translated into individual responsibilities.

My final conclusion is that a confrontation of cognitive knowledge with the self-evident suppositions of everyday life, which are rooted in the affective domain, will not immediately change the behavior of children, but it will sharpen and enhance their critical potential. It is important for children to discover that many problems cannot be solved immediately in the realm of our dominant scientific logical language but that often complex strategies must be developed that include the affective and action domains. Sometimes it will be necessary to start with a reconstruction of the learning environment by giving children more power and responsibility for the immediate area of the family, the school, and the society (van der Weijden 1998; de Winter 1995).

The idea of knowledge as a conglomeration of experiences within the different domains calls for different forms of communication and mediation of culture. This implies a new challenge for educators. They should make an effort to understand children's interpretations of the world and in doing so to help them to better understand how they can contribute to the task of building a humane future. This understanding requires sympathy for children, respect for their developmental struggle, a helping attitude, willingness to wait if they need more time to gain their insights, and hope for the possibilities of a positive approach. Teaching in this spirit can never become a mere technical activity. Evidently teachers will use techniques to explain things to children; they will employ strategies based on experiences of what is helpful and what is not, and certainly they will use the possibilities of the modern communication media. But the essence of the teaching and learning process cannot be grasped instrumentally; techniques acquire their meaning within a context of human dialogue and personal experience.

In the last part of this chapter, I shall present three Dutch peace education projects that are based on such a person-oriented approach. I shall demonstrate how these projects try to integrate the affective, the cognitive, and the action domain, thus allowing for children of different ages to be confronted with peace problems at their own level.

FIRST PROJECT: LITTLE BEAR BROM

The project of Little Bear Brom is written for children ages four to six. It is based on the Russian cartoon "Adventures of a Little Bear," which was broadcast on television in the 1970s. This simple story tries to familiarize children with aspects of fear and escalation of aggression. People often react automatically to fear, either by trying to flee or by becoming aggressive. The aim of the project is to help children recognize that fear is often generated in one's own mind and that solutions are often found within oneself. Here is the story:

A little bear is walking through the forest. He is singing a song. He feels happy. It is his mother's birthday. Then he meets the fox who asks him where he is going and why he is so happy. Our little bear answers that he is on his way to the other side of the river to pick flowers for his mother. The fox warns him: "You can't go to the other side of the river. That's dangerous!" "Why?" asks our little bear. "I can walk over the bridge." "But there is a monster in the water under the bridge," the fox says. "Don't do that!"

Our little bear walks on, but his singing gets softer and softer, and by the time he has reached the bridge, he is silent. Is the monster there or not? Is it awake or asleep? He takes his first careful steps, and then he sees something in the water. He is frightened and runs back to the safe riverbank. After a while he thinks: "I can try to cross the bridge with my eyes closed. The monster will not

see me." He tries, but it is impossible to do this. And when he opens his eyes, he sees the monster in the water and runs back as fast as possible.

Then the fox comes to the riverbank. The fox understands the problem and tells our little bear to look at the monster very angrily. Of course this results in the monster looking angrily at our little bear, so he still does not dare to cross the bridge. The wolf has stronger advice: "Take a stick and beat the monster!" but the enemy turns out to be armed too. Nothing helps until the wise owl recommends our little bear to smile at the creature in the water, then the creature will be kind to him. This turns out to be the solution to the problem. Now our little bear can pick flowers for his mother and he thanks the wise owl for his advice. The owl laughs heartily at his success.

For the project our little bear was given the name Little Bear Brom, and his story was drawn on working sheets, which illustrate five project themes. The children have to reflect on what Little Bear Brom sees in the water under the bridge. The first theme is making friends, the second the challenge of the water, the third being angry, the fourth a weapon, and the final image shows the happy solution. Every picture offers ample

opportunity to discuss the children's ideas, their own experiences, their feelings. In addition, there are songs and activities like making masks, acting out the story, and playing mirror.

This project combines an affective, cognitive, and action approach. The children are confronted with their own feelings, values, and unreflective behavior in a narrative way. This is the basis for cognitive reflection and other activities. Although the project was not systematically evaluated, teachers reported that the children liked it and were involved in the problem. The teachers favored the project because it did not involve conclusions. The children should discover the conclusions by themselves.

SECOND PROJECT: PEACE AND WAR AS THE CHILD'S PROBLEM

The second project. Peace and War as the Child's Problem, was developed as an application of a research project about children's real-life

experiences of peace and war. In this research project a phenomenological description is made of the perceptions, ideas, interpretations, and
visions of 6- to 12-year-old children about problems of war and peace.
The project made clear that war and peace are an undeniable and often
problematic part of the modern child's world. Children are continuously
confronted with problems of war and peace in the adult world, but they
cannot incorporate them in their own "child culture." In the research
project, we found that children use the words *peace* and *war* as often as
adults but that *peace* has more than 40 different meanings and war more
than 50. Besides, we found enormous differences between boys and girls.

The idea behind the project was that it would be interesting for teachers to gain insight into pupils' ideas about war and peace. This can be
valuable for a process of elaborated communication and reflection.
Teachers can use this information when they want to teach peace and
war issues, and it will prevent them from thinking too easily that children understand the information in the "right" way.

The project contains at least three different sources of information:
essays written by children about their vision on the future; drawings of
peace and drawings of war; and a group discussion, a mutual exchange
of ideas about war and peace based on the essays and drawings. The
success of the project largely depends on the willingness of the teacher
to "analyze" the essays and drawings before the group discussion. The
information from these products offers the teacher an opportunity to
understand what is going on in the minds of children, to take their ideas
seriously, and to structure the discussion. If the teacher can discuss these
results with colleagues, they can plan new activities, develop themes,
and so on. Schools can also use the drawings to organize an exhibition
to offer parents a "mirror of the world of their children."

As an illustration I offer an example of an essay of a 10-year-old girl
and the analysis that was used for the project.

> When I am a grown up I would like
> the world not to become more modern.
> For, if everybody drives a car and uses
> other things that pollute our air, we will
> die ourselves. And if I could choose a
> place to live I would prefer to live in a
> sociable and quiet village.

> When I am a grown up I want to do
> work which has something to do with
> animals, because I don't like all that
> computer stuff. For, after a while you get
> over-strung. But not in nature, there you
> always find something new.

In fifteen years time I hope there
will be no war, no rows, and no
discrimination.

For the analysis, we borrowed the following questions from the original research project:

- What is the child's idea of peace?
- What is its idea of war?
- Is the child optimistic or pessimistic about the future?
- What other remarkable points can be discovered?
- What is my conclusion and what does it mean for our common situation?

The short analysis of this essay offers the following themes:

- *Idea of peace*: quietness and harmony in nature, something like a hidden peace perspective.
- *Idea of war*: threat and fear.
- *Optimism or pessimism about the future*: no clear choice, but there is a longing for a clean and livable world and hope that there will be no war anymore.
- *Striking points*: aversion of technology; preference of rest and order.

A first *conclusion* can be that this child expresses a need for rest and order. Second, attention can be paid to the advantages and disadvantages of the computer.

We advise teachers to take all the essays of the children in the class into account. This can be useful for the planning of the rest of the project. Furthermore, we warn against easy interpretations based on old knowledge ("Of course this child does not like computers—she does not know how to use them") or based on old ideas about what the child is like ("She is reproducing the views of her parents, those environment freaks!") For the use of the drawings and the group discussion, we also offer a number of recommendations that can be helpful for the teaching and learning practice.

The main value of this project is the integration of cognitive and affective reflection, not only for the children but also for the teachers. Reflection is used here as a "technique" to become aware of self-evident values, norms, conceptions, ideas, and so on, that can be confronted with other ideas and knowledge.

THIRD PROJECT: THE COMMON-STRANGE TRAIN

The Common-Strange Train is a mobile game for 10- to 12-year-old children about prejudices, scapegoating, and the most valuable treasure in the world. It was developed by the Stichting Vredeseducatie (Foundation for Peace Education) in Utrecht and was funded by nine public and private financiers in the Netherlands and two in Belgium (Visser and Tuinier, 1996). It is housed in a special bus, which travels through the Netherlands and Flanders. The project consists of 33 tasks that confront children with the following eight themes: true or false; fact or opinion; common or strange; yes or no; prejudices; the scapegoat; fugitives; and it depends on your perspective. The children are given a participation ticket that gives access to a playful discovery trip. In approximately one hour they go from one task to another until they reach their final discovery: the nicest person on earth.

The aim of the project is to contribute to a positive intercultural education by accepting one's own identity. It tries to reach this goal by confronting children in a nonmoralistic way with the fact that everyone has prejudices. Then children discover that negative prejudices are often based on fear and insufficient information and can be very persistent. They learn that this mechanism can become a basis for discrimination and scapegoating of other people, mostly the weak.

The project has three phases. It starts in the classroom with some activities to be prepared by the teacher. For the children, it begins with a letter that invites them to visit the project bus. However, this letter is tricky and divides children into two groups: the "clever" and the "stupid." Of course, this division is completely arbitrary and only for the "learning moment" of the project. The "clever" children receive a normal letter; the "stupid" children receive a letter in mirror writing. Subsequently, the experiences of being "clever" or being "stupid" are discussed with questions like "How do you feel?" and "Can you imagine an experience like this in a foreign country?" After this the visit to the Common-Strange Bus is announced.

Common or Strange?

People who eat raw fish.

In The Netherlands many people like to eat herring, which they eat as raw fish.

Cleaning your nose with a handkerchief.

In India people do not use handkerchiefs. They feel that this is not hygienic.

Two discussions from the common-strange play that is part of the project.

The second phase is the visit to the bus. Here the children are very active with the teacher who is around but at a distance.

After the visit the trip is evaluated. The project requires a minimum of one hour to discuss the children's experiences. But it offers a lot of questions and suggestions for every phase in the game.

When we look at this project, we see a nice integration of the three domains of learning. The focus is on the action domain, which is justified by the idea of children as active learners in a challenging learning situation. But the project as a whole creates a very relaxed atmosphere around difficult topics of everyone's own life. Knowledge is important but only as an incentive to discover that many of our evidences are questionable. It offers many opportunities to discuss values and norms and their variations in different cultures. The whole project centers around fundamental peace values and norms.

CONCLUSION

In this study I explored a broad paradigm of learning, teaching, and education, which form the basis of peace education in different cultures and are probably an important basis for all human learning. Learning is primarily a social process of imitation and identification that starts in the affective domain as a confrontation with lived values and norms that structure experiences. But the same can be said about learning in the later phases of a person's life: Acquisition of knowledge starts in the affective domain; it is intuitively motivated at the precognitive level and value oriented. The cognitive domain is a culture-bound superstructure that shapes our unreflected experiences for intersubjective communication.

This does not only mean that the importance of the affective domain lies in the necessary connection of knowledge with values. It converts our common ideas about educating and teaching children as a cognitive introduction into the meanings of our culture. The focus on the cognitive domain is a misperception of our scientific rationalized culture, a misperception that has almost captured our world. But our world is not a product of logical constructs, and therefore it is only partly the outcome of logical *re*construction. It seems that this misperception is not a neutral phenomenon. It prevents people from growing up with a good balance between the cognitive and the affective part of their identities. However, a disturbed balance can lead to action in which the consequences are insufficiently taken into account. This is not only a personal problem; too many of these kinds of actions can finally dehumanize the whole planet.

The description of the three peace education projects shows that it is possible to integrate the affective, the cognitive, and the action domain in the teaching situation. Although these projects are not presented through a broad paradigm of learning and teaching, they offer insights into the possibilities of such an approach.

REFERENCES

Bloom, B.S. (Ed.). (1956). *Taxonomy of Educational Objectives. The Classification of Educational Goals. Handbook I: Cognitive Domain.* New York: David McKay.

Deboutte, G. (1997). *Geweld genoeg!* Brussels: Jeugd en Vrede.

de Winter, M. (1995). *Kinderen als medeburgers. Kinder- en jeugdparticipatie als maatschappelijk opvoedkundig perspectief.* Utrecht: De Tijdstroom.

Freire, P. (1972). *Pedagogy of the Oppressed.* New York: Herder and Herder.

Galtung, J. (1973). Probleme der Friedenserziehung. In C. Wulf (Ed.), *Kritische Friedenserziehung.* Frankfurt am Main: Suhrkamp.

Galtung, J., Kinkelbur, D., and Nieder, M. (Eds.). (1993). *Gewalt im Altag und in der Weltpolitik.* Münster: Agenda.

Krathwohl, D.R., Bloom, B.S., and Masia, B.B. (1964). *Taxonomy of Educational Objectives. The Classification of Educational Goals. Handbook II: Affective Domain.* New York: David McKay.

Lyotard, J.F. (1983). *Le différend.* Paris: D. de Minuit.

Mollenhauer, K. (1986). *Vergeten samenhang: Over cultuur en opvoeding.* Meppel: Boom.

Nossent, S.P.M. (1995). *Een beweeglijke psyche.* Thesis Utrecht University. Kampen: Kok Agora.

Rorty, R. (1989). *Contingency, Irony and Solidarity.* New York: Cambridge University Press.

van der Weijden, H. (1998). *Leren samenleven. Een sociocratische werkwijze voor basisscholen.* Thesis, Utrecht University. Assen: Van Gorcum.

Visser, G. (1988). *Vredes—En ontwikkelingseducatie.* Werkboek 4 tot 12-jarigen. Utrecht: Vredesopbouw.

Visser, G., and Tuinier, J.D. (1996). *Gewoon—vreemd express: Een mobiel spelencircuit over vooroordelen, de zondebok en het aardigste kind van de wereld.* Utrecht: Vredesopbouw.

Vriens, L.J.A. (1988). *Pedagogiek tussen vrees en vrede: Een pedagogische theorie over vredesopvoeding.* Thesis, Utrecht University. Antwerpen: Internationale Vredesinformatiedienst.

Vriens, L. (1994). *In the Past Lies the Future. The Necessity of a Peace Tradition as a Contribution to a Humane Future.* Paper presented at IPRA XV General Conference, Malta, October 31–November 4, 1994 (Peace Education Commission).

Vriens, L. (1996). Postmodernism, Peace Culture and Peace Education. In R.J. Burns and R. Aspeslagh (Eds.), *Three Decades of Peace Education around the World: An Anthology.* New York: Garland.

Vriens, L., and Aspeslagh, R. (1985). Peace Education as Alternating between the Person and the Structures. *History and Social Science Teacher,* 20(3–4): 11–19.

PART II

Case Studies

CHAPTER 6

Can Educational Improvement Equalize Minority Economic Opportunities? The Case of the United States

MARTIN CARNOY

Neoclassical economists have argued consistently for the past 25 years that market forces—the supply and demand for skills—determine how minorities fare economically and socially. By implication, this means that the educational choices minority families make in providing learning environments at home and motivating their children to do well in school are the principal factors in how much income their children will earn in the future. There is indeed considerable evidence showing that "good" choices do result in better outcomes for minorities. But it is argued that for minority groups in general, and for some particularly, making the right educational choices is probably not enough. For better or worse, government has been a major player throughout history in defining how these groups (and women) participate in the economy and society. Political decisions whether to continue to intervene in the future to compensate disdvantaged minorities educationally and in labor markets should make a significant difference in how these groups do.

The United States provides a rich source of data to examine whether improved education alone is likely to equalize minority economic opportunities, all else unchanged. African Americans and Latinos, the two largest disadvantaged groups, now comprise about one-fifth of the U.S. population, and in many states, the proportion is much higher. In the past, they earned significantly less than Anglo white Americans, in part because they had much lower levels of educational attainment and even with the same level of education. A generation ago, most Americans felt that past slavery, Jim Crow laws, Japanese exclusion laws, and segregated education were highly prejudicial and required remedies through new kinds of "good" government interventions that would correct previous "bad" interventions. This included increased spending on minority K–12 education, breaking down access barriers to white universities, and affirmative action in labor markets. But today the white community tends to believe that past discrimination has been essentially corrected by more recent government remedies, that free and unfettered labor markets are now fair and efficient in allocating and paying workers of all ethnic groups and genders, and that continued intervention, even if intended to be helpful, makes conditions worse for all Americans, including minorities.

This shift back to a "merit-based" system, where merit is measured by achievement test scores, implicitly assumes that disadvantaged minorities get lower-paying jobs because they do not score as high on tests as whites (and Asian Americans), and they do not score as well on tests largely because they go to "bad" schools and do not get proper work habits at home. These arguments are logical and can be supported by evidence: Many urban schools catering to disadvantaged minority students appear to be doing a poor job in teaching them to read and do even simple arithmetic, and disadvantaged minority families living in poverty do not generally provide an environment amenable to learning.

But how much would improvement in schools change this situation? My argument is that whatever the philosophical debate on government intervention in access to higher education and labor markets, the empirical evidence shows that these markets, allegedly based solely on merit, are rife with imperfections, that government interventions in the recent past have worked to reduce differences in the way these markets treat minorities of color but that these differences persist, and that failure to continue intervening could very well make things worse for minorities.

I argue that (1) affirmative action has made a major contribution to equalizing incomes between whites and disadvantaged minorities; (2) for some minorities of color in the United States, such as Latinos and Asian Americans, equalizing education differences goes far in equalizing opportunity, but (3) for others, such as African Americans, the evidence suggests that poverty and discrimination in labor markets work against the educational argument and that political action in labor markets is necessary to overcome these imperfections.

IS THERE A CASE FOR AFFIRMATIVE ACTION?

Affirmative action, legislated by the Civil Rights Act of 1964 and implemented in a series of Supreme Court decisions and agreements between the Equal Employment Opportunity Commission (EEOC) and major U.S. companies, has been the major remedy for past unequal treatment of minorities in education, the political system, and labor markets. It mandated an end to unequal education and to discrimination in hiring, not only for African Americans but for all ethnic groups and for white women. The underlying assumption was that such inequality and discrimination were indeed part and parcel of a segregated educational system and of the labor market. If education and workplaces were not marked by unequal access and discrimination, it would be difficult to make the case for affirmative action.

One of the problems in arguing for affirmative action today is its past success. A good case can be made that affirmative action was key to improving access to higher education and the jobs and incomes of African Americans and Latinos in the 1960s, 1970s, and 1990s and of women in the 1980s and 1990s. Yet the widespread belief that access to higher education has been equalized for disadvantaged minority groups, that differential access is now mainly a matter of social class, not race or ethnicity, that racial, ethnic, or gender discrimination in labor markets has been eliminated, and that differential pay is now mainly a matter of capability are not correct, as we shall show.

Education

It is impressive how rapidly African Americans and Latinos (and Asian Americans) were able to close the educational attainment gap with whites when given an opportunity. Over the past 15 years, African American young men and women who work have essentially equalized the amount of education they have compared to non-Hispanic whites when it comes to high school completion and some postsecondary education. Forty-nine percent of employed young black men and 54 percent of young black women have taken some years of college education or more (see Table 6.1). Although a wide gap still exists in the proportion of African American and white men and women who have completed college, employed black men continue to gain on their white counterparts.

The past 15 years only tell part of the story. In 1960, before the Civil Rights Act, only 31 percent of 25- to 34-year-old employed African American males nationwide had finished high school or more, and only 12 percent had any postsecondary education. And even in 1970, a generation ago, only 53 percent had finished high school or more, and only 15 percent had some college or more. So the gains since 1970 have been nothing short of transformational.

The educational gains for Latinos and Latinas are much lower but heavily influenced by massive new immigration since 1970. The figures in Table 6.1 reflect the low educational levels of young immigrants, many of labor force age arriving in the United States without high school education or dropping out of high school even if coming here as young adolescents with their families. Considering only Latinos who are native

Table 6.1
United States: Educational Attainment of 25- to 34-Year-Olds, All Workers
with Income, 1980–1995 (in percent)

	Non-Hispanic Whites			Latinos			African Americans		
Male	*1980*	*1990*	*1995*	*1980*	*1990*	*1995*	*1980*	*1990*	*1995*
HSG or More	89.7	90.4	93.0	58.3	56.2	59.6	76.6	86.4	90.9
SC or More	55.0	49.2	58.5	30.5	23.4	29.3	37.4	38.0	48.7
CG or More	29.9	27.9	30.6	11.1	8.0	9.9	13.0	14.8	17.8
Female	*1980*	*1990*	*1995*	*1980*	*1990*	*1995*	*1980*	*1990*	*1995*
HSG or More	91.9	94.4	94.9	68.5	71.8	74.4	83.8	88.0	91.1
SC or More	51.8	54.2	64.4	33.9	33.2	40.7	41.0	42.3	54.3
CG or More	27.9	30.5	32.9	10.9	13.4	14.3	15.2	17.8	17.2

Notes: HSG = High School Graduate; SC = Some College; CG = College Graduate (in 1980,
college graduate defined as individual reporting 16 years of schooling completed,
which tends to overestimate the percentage of college graduates in that year); "White"
= Non-Hispanic White.

Source: U.S. Department of Commerce, Census Bureau (1995).

born, attainment gains are more positive, particularly for women, and
levels of attainment are much higher than for the totality of the young
Latino labor force. For example, in California, where educational attainment among native-born Latinos and Latinas is considerably higher than
nationally (Carnoy, 1994), data are not available in 1995 for native-born
separately, but in 1990, 79 percent of 25- to 34-year-old native-born employed Latino men had completed high school or more, 48 percent had
completed some college or more, and 12 percent had graduated from
college or more, with the main (small) gain over 1980 coming in the
proportion who had some college (48 in 1990 versus 44 percent in 1980).
The gains for Latinas were much larger: In 1980, 82 percent had completed high school or more, 39 percent some years of college or more,
and 10 percent college graduation or more; by 1990, the proportions had
jumped to 86 percent, 57 percent, and 14 percent, respectively. But even

Table 6.2
Total Undergraduate Enrollment in Institutions of Higher Education, by
Race, 1976–1994 (in thousands)

Year	White Non-Hispanics	Black Non-Hispanics	Hispanics	Asian/Pacific Islanders
1976	7,740	943	353	169
1980	8,481	1,019	433	249
1984	8,484	995	495	343
1988	8,907	1,039	631	437
1990	9,273	1,147	725	500
1991	9,508	1,229	804	559
1992	9,388	1,281	888	613
1993	9,100	1,290	918	634
1994	8,916	1,317	968	674

Source: National Center of Educational Statistics (1996): table 203.

with these higher numbers for the native born, Latinos remain the least educated major minority group nationally.[1]

Undergraduate enrollment data for recent years suggest why African Americans' educational attainment gains slowed down at the college level. Black undergraduate enrollment in four-year and two-year colleges combined increased only slightly in the 1980s from about 430,000 to 450,000 (Table 6.2). This did represent an increase in the percentage of black high school graduates going to college, but not nearly as great as the white increase (Table 6.3). Also, all of the increase in absolute and relative black enrollment came in the last two years of the 1980s. After 1988, however, blacks began going to college again in large numbers, duplicating the increases of the 1970s. White undergraduate enrollment, in contrast, rose rapidly until 1991 and then dropped rapidly. The drop in white enrollment after 1991 is mainly connected to the end of the baby boom. Although Hispanic absolute enrollment increased as their numbers in the population increased, the proportion of 18- to 24-year-old Hispanics in higher education only rose after 1991, essentially showing the same trend as for blacks. One explanation for the lag in black and Hispanic college enrollment is economic. It may not have been until the late 1980s, five years after the end of the early 1980s recession and the Reagan administration's reductions in financial aid, that young people from these low-income groups could afford to go to college in larger numbers.

Financial and other, more complex and subtle barriers to entry in higher education in the United States continue to exist, even though af-

Table 6.3
Total Enrollment Rates of 18- to 24-Year-Olds in Institutions of Higher Education, by Race, 1976–1994 (percent of high school graduates)

Year	White Non-Hispanics	Black Non-Hispanics	Hispanics
1976	32.1	32.1	34.7
1980	31.0	26.0	27.6
1984	32.6	25.6	28.8
1988	37.4	26.8	29.1
1990	39.2	30.4	26.8
1991	41.0	28.2	31.4
1992	42.8	33.9	37.5
1993	42.6	32.8	36.1
1994	43.7	35.6	33.1

Source: National Center of Educational Statistics (1996): table 203.

firmative action did a lot to improve access in the 1970s and even though black and Latino enrollment growth eventually recovered to keep pace with white enrollment in the 1990s. These more complex barriers have to do with academic expectations in primary and secondary schools, the broad issue of test scores as a valid measure of capacity to do well and what they convey to students about their own capabilities, and the over-all relationships between races and ethnic groups in higher education institutions.[2]

Income and Wages

Nationally, not only did young African Americans increase their educational attainment rapidly in the 1960s and 1970s, entering colleges and universities in record numbers and giving them access for the first time to a wide range of professional jobs, but blacks with the same level of education as whites earned steadily higher relative incomes. The median income of full-time employed young (25- to 34-year-old) African American men who were high school graduates rose from 70 percent of white male incomes in 1959[3] to 80 percent in 1979. African American male college graduates' incomes began their rise in 1969, again from less than 70 percent to 82 percent of the income of white male college graduates by 1979 (Table 6.4). As important, large numbers of young African Americans entered universities for the first time in the 1970s. The 1964 Civil Rights Act, subsequent court cases, and the compromises regarding business compliance reached between corporations such as AT&T and

Table 6.4
United States: Minority-White Income Ratios, by Age, Gender, and Education, 1979–1994 (in percent of white income)

	1979		1989		1994	
Males	*Latinos*	*Blacks*	*Latinos*	*Blacks*	*Latinos*	*Blacks*
16- to 24-year-old HSG	92	80	89	89	97	80
16- to 24-year-old SC	83	85	88	91	96	86
25- to 34-year-old HSG	89	80	80	77	83	78
25- to 34-year-old SC	95	88	86	81	91	87
25- to 34-year-old CG	88	82	79	72	87	80
Females	*Latinos*	*Blacks*	*Latinos*	*Blacks*	*Latinos*	*Blacks*
16- to 24-year-old HSG	94	97	98	105	106	90
16- to 24-year-old SC	99	93	89	99	90	99
25- to 34-year-old HSG	93	95	97	90	98	92
25- to 34-year-old SC	96	99	95	92	97	92
25- to 34-year-old CG	94	95	102	90	89	89

Notes: HSG = High School Graduate; SC = Some College; CG = College Graduate.

Source: U.S. Department of Commerce, Census Bureau (1995).

the EEOC were major factors in defining the upward mobility of young African Americans and Latinos in the late 1960s and in the 1970s.

In the 1980s, conspicuous inattention by the Reagan administration to enforcing antidiscrimination laws, particularly when applied to minorities, also had an impact: African American's incomes fell behind. The relative drop was especially great among young male college graduates, the group that had most benefited in the 1970s from affirmative action. Table 6.4 shows that their incomes fell back to 72 percent of white male incomes. Latino incomes relative to whites also fell in the 1980s, although at least part of this decline was due to continued rapid immigration from Latin America and the fact that many of these new immigrants spoke imperfect English. Minority enrollment in universities also stagnated, particularly for African American males, as federal student loans and grants became more restricted and poverty rates rose.

But the 1980s saw significant economic gains for women when compared to men. This was particularly true for non-Hispanic white women. In 1979, the average full-time employed white woman, 25- to 34-year-olds, who had completed high school earned only 64 percent of her counterpart male worker. By 1989, this had risen to 70 percent. For women college graduates, the proportion was 68 percent in 1979 and 78 percent in 1989. Although Latinas kept up with white women, African American women fell behind, although they did gain compared to white men and especially African American men.

In the 1990s, both men and women disadvantaged minorities again began to make gains compared to whites, so that African American men now earn about 80 percent of white male incomes. One reason could well have been the return to enforcement of antidiscrimination laws, mildly by the Bush administration and much more strongly in the Clinton years. White women high school graduates, 25- to 34-year-olds, employed full-time, increased to 74 percent of corresponding male incomes by 1994, and women college graduates, up to 82 percent. Yet even with black women holding steady relative to white women, at about 90 percent of white women's income, this means that black women currently earn 68 percent to 73 percent of white male median income.

Without continued affirmative action previous gains made in the 1970s and current gains in the 1990s by minorities and women would probably not have been as great and may not have occurred at all. Thus, affirmative action may have contributed as much as 10 percentage points of white male income to black earnings (about $2,400 in 1995 dollars) and reduced younger male African Americans' probability of earning a poverty wage or less from about 41 percent to about 33 percent.

Minority Achievement Gains and Relative Incomes

A counter to the argument that wage differences between blacks and whites are susceptible to legislative remedies such as affirmative action is that blacks (and Latinos) score lower on achievement tests than whites, hence properly earn less for the same level of schooling. This counter-argument was taken to its logical extreme in *The Bell Curve* (Herrnstein and Murray, 1994), yet its implication even in less eugenic terms is that those with lower achievement test scores are less capable, hence less productive, and *should* be paid less in the labor market.

It is clear that those with higher test scores are more likely, on average, to attain higher levels of schooling than those with lower levels of schooling. Data from the National Longitudinal Study (NLS) survey, which followed 1972 high school seniors for 14 years, and the High School and Beyond (HSB) survey, which followed 1980 seniors for 12 years, both show that those who attend college have higher high school test scores than those who do not (Murnane, Willett, and Levy, 1995). Depending on gender and the survey (NLS or HSB), college graduates averaged about 0.8 to 1 standard deviation higher high school test results than those who graduate high school but did not go on to college. In that sense, higher test scores in high school do lead to higher incomes, and it can be argued that college degrees are primarily a *signal* to employers of cognitive knowledge (Groot and Hartog, 1995: 3438).

However, if test scores reflect labor market value, we would expect a strong relationship to exist between achievement test score and wages for those with the *same* level of education. Then *changes* over time in relative test scores between different ethnic/gender groups with the same level of formal schooling should also be reflected in changes in relative wages over time. This relationship is much more difficult to show either in static or dynamic terms. Murnane, Willett, and Levy (1995) estimate that, holding education constant, a 1 standard deviation difference in high school math test score was associated with an average 5 percent difference in wages six years after high school graduation for the 1972 cohort and a 7 percent difference for the 1980 cohort. When I and my colleagues at Stanford reestimated their results dividing into high school and college graduates, we found that the returns to a 1 standard deviation higher test score were negligible for high school graduates but were about 7 to 10 percent for college graduates, lower in the 1970s and higher in the 1980s (Carnoy and De Angelis, 2001). This suggests that very large differences in test scores result in very small differences in wages *among those with the same level of schooling*.

Now let's compare African Americans' test scores to white test scores nationally. The graph in Figure 6.1 shows that black males have reduced the gap between their mean Scholastic Aptitude Test (SAT) math scores

Figure 6.1
SAT Math Scores, by Race, 1975/1976–1994/1995

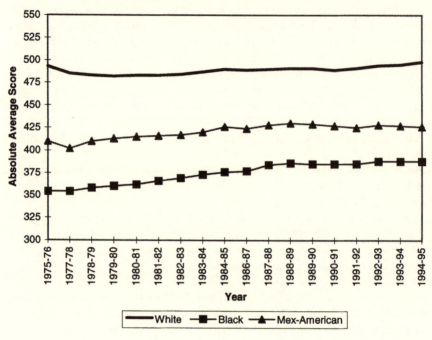

and those of whites between 1976 and 1990, and the gap has increased somewhat since, possibly because of the severe recession and increased poverty levels in the early 1980s, when the cohort taking the SAT was six and seven years old (see Carnoy, 1994: ch. 4). Yet the fact that SAT scores went up so rapidly for blacks relative to whites is particularly impressive because a larger (and thus less elite) group of African American students took the test in the late 1980s than in the 1970s. Despite the expansion of the pool, test scores rose.[4]

The graph in Figure 6.2 compares math scores by race for a random sample of 17-year-olds tested under the National Assessment of Educational Progress (NAEP). The NAEP distinguishes five levels of math scores. Students with a score of 150 can recognize simple situations in which addition and subtraction apply. Those at the 200 level also know basic multiplication and division and can read information from charts and graphs. Students at the 250 level can apply addition and subtraction skills to one-step word problems, can compare information from charts and graphs, and can analyze simple logical relations. Those at the 300 level perform moderately complex procedures and reasoning, like compute decimals, fractions, and percents, interpret simple inequalities, evaluate formulas, and solve simple linear equations. Students at the 350

Figure 6.2
NAEP Math Scores, by Race/Ethnicity, 1973–1992

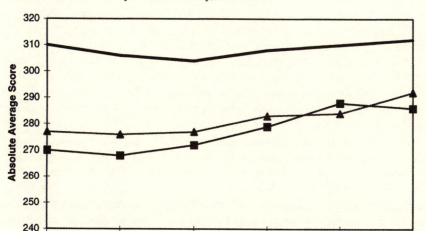

level can solve two-step problems using variables, identify equivalent algebraic expressions, and are developing an understanding of functions and coordinate systems.

NAEP math score differences between black and white students behave similarly to SAT score differences (the NAEP math score difference drops from about 1.1 standard deviations lower for blacks in 1978 to about 0.8 in 1990, before also rising to about 1 standard deviation in 1992).[5] Average math NAEP scores of white 17-year-olds were 310 in 1973, 306 in 1978, 308 in 1986, and then back at 310 in 1990, and 312 in 1992. For African American 17-year-olds, again there was a relative gain, from an average math score of 270 in 1973, to 279 in 1986, to 288 in 1990, but then down to 286 in 1992. For Latinos, the scores went from 277 in 1973, to 283 in 1986, to 284 in 1990, and then shooting up to 292 in 1992 (Mullis et al., 1994: 80, fig. 4.2).

Nationally, the average NAEP reading proficiency score of white 17-year-olds went from 291 in 1971 to 295 in 1988. For African American 17-year-olds, the gain was greater, from an average of 239 in 1971 to 274 in 1988. For Latino 17-year-olds, the gain was from an average score of 252 in 1975 to 271 in 1988 (Mullis et al., 1994: 137, fig. 7.2). NAEP scores represent a range of reading abilities. A score of 150 reflects an ability to follow brief written directions. A score of 200 reflects an ability to combine ideas and make inferences based on short, uncomplicated passages. A score of 250 reflects an ability to make inferences and reach generalizations from passages dealing with literature, science, and social studies. A score of 300 reflects an ability to find, understand, summarize, and explain relatively complicated information. And a score of 350 reflects an ability to synthesize and learn from specialized and complex texts such as scientific materials, literary essays, and historical documents. Thus, while average white scores remained higher, the average scores of all three groups in 1988 reflected the ability to make inferences and reach generalizations from passages dealing with literature, science, and social studies.

These are highly significant gains. In 1978, the gap between white and African American mathematics 17-year-old NAEP scores was over 1.1 standard deviations, meaning that the average African American score was 37 percentile points lower than the average white score. By 1990, the gap had been reduced to 0.6 standard deviations, or about 21 percentile points. On the verbal test, the gap was reduced from 1.2 standard deviations (about 41 percentile points) to 0.7 standard deviations (about 24 percentile points). Thus, the gap between white and African American NAEP scores was reduced by about 40 percent from the 1970s to 1990 (Grissmer et al., 1994: 16–17).

Gains, though of smaller magnitude, were also posted by Latinos. (NAEP score reports do not distinguish between the scores of native and foreign-born students, although we are less concerned with the distinction here, since NAEP scores are only reported for students in high schools and so would not be affected by immigrants who never attended school in this country.) In mathematics, the white-Latino gap for 17-year-olds was reduced from about 0.9 standard deviations (about 31 percentile points) to about 0.8 standard deviations (about 27 percentile points). On the verbal test, the gap was reduced even more—from about 0.95 standard deviations (about 32 percentile points) to about 0.5 standard deviations (about 17 percentile points) (Grissmer et al., 1994).

In the case of both reading and math, therefore, the gap between NAEP minority and white scores narrowed nationally, while students preparing for the labor market in 1980, 1990, and 1995 were still in school. In sum, although conclusions must be tentative, there is nothing in the NAEP results to suggest that young minority workers aged 25 to 34, participating in the labor market with higher rates of high school graduation in 1995 than in 1990 or in 1980, did so with less academic preparation. On the contrary, based on what we can infer from these data, the narrowing of the attainment gap is probably paralleled by a narrowing of the achievement gap as well.

If the increases in black high school graduates' achievement compared to whites in the 1980s reflect capacity to be productive, we would expect that the wages of young blacks should have increased significantly compared to the wages of young whites. Since Latinos' test scores also rose relative to whites in the 1980s (but much less than blacks' scores), we would expect a similar increase in young Latinos' relative wages. But going back to Table 6.4, we find no evidence that 18- to 22-year-old black and Latino males and females who had graduated high school earned relatively more in 1989 than in 1979. There is evidence of rising black relative annual incomes among full-time employed 16- to 24-year-olds nationally, but when the comparison is made among *hourly earnings* for all workers (both part-time and full-time) with income in this age group, there was no increase in relative hourly earnings in the 1980s, either for black men or black women or Latino men or women (Carnoy, 1994: table 4.7). Rather, the national relative wage data for young minorities seem to have risen and fallen with the business cycle during the period 1973–1991. Indeed, when the relative incomes for blacks began to rise in the 1990s, it was concomitant with declining black test scores compared to whites.

Labor Markets Based Only on Merit?

If proponents of the merit theory of labor markets hope to make their case, they must show that improved performance in achievement tests really does pay off in higher wages for young minorities and women with the *same level of education* as white men. The evidence that this is the case is not powerful. We know that those students who complete college have higher high school test scores than high school graduates who do not go to college. College graduates earn higher wages than high school graduates, and part of their higher wages are due to their higher achievement in high school. Yet the evidence suggests that employers are much more sensitive to "sanctioned" higher achievement, where applicants have degrees that "prove" that they are capable of more complex tasks, than of test scores themselves. We also know that those with the same level of schooling may get a small premium if they are a lot better in math. But if a 1 standard deviation in high school math test score produces only a very small difference in wages, why do both black high school and college graduates get paid so much less than whites with the same education?

Similarly, we have been unable to find a relationship between changes in minorities' relative high school test scores, even when those changes are large, and changes in minorities' relative wages. While no single statistic is sufficiently reliable to prove a case, the broad trends are remarkably consistent in their direction—the data show that the educational attainment and achievement of minority 17-year-olds, relative to the attainment and achievement of comparable whites, improved steadily and, in some cases dramatically, from 1973 to 1988. Yet when these youths entered the labor market, their improved relative qualifications did not result in improved relative wages. On the contrary, these more educationally qualified minority workers found that when they were in their late twenties and early thirties, their wages were lower, relative to their comparably educated white coworkers, than were the wages of previous cohorts.

Thus, we can reasonably conclude that the labor market is not working perfectly, at least with respect to compensating minority workers more equally relative to their educational qualifications. An evaluation of affirmative action in hiring or promotions to determine whether it is the most appropriate response to this market imperfection is beyond the scope of this chapter. However, we can say that, contrary to the stated fears of its opponents, continuance of affirmative action in employment would not likely serve to distort the efficiency of the labor market; rather, based on the evidence we examined here, affirmative action would likely make the labor market more efficient, by putting pressure on wages to have a more consistent and rational relationship to workers' educational qualifications.

Much more convincing is that labor markets have "job and salary structure cultures" that slot people into certain kinds of jobs and job ladders *partly* on the basis of race, ethnicity, and gender. Educational attainment is also an important variable in allocating people to jobs and in determining the wages they receive. Yet if noneducation and experience factors influence individuals' opportunities in the labor market, then that alone allows for "culture-altering" interventions with insignificant impact on overall productivity. These interventions are capable of changing employer hiring and wage-paying behavior and therefore the wage structure without economic costs to the economy as a whole (although some groups may feel that they are worse off as they lose preferences).

The data we have presented suggest strongly that such job and salary structure cultures continue to exist and that these cultures continue to leave African Americans, Latinos, and women worse off than white men. With that in mind, it is hard to avoid the conclusion that moving to a purely test-score based "merit" system and discarding affirmative action at this point in history would likely leave African American men stuck at 80 percent of white male incomes and African American women at about 90 percent of white women's income, in addition to both having an increasingly lower probability of graduating from college than their white counterparts. In 1994, the average black male in California who had graduated high school or taken some years of college (but not graduated), 25–34 years old and *employed full-time*, earned less than $20,000. With all male incomes falling steadily in real terms, this can only mean that by the year 2003, a higher percentage of African American males than now—even those lucky enough to have full-time jobs—will be close to poverty. A 20 percent lower income for blacks from a white male base of a median $25,000 means that 33 percent of black males in this age group and with this level of education are likely to earn $14,000 or less (a low estimate of urban poverty), instead of about 16 percent of white males likely to earn a poverty income. Equalizing incomes of blacks and white males with the *same* amount of education would therefore go far in reducing the chance that blacks would be poor.

For 25- to 34-year-old African American women who earned a median full-time income of about $18,000 in 1995 (and not much more at 40 years old), it was probable that almost 40 percent earned less than $14,000 annually. Since such a high proportion of African American women are single heads of households, this often represents the total family income. And their real wages declined in the 1990s, implying that this probability of earning a below-poverty-level income could even increase, should efforts to enforce affirmative action be reduced.

The other side of the coin is that educational policy alone would not be enough to resolve these differences and what they imply for the poverty levels of disadvantaged minority groups. Obviously, if minorities can attain equal levels of education with more favored groups, they can overcome much of their economic disadvantage. Such is the case of Asian Americans in the United States, who actually have much higher attainment levels and high school math scores than whites. But the case of educationally disadvantaged groups is complicated by a vicious circle of family poverty, poorer performance in early schooling, and low educational and economic expectations. Educational improvement policy alone provides only a partial remedy to this complex set of negative forces. Educators need to impress on voters and government leaders that for educational improvement to be successful it must be part of a larger program of poverty reduction and labor market interventions that eliminate discriminatory practices.

NOTES

I thank Richard Rothstein and the Economic Policy Institute for their collaboration.

1. There exist significant differences among Latino groups, however, with Cuban Americans the highest educated and Mexican Americans with the lowest levels of education.

2. See, for example, Steele (1992).

3. The data on annual income from census data refer to income for the year previous to the year in which the census was taken. So income data from the 1960 census refers to 1959 incomes, from the 1970 census, to 1969 incomes, and so forth.

4. This translates into a decline in the math score gap from 1.2 standard deviations lower in 1976 to 0.97 lower in 1993, and a decline in the test score gap

in their verbal score difference from 1.25 standard deviations lower in 1976 to 0.95 lower in 1993. In historical terms, these are very large gains.

5. The difference in the NAEP reading score drops to 0.5 standard deviations in 1988 from 1.2 in 1980, but then it rises again to almost 1 standard deviation in 1992.

REFERENCES

Carnoy, M. (1994). *Faded Dreams*. New York: Cambridge University Press.

Carnoy, M., and De Angelis, K. (2001). *Does Ability Increase Earnings, and If So, By How Much?* Stanford, CA: Stanford University School of Education. Mimeographed.

Grissmer, D., et al. (1994). *Student Achievement and the Changing American Family*. Santa Monica, CA: RAND Corporation.

Groot, W., and Hartog, J. (1995). Screening Models and Education. In M. Carnoy (Ed.), *The International Encyclopedia of Economics of Education* (2nd ed., pp. 34–38). Oxford: Elsevier Science.

Herrnstein, R., and Murray, C. (1994). *The Bell Curve*. New York: Free Press.

Mullis, I.V.S., et al. (1994). *NAEP 1992 Trends in Academic Progress*. Washington, DC: U.S. Department of Education, Office of Educational Research and Improvement, Report No. 23–TR0.

Murnane, R., Willett, J., and Levy, F. (1995). The Growing Importance of Cognitive Skills in Wage Determination. *Review of Economics and Statistics* 77(2) (May): 251–266.

Steele, C. (1992). Stigma: Race and the Schooling of Black Americans. *Atlantic Monthly* (April): 68–78.

CHAPTER 7

Cultural and Religious Minority Education in France: Limits to Diversity and Equality

LESLIE LIMAGE

Educational policy debates on the limits to diversity and equality promotion by schools can be approached by two models. Both the federal/decentralized approach of targeting forms of inequality with compensatory or affirmative action in the United States (see Jencks et al., 1972; Jencks and Peterson,1991; Tomasson et al., 2001; Vega, 1999) and the more centralized French republican model of equality through identical treatment are becoming less clear-cut and increasingly questioned. These models have been exported through international organization and bilateral aid or foundation projects aimed at democratization and/or poverty alleviation. Thus, a discussion of these models' origins and development can be useful to a more global debate.

The most constructive models for individual and social promotion include recognition of multiple identities and mutual respect, but the contours of political recognition of cultural pluralism are shifting. Public national and international educational policies cannot be grounded in a relativistic "multiculturalism" nor in a rigid notion of "republicanism." Lessons learned from both perspectives reviewed in this chapter lead to the conclusion that technical solutions, however generously inspired, to fundamentally political questions may have limited value. They are certainly increasingly questioned in a world challenged by increasing conflict and pressing need for peace. This chapter addresses the French republican model of treating diversity and equality.

EQUALITY AS IDENTICAL TREATMENT: FRANCE IN HISTORIC PERSPECTIVE

This section of the chapter examines the French republican principles that have long governed the role of schooling, relations between the state and its civil service (ministers, ministries of education, teachers), and the public (parents, children, and all "outside" influence). It situates the official discourse that, on the one hand, proclaims that the state and its schools promote a secular and equal opportunity for all and, at the same time, makes limited allowance for cultural, linguistic, religious, or socioeconomic diversity. It looks at the situation of immigrant populations since the mid-1960s in French schools and the role of governments of countries of origin in responding to economic and political emigration. It clarifies the heterogeneity of what is meant by immigrants from the Maghreb. It then turns to the more recent attempts by French governments since the mid-1980s to address the longer-term needs and aspirations of immigrant populations of Muslim origin as it becomes clear that these populations are massively becoming French citizens and have no further plans to return to countries of origin. It traces the attempts to maintain a secular (*laïque*) position while offering some recognition of the diversity of Islamic expression in France. The chapter concludes with reflections on the specificity of the French approach to linguistic and cultural diversity in a context of equality as identical treatment. Above all, it emphasizes a certain unity of view across political parties and communities that this specificity, although in crisis, does not require adoption of another radically different model than the traditional republican approach.

Three issues in 2001 crystallized concerns about this approach without seriously shaking confidence in it. The three issues are introduced here: (1) equality and affirmative action: the Institut d'études politiques (Sciences Po); (2) regional languages and schooling; and (3) violence and schools.

AFFIRMATIVE ACTION AND ELITE HIGHER EDUCATION

In March 2001 the prestigious Institut d'études politiques of Paris announced that it would admit a number of secondary school pupils from recognized disadvantaged educational priority zones (ZEPs—*zones d'éducation prioritaire*) without the usual obligatory competitive examination. This decision provoked an enormous outcry, especially among actual students, unions, intellectuals throughout the university, research communities, and of course, all political persuasions (Bernard, 2001). The notion of affirmative action is fairly foreign to French principles of equality, as is discussed later in this chapter in considerable detail. The measure is considered to be a failure from the outset. The competitive examination system will continue for the majority of candidates. Those students admitted based on their files and reports by head teachers in certain secondary schools are doomed to failure according to the majority of observers. There are concerns that the pupils are selected on the basis of their location first and foremost. Hence, parents will move their families to these zones in order to have a better chance of ensuring entry to the prestigious institution. This flight will mainly concern families who are already privileged, especially families of education professionals. Pupils selected may also find that they cannot survive once they arrive at Sciences Po. They will be recognizable by their lack of preparation for such studies. They will lack the reading, writing, and oral expression skills that those who have successfully passed the examination system master. They will be stigmatized precisely because of the privileged treatment they have enjoyed and will be further marginalized within the institution itself. Over 80 percent of students in the parallel prestigious grandes écoles system in France are from the highest socioprofessional background families. The concerns about the social reproduction of elites are not new in France of course, but the solutions along the American model have little or no support.

By the beginning of the academic year in autumn 2001, the first group of 18 secondary school graduates admitted without the competitive entry examination began their studies at the Institut d'études politiques with mixed feelings and a mixed reception. The admittance process had only been completed after several of them had already received places in the French university system and begun another course of study. The experiment in using a parallel admittance system to ensure socioeconomic and/or cultural diversity in this institution is thus too recent to evaluate in terms of the reservations in the larger education community (Guibert, 2001b).

REGIONAL LANGUAGES AND SCHOOLING

Schools are the focus of most larger social debates in France. A major example of concern to this chapter is the role of regional languages. In April 2001, Jack Lang, minister of education, announced that there was no need to await French ratification of the European Charter of Regional Languages in order to improve the status of those languages in the country (Guibert, 2001a). The minister of education was responding to President Jacques Chirac's veto of ratification of that charter by French Parliament in June 1999 based on an opinion given by the French Constitutional Council. Lang proposed a new framework for teaching the "languages of France," a special competitive examination to recruit teachers and an improved partnership with local authorities. His position is said to be based on several principles: a political will to preserve these languages as part of the French cultural heritage, a contribution to recognition of cultural diversity, and the need to provide continuity of instruction throughout schooling. According to the report released at the same time, more than 152,000 pupils learn a regional language during their primary or secondary school years through public, private, or association classes. Some 72,000 learn Occitan, 28,000 learn Corsican, 21,000 learn Breton, 9,000 learn Basque, 9,000 learn Catalan, 7,500 learn German or Alsatian, and nearly 6,000 learn the languages of the Moselle region of France. Among those pupils, about 28,000 have some type of bilingual education.

Lang then proposed a first Administrative Circular (a ministerial document that provides the directives to the French education system) for a development plan for modern languages in primary school in May 2001 that included regional languages. Regional languages were to have up to three hours per week in primary school on an equal footing with English. In lower secondary school, where two languages will be obligatory starting in 2005, regional languages can also be an option on an equal footing with other foreign languages. Teachers will receive further training in regional languages. Starting in 2002, special competitive examinations will lead to recruitment of teachers who can already teach regional languages or provide instruction in another subject through the language. A decree will set up these competitive examinations for teachers of eight languages (Basque, Corsican, Breton, Catalan, Creole, and Occitan and the languages of Alsace and the Moselle). Lang's policy goal was some form of bilingual education starting at *the maternelle* (nursery school) level for France. His ambitious goal was to provide children with equal fluency in French and the regional language by *CM2* (the third year of primary schooling). The opening of sections in primary schools would be based on sufficient parental demand, and at secondary level, along the model of European language international sections (two subjects taught in the regional language and the language itself with the exception of mathematics, history/geography, and physical education). These sections will be mentioned on the Baccalaureate (secondary school examination and diploma). Lang even floated the idea of immersion programs at a future date. With a daring usually not seen in French educational debates, the minister proposed to include private schools in contributing to modern languages instruction, referring particularly to the classes provided by specific regional language and culture associations. This last gesture provokes the republican secular or *laïque* majority in French society.

The response by Alain Bentolila, professor of linguistics at the University of Paris V and a strong critic of the work of the French interministerial body for literacy in France (Groupe interministerielle permanent de lutte contre l'illettrisme), in an article in *Le Monde* summarizes the position of much of the French education community. He considers that the role of the school in the French republic is to equitably distribute linguistic power among all children. That means that schools must prepare children to use the national language, French: "For that is the priority, to give all pupils the means to speak correctly, to read correctly and to write correctly in the national language" (Bentolila, 2001: 16; translated by the author). For Bentolila, effective mastery of French does not mean lack of respect for regional languages. But he does believe that the school cannot change the balance of sociolinguistic power in society. He does not believe that regional languages, with fewer speakers, can acquire the power and dynamism they lack in society in this way. His position is widely shared. It is certainly for that reason that the sections mentioned in the ministerial circular will not be allowed to teach mathematics (the most important subject for selection in French society) or history-geography (the subject most fraught with political meaning) in regional languages.

President Jacques Chirac once again addressed this issue on October 15, 2001, in a plenary speech to the 31st UNESCO (United Nations Educational, Scientific, and Cultural Organization) General Conference in Paris. He lauded the preparation for debate of a "Draft Universal Declaration on Cultural Diversity" and called for greater attention to cultural and linguistic diversity worldwide. He was referring, however, to the use of French in international exchange and greater use of minority languages outside France. He had not changed his position on the use of regional languages within the French public school system. In fact, the French Constitutional Council had once again reiterated its position earlier in October (Chirac, 2001: 18).

VIOLENCE IN SOCIETY AND SCHOOLS

Over the past three years, violence has become a major preoccupation throughout Europe and North America, especially with respect to schools. A major crisis occurred in France in 1999 to which former Minister of Education Claude Allègre responded with a national action plan against violence in schools. He was forced to resign. It was in this setting that Jack Lang was named minister. And he has made security the number-one political issue with respect to education.

Among thoughtful observers of the French climate, Hugh Starkey (2001) noted: "The school is one of the central institutions of the French Republic and violence directed against the school is, as well as a symptom of crisis, a direct attack on the State by its youngest citizens who are also its future." However, Starkey, along with the author of this chap-

ter, notes that the French republic was founded on the basis of a particular view of citizenship, and that view is still the dominant one. The
French model is based on the undifferentiated citizen, whose public and
private lives are quite distinct. These spheres in a society that recognize
its multicultural or linguistic and cultural diversity are not so watertight.
Starkey goes so far as to affirm that education for citizenship in the
twenty-first century cannot be effective in outmoded institutions. He
states "that Republican schools need therefore to be based not just on
the transmission of a culturally hegemonic body of knowledge but on a
recognition of and respect for the varied communities in which their
pupils live. That in itself would constitute something of a revolution"
(Starkey, 2001: 2).

National reports for government have been commissioned by the Ministry of Education since the early 1990s on violence in schools or difficult
schools. A European Observatory of Violence and Schools is currently
housed in the University of Bordeaux led by Eric Debarbieux, a well-
known French specialist on violence and education issues. But in fact, as
Debarbieux and other observers outside the French media would argue,
violence is concentrated in a smaller number of schools than appears to
be the case. Also, the nature of institutional violence or the violence and
lack of respect for pupils by the school system and its actors is almost
never taken into account, much less the dimensions of direct, indirect,
repressive, or alienating violence education might perpetrate, which
could be analyzed in the holistic framework developed by Salmi (Salmi,
2001).

Also, as Debarbieux (1996) argues, the perception of violence in
schools by pupils and staff increases, the more attention is focused on
the issue. The percentage of pupils and teachers feeling insecure in
schools is on the increase. A growing number of pupils no longer have
confidence in the school as a safe and effective place. Michel Wieviorka
(1999), sociologist, wrote that teachers and their unions also orchestrate
perceptions of violence. Since French schools are structured so that teachers are not responsible for any pastoral care or discipline, they are loathe
to give up their free time for any noninstructional activity outside class
time. They are of course the least likely to provide a model of mutual
respect for pupils, as is discussed later in this chapter.

A very few observers are sensitive to the lack of democracy and mutual respect in schools as institutions. Bernard Defrance (1993) and sociologists François Dubet and Marie Duru-Bellat (2000) are among the
rare authors to raise such issues. Defrance argues that children and especially adolescents attend schools where they have no voice whatsoever. They have no independent authority to whom they can submit
cases of perceived injustice at any level. School councils function to the
advantage of teachers, and parent or pupil concerns must be humbly

expressed. Head teachers or principals lack the authority and the will to arbitrate fairly, and sanctions vary from teacher to teacher. They are also frequently unjustified, nor is there any mechanism to ensure that sanctions are commensurate or even related to the actual misdemeanor. For example, a teacher may arbitrarily give a pupil a zero on an examination because of his or her being late for class. In any case, teachers consistently consider students or their families or their home environment to be at fault and rarely question their own pedagogy.

Studies by Limage (2001) and Starkey (2000a) draw attention to the republican origins of this apparently unfair situation in an attempt to look at the strengths and weaknesses of different models of schooling for the promotion of democracy. The French model appears assimilationist rather than integrationist. The basis of state education goes back to the French Revolution and involves initiation into a common culture through a single curriculum. It does not recognize difference. The republic should guarantee equal treatment to all citizens. The curriculum is therefore undifferentiated, and although equal resources are to be allocated, the fact that they are allocated to a diverse group of pupils with diverse abilities, with consequent inequality of outcome, remains largely undiscussed. Only in rethinking the educational priority areas or ZEPs has there been a discourse about greater community and family participation in the nonpedagogic aspects of schooling or differentiated teaching and learning (Simon and Solaux in Koubi and Gugliclmi, 2000).

There is enormous resistance to any notion of pluralism. The overriding concern remains a fear that society may break up into ghettos of religious, ethnic, or cultural and linguistic communities. This fear is clearly summarized in the discussion of the Islamic headscarf issue later in this chapter. It was also in the forefront in June 1999 when the European Charter of Regional Languages was declared unconstitutional by the Constitutional Council of France and when it reiterated its opinion in October 2001. Both issues test the limits of the republican model. But the historical conditions in 1792 and the need for national unity are clearly not the same as those in an era of globalization. It is useful, therefore, to retrace the path that has been traveled.

LIBERTY, EQUALITY, FRATERNITY: A CENTRALIZED SCHOOL SYSTEM INTENDED TO PROMOTE EQUALITY

Since the first condition of all instruction is to teach only truths, institutions established by the state (public power) must be as independent as possible of any political authority. . . . [T]hat independence is best ensured by the assembly of representatives of the people, because it is the least prone to corruption . . . and the least likely to be an enemy of enlightenment and progress than any other power. . . .

Thus, instruction should be universal. . . . It should be distributed with all the equality which available resources allow. . . . No public institution should have the authority or even the possibility to prevent the development of new truths, the teaching of theories which contradict its particular policies or its short-term interests. (Extracts from the "General Organization of Public Instruction Report," Condorcet, April 1792, quoted in Allaire and Frank, 1995; author's translation)

The highly centralized French school system has always been perceived to offer the best means to promote equality and national unity. The notion of the state in the Enlightenment sense began to take form with the French Revolution in 1792 (Furet, 1978). The France of the late eighteenth century was a linguistically and culturally diverse collection of regions and divergent interests. Contemporary France is still fundamentally diverse in spite of 200 years of centralization, imposition of the French language, and enormous efforts to promote a unified notion of equality in a single state, administered in a superficially equal manner (De Certeau, Julia, and Revel, 1975).

It has long been thought that only a highly centralized system could and would effectively redistribute the nation's wealth to reduce regional disparities and special interests. This view extends, of course, well beyond France and in centralized countries/systems of schooling and is only marginally challenged from within. While globalization, the expansion of multinational corporations, and the movement toward a more politically and economically united Europe proceed at one level, the basic principles upon which the French state was founded and the school system that it built to support those principles continue fairly untouched by outside influence.

Social science research of the 1960s and 1970s such as that of Pierre Bourdieu demonstrating the social reproduction role of this centralized system has had little long-term impact on how French schools are administered, how French teachers teach, or how schooling is organized. Other research demonstrating that the school system straightforwardly contributes to wastage and underachievement by arbitrarily creating failure at an early age (échec scolaire), such as that of Baudelot and Establet (1989), still has little impact on how equality of opportunity is best defined. Even very recent studies about the actual disparities between resources allocated by the central state school system to different regions has little effect on philosophical debate about the role of schooling (Dubet and Duru-Bellat, 2000). The fact that conditions of teaching and learning at a material level vary from one part of the country to another, that in spite of basic principles inequality of resources actually dominates school provision in France, has little impact on how decision makers, intellectuals, trade unions, and the school administration see matters.

Parents and pupils are rarely heard (Fernoglio and Herzberg, 1998; Gurrey, 1997).

Stasse (1997) finds the origin of the notion of equality before the law in the "Declaration of Human Rights and Those of the Citizen" of 1789 in the statement that "all men are born and remain free and equal under the law." The notion of equality progressively comes to mean that all citizens confronted by a similar situation should be treated *identically* under the law. This means that no distinction can be made between citizens on the basis of race, religion, or origin.

The critical definition of positive discrimination has a basic weakness. The concept of equality before the law has had little impact on reducing economic, social, and cultural inequalities in France (or elsewhere). The State Council recognizes the weakness of the simple principle of equality before the law and begins to address equality of opportunity as a form of social solidarity. Most of the social welfare measures of the post–World War II period and those currently under debate or criticism today have been developed with this second concept in mind. And even more recently, equity as equality of condition enters the arena of political debate. The implications for schooling are critical, but the response is extremely hesitant. On the one hand, the overriding principle that equality should mean providing everyone with the same instruction or knowledge (with respect to schooling) does little to address the issue of inequality of ability or interest to take advantage of that body of knowledge or instruction. The French school system was founded in the latter part of the nineteenth century on the principle of equal access to the same education for all at the first stage (primary school). But it has taken nearly a century for the notion of positive discrimination to gain any ground. Educational priority areas (ZEPs) based on the British model have been developed with the rationale that more educational resources (numbers of teachers, ancillary staff, and necessary security personnel or building repairs) need to be provided to particularly disadvantaged areas.

But these measures are seen as temporary and fraught with the risk of further stigmatizing or marginalizing the populations they are meant to serve. The argument in France remains that special measures must lead back to the mainstream view of equality, the ability to participate on the same footing with all other young people, regardless of socioeconomic origin, with the same access to the same body of knowledge.

An understanding of this philosophical position is critical to understanding why and how French schools actually operate and the contours of debate about schooling. It plays a critical role in the experience of children of immigrant origin in French schools and frames the discourse concerning "integration" of populations of differing religions, geographic origins, and socioeconomic status.

TEACHERS IN FRANCE

Most teachers in France are civil servants. It has long been a corollary of the basic principle that the state is responsible for providing equal instruction for all that the best way to ensure that responsibility is through a civil service. The civil service is viewed as the best means for ensuring that teachers remain independent of outside pressures, be they of passing political views, the voices of families or children, or religious positions. The French primary school teacher of the late nineteenth century was seen as a moral authority to promote the republican ideas of liberty, equality, and fraternity in an atmosphere of secularity and complete neutrality. And if we return to the earlier quotation from Condorcet as he addresses the National Legislative Assembly in 1792, the roots of this view of teachers are already present. Condorcet refers to a system of instruction free of all outside influence in which all have access to a body of knowledge based on the truth as it is understood in a specific historic context. There is full agreement that a single idea of truth is to be taught by schools although what constitutes truth will change over time. But the school system and its teachers will remain the best neutral judges of what is best to include in the body of knowledge to be conveyed.

The history of French unionization of teachers reflects this very particular perspective. Initially, teachers did not have the right to organize, but as they did begin to do so, many tendencies of a political nature arose to distinguish between different views of what it meant for civil servants to unionize. According to André Robert (1995), early forms of organization have simply been intended to protect and promote better conditions of service rather than question in any way the content of education or its transmission. This was not a difficult decision since a strong distinction has long been made between what constitutes school-based knowledge and instruction and a larger role that has not been that of the school, namely, to educate.

French teacher unions of all tendencies question salary and working conditions, allocation of positions in different parts of the country, insecure conditions and violence, and attempts to ask them to take on additional tasks that are not purely instructional tasks and any nonformalized contact with parents or pupils. They do not take on pastoral care or organize clubs, for example, as do teachers in many other countries, with few exceptions.

Parent associations are welcomed solely to support teachers in their demands for better conditions of service and are no way considered as partners in what goes on within the classroom. Parents and teachers as well as pupils have been united in major demonstrations in very recent times on maintaining a secular school system (in the 1980s, a confrontation between greater control over private, essentially Catholic schools; in the mid-1990s, against an attempt by the conservative government to allow state resources to be spent on improving private school buildings, again essentially Catholic). In 1995 and again in 1997 and 1998, teachers, parents, and pupils have gone on strike to protest violence in schools. André Robert (1995) found that teacher preoccupation remains resolutely the same over time. Teachers "instruct." Parents "educate." Pupils receive successfully or otherwise "knowledge."

SCHOOL-BASED KNOWLEDGE AND CIVICS

Since school-based knowledge remains exclusively the domain of the state, and it is "transmitted" by teachers, there is only highly formalized means for including new or alternative issues, events, or changes in French society. History and civics education are the content areas in a highly compartmentalized system of disciplines that are of particular interest in this context. For the past 15 years or so, successive ministers of education wanted to give civics education a real place in secondary school programs. At present, civics education is hidden at the lower secondary level in a short course on the institutions of the Fifth Republic and general moral principles of the secular French system of government. But the content of a renewed and enlarged program has beaten each minister.

Minister of Education Jack Lang, like his predecessor, proposes that civics education have a place throughout all schooling and that it be based on the principles of tolerance, responsibility, respect for rights and obligations, secularity, solidarity, and courtesy. Since no one can be opposed to these generalities, the problem lies in how one takes the step from general principles to a syllabus.

Civics education has consistently been the content area the most difficult to define in French schooling for these reasons. There is no question of "social studies" or "current events" periods American style. There is certainly no place for examination of cultural, religious, or linguistic diversity or tolerance. The only content that has appeared noncontroversial has been the study of the institutions of government in a fairly formalized manner. Another major stumbling block is already inherent in the institutional context of schooling. There is no space for the practice of democracy in the school as institution, the classroom in particular. Parent bodies, as already mentioned, are outside the school and negotiate from the exterior. Parent representation on school councils that meet several times a year in no way allow parents or their representatives to discuss pedagogical matters. Similarly, student representatives on these councils and student organizations are simply formally present to ask polite questions and receive decisions taken by teachers about their classmates. They are not the site of dialogue.

The practice of democracy and participation has little place in the schools. It is quite customary for teachers to insult their pupils of all ages with vague accusations of how stupid they are and how incapable. School report cards in the French tradition frequently are noted: "doesn't have the level (*niveau*); lazy, unmotivated, incapable, needs to make a greater effort." And teachers are not accountable for these vague comments, which follow a pupil throughout his or her school career. Again, the impunity of teachers and the school administration makes it very difficult to envisage a civics education based on a shared view of individual and collective responsibility. The imbalance of power is too flagrant. The only response possible to many young people is to retreat into indifference or insolence (Defrance, 1993; Gurrey, 1997).

EQUALITY THROUGH EXAMINATION-BASED SELECTION

Another major constraint to developing a sense of individual and collective responsibility in French schools has to be mentioned, although not fully developed in this chapter. The French system is an examination-oriented system of education. Although overt selection after primary schooling has been eliminated, orientation and instruction at the secondary level are bound and structured by the examination pupils will take in different forms of post lower-secondary schooling. While the syllabus for all schooling is decided centrally, so too the examination system dictates what will be taught and how it will be taught. As long as a particular form of writing is critical to success in the philosophy examination at the baccalaureate examination or another in the French-language examination, all instruction focuses on those formalized rituals.

The goal remains in terms of equality to offer pupils equal opportunity to learn how to successfully express themselves in terms of a highly codified means of expression at oral and written examination time. The form of expression is considerably more important than the content, and outside knowledge that has not been transmitted by the teacher (or obtainable in the families of middle-class households) is anathema (*hors sujet*).

PRINCIPLES OF SECULARITY, NEUTRALITY, EQUALITY, AND PRIVATE SCHOOLING

While the philosophical foundations of French society and schooling are intended to offer equality before a body of knowledge, they allow for limited diversity, let alone pluralism. There is little acknowledgment of the cultural and linguistic diversity that make up the school populations of France and French society in general. Since the French Revolution, the effort to impose the French language on all other dialects and languages has been seen as the best way to convey republican principles and develop national unity. Hence, the languages and cultures of immigrant populations of first, second, and third generations as well as the regional languages of France have little place in schools. For a very long period, the latter were actually forbidden even on the school playground. The terms *multiculturalism* or *preservation of cultural identities* have no place in schools, other than the exceptional look at recipes or songs or folklore of other cultures at the primary level. Foreign-language instruction at the secondary level is usually restricted to traditional English, German, Russian, Spanish, possibly Greek, Latin, or Portuguese. Students wishing to take Arabic or less-often-spoken languages may do so with special authorization by taking outside or distance education courses only. The very recent circular of regional languages in schools introduced earlier in this chapter has yet to be implemented.

Respect for secular (*laïc*) schooling is perhaps the strongest normative pillar of French political philosophy. The historic attempt to separate church and state has deep roots and awakens a passionate response whenever perceived as being threatened. The long negotiations with the Catholic Church over nearly two centuries have culminated in a delicate balance that can be upset easily. The historic battles between the Catholic Church and successive French governments have been referred to as *guerres scolaires* quite literally. With respect to more recent "battles," an attempted reform under Minister of Education Alain Savary in the early 1980s to create greater state control over Catholic schools led to such protest by Catholic families and politicians that the minister was forced to resign, and President Mitterand had to withdraw the proposed legislation. Even more recently, teachers, parents, students, and politicians committed to secular education took to the streets to protest a proposed law allowing state monies to be used by the regions to repair and improve Catholic school buildings under contract with the state. That proposed law was not enacted.

The major piece of legislation that defines the role of private (essentially Catholic) schools, the Debré Law (Loi Debré) was enacted in 1959 after World War II. In the post–World War II period, the Debré Law (finally adopted after long negotiations with the Catholic Church and the powerful pro-Church groups in France) became a compromise. The state funds teachers' salaries in the religious schools, but in exchange, the schools should be open to all pupils in the area and should respect the freedom of religious conviction of each individual. The state also determines, as with secular public schools, the basic syllabus. The Debré Law was weakened by two later pieces of legislation. Under Minister of Education Olivier Guichard (1971), the state entered into a simple contract with Catholic schools and committed greater funds to teacher training. With the Guermer Law (1977), further advantages were granted to Catholic schools without a demand for reciprocal responsibilities (Allaire and Frank, 1995).

In spite of the major concessions made to religious schooling in terms of Catholicism, the overriding discourse concerning French public schooling remains more than ever committed to a secular and neutral system. The most recent reaffirmation of this commitment is contained in the Circular of December 12, 1989, signed by then Minister of Education Lionel Jospin, as a result of the State Council's verdict concerning the wearing of head scarves in school by girls of Islamic origin. The actual conflict will be looked at in some detail later in this chapter, but it is important to cite the introduction to this ministerial circular to emphasize basic principles:

Secularity, a constitutional principle of the French Republic, is one of the pillars of the public school. At school like elsewhere, religious beliefs are a matter of individual conscience and freedom. But since all children come together in school without any form of discrimination, the exercise of freedom of belief with the public service's responsibility for respect for pluralism and neutrality, means that the entire educational community should be protected from any form of ideological or religious pressure. (Lionel Jospin, Introduction to the Circular of December 12, 1989, cited in Allaire and Frank, 1995: 246–247)

IMMIGRATION IN FRANCE: AN OVERVIEW

France has a long history of political and economic immigration. The pace and scale of immigration from former colonies and other countries of the Mediterranean Basin accelerated after World War II. Each group, depending on its origin, motivations for emigration, and similarity to French cultural norms and practices, has had a different experience. It is misleading to consider central and eastern European immigrants or Spanish, Italian, and Portuguese alongside immigrants from North Africa or sub-Saharan Africa. It is also quite misleading to assume that all immigrants holding some Islamic cultural heritage have come to France under similar conditions or with similar expectations or have found a similar response to their needs and aspirations. A large research-based literature has developed, especially since the late 1960s, concerning immigration to France and other western European countries (e.g., see Limage, 1984, 1985; Minces, 1973; OECD–CERI, 1983).

France's declining demographic situation since the turn of the twentieth century, however, made it a more likely destination for both political and economic immigration than many other western European countries. The need for an enlarged workforce led to a continuing growth of clandestine as well as official immigration until the early 1970s. Across nationalities and at the risk of oversimplification, however, economic immigration usually meant that emigrants had a plan to return to their countries of origin once their material conditions allowed. Among immigrant groups who have maintained this plan as dream or concrete project, Portuguese, Spaniards, and Italians have been found to be most likely to foresee a possible return. Political and economic refugees from central and eastern Europe have been least likely to consider return migration. In a first period, North African (Tunisia, Morocco, Algeria) and sub-Saharan African immigrants came with plans to return and forwarded earnings to families left behind. As economic conditions and, in many cases, political conditions have deteriorated, both in Europe and in countries of origin, the plan to return has seemed less and less likely.

With the onset of economic crisis in the early 1970s, most European countries drastically limited immigration. France was among the last to place such restrictions and confine further immigration to family reunification (especially among North Africans and, to a lesser extent, sub-Saharan Africans from former colonies). France has also been seen, when compared with other European countries, especially Germany, as one of the most open to, first, immigration and, second, the possibility of acquiring citizenship. Germany has always been seen as the country with the most restrictive immigration policies, calling economic immigrants *Gasterbeiter* (guest workers), reinforcing the temporary nature of their stay and welcome. Sociologists in the 1970s and 1980s easily discovered that immigrants were most likely to seek permanent residence in countries that welcomed them (at least at an official level) and least likely to do so where both reception and conditions of stay were most restrictive (Germany) (Césari, 1997a; Charlot, Lauran, and Ben Dhiab, 1978; Granotier, 1970; Limage, 1975, 1984, 1985).

Both countries of origin and countries of immigration have attempted to regulate movements of populations with varying degrees of success. As it has become clear that the political and economic conditions on a global scale have continued to deteriorate, these attempts have taken the forms of incentives measures (sums of money to encourage voluntary departures) and more spectacularly in very recent times in France with forced departures for clandestine immigrants or those whose residence and work permits have expired. Countries of origin have long sought ways to maintain contacts with their expatriate populations without encouraging return migration. These means have included formal agreements with the host country (France in this case) to organize language and culture classes, *amicales* or associations for mutual support and celebrations, and to some extent, assistance in developing places of worship.

These measures will be discussed in some detail with respect to populations of Islamic origin.

IMMIGRANTS OF ISLAMIC CULTURE: DIVERSITY OF POPULATIONS, DIVERSITY OF ASPIRATIONS

Before looking at the educational response to immigrants of Islamic origin, it is essential to recognize the diversity this title actually represents.

Moroccan and Tunisian immigration is more recent than that of Algerians. Moroccans came to France essentially during the 1960s until about 1973. Tunisian immigration began in the mid-1960s and also ended around 1973. It has always been on a much smaller scale. Tunisian immigration also has a fairly specific socioeconomic character. Tunisians have been more likely to run small businesses and shops. Similarly, Moroccans have also been more likely to arrive with a small amount of capital to start a business. Algerian immigration, on the other hand, has been on a much larger scale over a much longer period of time and with a much larger impact on French society (Geisser, 1997).

It has taken considerable time, however, for official French society to recognize that impact fully. Each North African country had a particular relation to France. Only Algeria was considered under the colonial period as an integral (if unequal) part of France and recognized as a *département*. Large numbers of Algerians volunteered in both World War I and World War II to fight alongside the French. But it was only in 1998 that the president of the republic, Jacques Chirac, publicly acknowledged the contribution of Algerians to the protection of the "metropole" during both world wars.

The category "French from Algeria" or "Maghrébins français," covers even greater diversity. For the purposes of this chapter, reference is made to all categories, but only those of Islamic origin are further discussed. First, a large French population settled in North Africa—Algeria in particular—over several generations. When forced to return to France at each country's independence, each population has constituted a group known as *pieds noirs*. A second category of North Africans of Jewish faith both were readily granted French citizenship and immigrated massively at the time of independence of each North African country. While these two groups have had some privileged treatment when compared to other North African immigrants, they have also encountered, nonetheless, difficulties in integration and assimilation. Berber populations (non-Arab) of Algeria (Kabylie) and Morocco have distinct migration patterns. The repression of their languages and cultures by the Arab elites has not contributed to bringing them closer to other Arab immigrants in France.

Nonetheless, the French public does not necessarily note the difference.

Probably the group that has encountered the greatest amount of misunderstanding and disappointment has been the "harki." Even the term *harki* covers a wide range of people and is frequently used in a pejorative sense. The North African, mainly Algerian, populations who composed the administration, officers, and soldiers working on behalf of France before Algeria's independence are known officially as RONA (Rapatriés d'origine nord-africaine). With either title, they have found least sympathy both in Algeria and in France. Their various motivations for working with the colonial power and then seeking asylum in France after being perceived as traitors by the victorious Algerian independence forces (National Liberation Front—FLN) have been the object of less publicity and even less justice in France (Geisser, 1997; Hamoumou, 1994). Hamoumou documents the diversity of motivations and backgrounds of Algerians who worked with the colonial power in some way, in many cases with no particular political attachment. The Algerian war of independence was undoubtedly the most violent on all sides and has left both Algeria and France with lasting bitterness along with lasting and current concerns over an equally brutal ongoing civil war. The Muslim populations who sought protection from the retreating French (for whom they had worked) were widely betrayed, and those who eventually reached France were placed in camps. Most of these camps were in isolated areas and remained homes to these populations for more than 20 years. Their children grew up in these camps and attended separate/ segregated schools for the most part, rather than being integrated with the rest of the French population and the children of other immigrants including Algerians. Unemployment among this population is estimated officially at 42 percent of the active population (and as high as 62 percent by those concerned), whereas official French unemployment is estimated at roughly 12 percent. (Bruno, 1997; Césari, 1997a, 1997b; Hamoumou, 1994).

Other immigrants of Muslim culture and Algerian origin who have immigrated over the past 50 years also must be distinguished by period of immigration, generation, and nationality. There are a considerable number of Muslims of Algerian origin who immigrated prior to the war of independence, that is, before 1962. They have, for the most part, taken French nationality and are difficult to count. Similarly, second- and third-generation Muslims of Algerian origin with French nationality are not considered as "foreigners," although they may feel some attachment to cultural roots. Each generation is also characterized by a socioeconomic background. The discovery of the 1960s and early 1970s was that of "slums," or *bidonvilles* (Granotier, 1970). The discovery of the 1980s and the 1990s has been that of decaying suburbs or *banlieues*. Multiple factors have led second- and third-generation Muslims of Algerian origin to develop new identities and a certain pride. *Beur* culture is a combination of distant ties to North Africa and current search for identity between an "official" French society and the reality of disadvantaged suburbs characterized by insecurity, violence, unemployment, and new forms of solidarity in gangs or community-based associations.

North African immigrants who have come as university students, intellectuals, and artists seeking freedom of expression or wider professional possibilities constitute elites who apparently find it easier to assume both their origins and their status in France. In a recent study carried out by Vincent Geisser (1997) of how North African elites act politically as they take French nationality and participate, especially in local government, has shown that the vast majority give priority to French republican ideals and processes and seek to mediate between the larger Muslim origin community and the French state. Geisser comes to the conclusion that these political elites are actually unable to serve the mediation role assigned to them. It is especially interesting that both Geisser and Césari (1997a, 1997b) have found a very complex political scene. While integration of Algerian immigrants (and other North Africans) has passed essentially through trade union movements, the attempts by the Socialist and Communist Parties to include and promote French of Muslim culture has been less successful than the more conservative parties and recent governments. It is beyond the scope of this chapter to speculate why this seems to be the case, but a considerable part of the response appears to be linked to the more conservative French government's recent attempts to create and control a distinctly French Islam with representative institutions (Bruno, 1997; Césari, 1997a, 1997b).

RECEPTION IN FRANCE: CONTOURS OF EDUCATIONAL RESPONSES TO IMMIGRANTS IN SCHOOL

After the effervescence of "mai '68" (May 1968) in France and student and worker uprisings across Europe and North America, the French left wing discovered the most disenfranchised population: the immigrant worker and, in some cases, his family. Numerous associations and solidarity groups were created to "accompany" and encourage this heterogeneous population. With respect to adults, the entire movement for adult literacy (called *alphabétisation de travailleurs migrants*) quickly developed to promote access to what was, in fact, French as a second language. This discovery of literacy issues among the immigrant population created both a service and a disservice. For the next 10 years, all literacy difficulties were officially associated with immigrants, especially North Africans, and no attention was given to the broader French public (Limage, 1975, 1986). The service was the creation of networks of training for adult immigrants to acquire rudiments of spoken and written French. Initially, the French Ministry of Education took some responsibility but quickly returned that responsibility to nonprofit and profit associations. The finance for most of these programs came from the Fonds d'Action Sociale (FAS), a fund composed of social welfare benefits withheld from mainly male immigrant workers whose families had not rejoined them in France. The FAS continues its work today, although it has broadened its clientele if not its resources. In her doctoral dissertation of 1975, this author identified over 200 associations offering some form of adult basic education called adult literacy or French as a second language (Limage, 1975).

As family reunification became the main source of official immigration from the mid-1970s onward, countries of origin of immigrants entered into bilateral agreements with France to offer instruction in "mother tongues" or official first languages of children of immigrants. The French Ministry of Education resolutely insisted that these classes were not their responsibility, and governments of countries of origin, eager to demonstrate their continued links with their expatriate populations, financed teachers and rented space in public schools in order to provide such instruction outside classtime (Limage, 1980; OECD-CERI, 1983). Thus, children whose families wished them to maintain some form of contact with the languages and cultures of origin attended and attend classes, essentially taking place outside regular school time with no cooperation from French teachers nor participation of French children of nonimmigrant origin. In the 1970s, some effort was made to make French teachers more aware of the backgrounds of immigrant pupils in their classrooms through in-service training. The number of teachers applying for such training (voluntary at the time) was minimal. For the most part, the response of the French school system to the linguistic and cultural diversity of its pupils has been rather homogeneous: grade repetition, placement in special education classes (when the issue is lack of language skills rather than individual handicap), and in some cases, special reception classes for special French-language instruction.

By and large, children of immigrant origin appear to have received the same treatment but to an even larger degree than French children of French background. The public school maintained its primacy concerning legitimate knowledge and the means to transmit it in the name of republican ideals of neutrality, secularity, and equality. The notion of individualized instruction or cooperative learning or making the school more responsive to the child has met with little response as diversity remains an out-of-school matter (Limage, 1980, 1990).

THE FRENCH GOVERNMENT AND THE DEVELOPMENT OF A "FRENCH ISLAM"

Origins of Interest in Islam in France: Dilemmas of Republicanism and Fear of Foreign Influence

The attempt to regulate or institutionalize relations between the French government and Islam in France has been a completely new experience for everyone concerned. Muslims are making their first discovery that they constitute a "minority," while French officialdom takes note of the impact of Islam in its many forms on French society. This process is in progress, and it would be extremely difficult to do other than trace the distance covered to date. As mentioned earlier, the first sign of an Islamic presence occurred when small groups of individuals sought and set up rooms in which to pray and hold meetings, either within their apartment buildings in distant suburbs or nearby. A second phase has involved the creation of various associations with differing motivations and goals, often in competition with each other. The most recent phase, the intervention of the French government in the 1990s, marked a turning point. There is a renewed effort in a sense of urgency since September 2001 to create the institutional arrangements for a coordinated Islamic body so that the complex communities may dialogue with the French government.

Initiatives, Policies, and Counterresponse

A law passed in 1981 removed obstacles to foreigners creating associations of their own and led to the creation of groups to support prayer rooms of a modest nature. These initiatives began as solely the prerogative of local groups neither supported nor hindered by outside, let alone foreign, influence. In a second phase, associations sponsored by North African governments have indeed offered financial or spiritual support. In the case of Algeria, the Mosque of Paris ("de Paris") officially sponsored by that government has made a concerted effort to extend its jurisdiction over local prayer groups and associations by offering temporary "imams" or spiritual leaders or through the consulates by offering Arabic-language teachers.

Local prayer groups supported either by outside associations or by limited local assistance tend to become community meeting places as much as places of prayer. They have also progressively taken on the educational role of language instruction or religious instruction. It is their educational role that seems to have had a soothing effect on local authorities. A great variety of prayer groups exist, very dependent for their activities on the personalities and ages of those who lead them. Young and educated Muslim community leaders are more ambitious, and their centers offer classes in calligraphy, music, and literature, help with homework for children, leisure activities, and sports.

After a number of years, the popularity of such prayer rooms and community centers has led to their inability to fulfill all that is expected of them. In the later 1980s and especially in the 1990s, in specific cities in France with high concentrations of Muslims, a demand to build actual mosques has emerged. This stage has been an extremely delicate one, with local sensitivities finally discovering the visibility of Islam. Many will argue that it is high time that Islam and its practice in France be allowed the same guarantees of religious practice as those of other faiths. One area of controversy is in fact misleading. The argument that local or national tax money will be spent on mosques if they are allowed is actually untrue. The state does not finance purely religious construction. That is why most mosques built over the last 10 years have had financial assistance from other Arab countries, especially the Gulf States and Saudi Arabia.

On the other hand, there has been an effort over the past 10 years to create some federation of Muslim associations, community centers, and mosques. A considerable number of actors in this struggle, and it does appear especially conflictual, are too diverse in their goals to work together. It is, however, possible to distinguish the role of countries of origin as well as that of the French government. First among the actors in this struggle is the Paris Mosque sponsored by the Algerian government. Given the size of the population of Algerian origin as well as the long history of close links with the country, it is not surprising that the French government has leaned toward the Paris Mosque and its spiritual and managerial leaders. This preeminence has led to a long history of conflict. In 1992, a rector of French nationality was named for the first time, Dalil Boubakeur. Until this nomination, the rectors have been Algerian.

A small number of fairly vocal federations of associations also exist, which while disagreeing among themselves on many matters do advocate an autonomous Islam in France, especially an autonomy in relation to the Paris Mosque. The best known of these federations of associations include the Fédération nationale des musulmans de France (FNMF) and the Union des organizations de France (UOIF). The former was created in 1985 through the initiative of a Frenchman converted to Islam, Daniel Youssouf Leclerc. After a rather tumultuous period, the organization seems to be under Morocccan influence. The latter, the UOIF, was created in 1983 by Tunisian intellectuals. It favors fairly strict obedience to Islamic rituals and customs while engaging in cautious dialogue with other religious groups in France. Other associations with other orientations are also growing and developing with support from many external sources.

The French government had been fairly indifferent to the practice of Islam in the country and to its organization in some way facilitating dialogue. That position has changed rapidly in very recent years. As the visibility of religious practice in prayer rooms (*salles de prières*) became more evident and as the financial backing for further growth, educational initiatives, and building increased, various actors in the French government and in the competing associations and federations of associations representing different interests surrounding Islamic cultures sought ways to dialogue in a more traditional manner. In a first instance, the French government attempted to compare the means of dialogue that developed with the French Jewish community through the Conseil représentatif des institutions juives de France (CRIF). The long history of French Judaism is beyond the scope of this chapter. It should be mentioned, however, that it has never seemed truly feasible to create the same institutional arrangements for the Islamic communities in France. In addition, international crises and internal security fears have created a more confused image of the reality of Islamic communities in France, further complicating policy positions based on anything more solid than temporary responses to immediate situations.

Until the early 1980s, the French government generally saw the extremely heterogeneous community of Islamic culture as an immigrant worker issue (as with educational measures discussed earlier in this chapter). In 1976, Paul Dijoud, the secretary of state for immigrant workers, took several initiatives to encourage the creation of prayer rooms in large factories or businesses in which Islamic workers were employed and encouraged flexibility with respect to observance of Islamic holy days. Later, in 1982, television and radio programs for the Islamic public were created.

International events in the early 1980s around the creation of Islamic movements in other countries of the Machrek and the Maghreb led to new attention to domestic Islam. Nonetheless, official interest in French Islam began to be mainly a security preoccupation. After the successful negotiation of freedom for French hostages in Lebanon by Algeria, French Minister of the Interior Charles Pasqua announced that the Paris Mosque issue was settled: It remained under Algerian jurisdiction. In 1988, Pierre Joxe, minister of the interior and also secretary of state for religious affairs, created the commission Conseil de réflexion sur l'islam en France (CORIF). This commission was intended to act as a source of advice and communication between the government and the Islamic communities on any and all issues that might be of mutual concern. In fact, this commission marked the entry of the French government into Islamic affairs in a concrete manner. The role of the government and its capacity to dialogue with a responsible and responsive partner seemed all the more urgent after the Salman Rushdie fatwa and then the head-scarf issue in French schools. Also, as Islamic communities wishing to obtain planning and construction permission for mosques in various cities in France became more and more problematic when left to mayors and city councils, the government felt obliged to step in (Bruno, 1997; Césari, 1997a, 1997b; Geisser, 1997).

It is interesting to note how the French government justified this intervention in religious matters. In a first instance, it was pointed out that the majority of Muslims in France were, in fact, French. On the other hand, the majority of imams, or religious leaders and teachers, were foreign. There was no facility in France for the training of imams. Hence, virtually all of them came from abroad. Nonetheless, CORIF gave every sign of representing a legitimate partner for the government, holding little credibility among the actual Islamic communities in France. In fact, with a change in political majority in the French National Assembly in 1993, this commission was disbanded. The alternative solution became a simple return to giving the Paris Mosque (still under Algerian tutelage) priority. The rector, Dalil Boubakeur, in turn, created another consultative body composed of the most visible associations and individuals in the Islamic communities (Conseil consultatif des musulmans de France). This new phase led to a long crisis in the Islamic communities who refused to accept the authority of the Paris Mosque under Algerian hegemony. Nonetheless, Minister of the Interior Charles Pasqua gave the Paris Mosque authority for the ritual killing of animals intended for consumption (*halal*). The council also developed a "Charter" for Muslim practice in France, although the actual text was authored by the Paris Mosque leaders. Since this document was intended to reconcile the Islamic communities with their French nationality and provide for their religious aspirations, the controversy was focused on the hegemony of the Paris Mosque rather than on the content of the charter.

Amid much debate and controversy, another body was formed on December 16, 1995: the Haut Conseil des musulmans de France, somewhat on the model of the Jewish CRIF. The debate, however, continues, and no unified voice appears to emerge from the various temporary alliances among Islamic leaders and intellectuals in France. Alliances occur over specific issues but re-form or disintegrate on the longer-term concept of a single body speaking for Islam in France. The French government continues to take initiatives that provoke further debate. For example, since 1996, a policy concerning the construction of regional mosques (Evry, Lyon) has led to further dissension in the communities intended as beneficiaries.

The very notion of the French government attempting to create a unified Islam in France, either through councils or by giving priority to the Paris Mosque (backed by Algeria), is a novel and problematic position for a society based on secular, neutral, and equal relations by its institutions with the public. Theoretically, some of the issues actually to be treated by the government with the Islamic community already have precedents in terms of the Jewish community: ritual animal slaughter for making meat kosher, charitable organizations and activities, special food considerations, and holy days. Even the creation of private Islamic schools is not an insurmountable problem. The obstacles are actually more political within the highly diverse Islamic origin communities (Bruno, 1997; Césari, 1997a).

The challenge remains to accommodate the very real links of Islam in France with its sources and inspiration abroad while ensuring respect for republican principles. Further, as Islamic practices are frequently perceived as more cultural than ritual, it is these practices that actually produce conflict. An apt illustration of this dilemma is the head-scarf affair of 1989, which still has its echoes in France.

Reaffirmation of Secular Principles: The *Foulard Islamique* Affair

Since 1989, the reaction of school authorities, parents, pupils, and the larger community in France to the wearing of head scarves in lower and upper secondary school by a handful of girls of Muslim origin has created both a political and a sociological debate. That debate remains unresolved, although the courts of France continue to hand down decisions concerning various appeals by families whose daughters have been excluded from school for wearing the scarf. The various cases and arguments are summarized here.

As the second part of this chapter has emphasized, the French state and its public schools are seen as the repositories of neutrality, secularity, and equality before the law of all citizens. Schools are intended to form pupils to become responsible citizens through access to the same knowledge. There should be no outside influence by parents, community groups, or political or religious organizations. Religion is considered a very private matter, and proselytism is absolutely forbidden in the institutions of the French republic. All the more, teachers and other civil servants are bound to adhere strictly to these republican values.

Thus, when a handful of adolescent girls in several cities in France began wearing head scarves to school at the instigation of their families, the reaction was immediate. In addition to wearing the head scarves in many instances, the girls refused to participate in physical education activities and were supported in their initiatives by Islamic organizations or associations. The reaction of *proviseurs*, or principals and teachers alike, was to request the removal of the head scarves and the insistence that the girls participate like all other pupils in the obligatory classes of the school program. The refusal to remove head scarves and/or participate led in most instances to the girls being sent home. In a few cases, they were temporarily grouped in school libraries. The first demonstrations for and against this sign of "religious" practice were tense and remain so, in spite of the legal decisions taken to date.

In a first instance, the State Council (Conseil d'Etat) rendered a judgment that reminded the French public that it is the civil servants of the state who must remain neutral in all their official responsibilities, not the clients or, in this case, the pupils. Religious affiliation may be discreetly displayed as long as there is no attempt to convert or disturb the public in any way. The State Council left it to the minister of education to advise schools how to deal with this phenomenon. The minister of education reaffirmed the principles of neutrality and the secular nature of the school system. He asked, however, that each school principal and teaching staff treat the cases on an individual basis. He advised discussion and consultation with the girls and their families and an attempt to find a negotiated solution.

Unfortunately, French school administrators, especially principals, are unused to authority over the teaching staff in French schools, let alone dealing with sensitive issues of cultural and religious conviction (Allaire and Frank, 1995; Gruson, 1978). The decision making had, however, been placed in their hands. This has meant that over the past 10 years a number of cases have reached the courts in which girls have been excluded for wearing head scarves. By and large, the courts overturn these exclusions unless the wearing of the head scarf has been accompanied by a refusal to attend physical education classes or been associated with protest by outside organizations (demonstrations, meetings, etc.) (Kessler and Bernard, 1997).

This continuing conflict is perceived from two perspectives in France. The first issue, that of religious neutrality and secular public space, is fairly understandable. The other and perhaps overriding issue is more sociological. The status of women in Islamic countries and cultures predates Islam and reflects a strong patriarchal social order. International crises, especially the civil war in Algeria where women and children are the first victims of rape, massacre, and humiliation, have a very strong influence on French public opinion. The wearing of the head scarf is interpreted as a sign of girls' and women's lack of equal rights with men in Islamic societies. Above all, it appears as a potential threat to hard-won human rights for women, as for the most part, North African women have been less frequently veiled, cloistered, or subjected to purdah than Islamic women in countries of the Machrek, Sudan, and sub-Saharan Africa. Nonetheless, all three Maghreb countries still maintain the Family Code based on the Sharia or Islamic code of conduct in which women have a clearly secondary status.

It is thus difficult for the French public to engage in cultural relativism with respect to young women living in France and probably of French nationality. It is obviously an impossible task to decide whether the young woman is wearing the scarf voluntarily, because of religious conviction, under force, or as a sign of expressing her complex cultural identities. What strikes public opinion most forcefully is the fact that head scarves were not an issue in earlier years. It is the rise of a stronger Islamic identity around the world with its associated conflicts and aspirations that seems to have created fear and suspicion. France, of course, is not alone in this reaction.

CONCLUDING REMARKS: CONVERGING APPROACHES TO EQUALITY

This chapter has focused primarily on the principles that have framed the creation of institutions and policies in France for two centuries and the impact on schooling. The larger context is the continued difficulty for the French state to provide equality and solidarity as official discourse has promised since the end of World War II. The same issue is an international preoccupation. High levels of unemployment and growing levels of poverty in France, the United States, and worldwide, coupled with reduced public spending and alternating attempts to turn countries into basically market economies, then to redress the situation, have taken their toll. The centralized state has not led to redistribution of wealth and resources, notably for public schools, nor has the highly decentralized approach in the United States. Equality defined either in terms of opportunity or in terms of outcome remains a moving and controversial target. At the same time, cultural and religious diversity are not promoted as an appropriate goal in French institutions. Mutual respect and understanding are seen to be best learned through thoroughly secular institutions. The school is still seen as both a "safe haven" for young people and the place to learn the values of "liberty, equality, and fraternity" as defined by the French republic. The challenge since the end of 2001 is greater than ever.

NOTE

The views expressed in this chapter are those of the author and in no way reflect the organization with which she is employed.

REFERENCES

Allaire, M., and Frank, M.T. (Eds.). (1995). *Les politiques de l'éducation de la France de la maternelle au baccalauréat*. Collection: Retour aux textes. Paris: La documentation Française.

Baudelot, C., and Establet, R. (1989). *Le niveau monte. Réfutation d'une vieille idée concernant la prétendue décadence de nos écoles.* Paris: Editions du Seuil.

Bentolila, A. (2001). L'école et les langues régionales: Maldonne. *Le Monde*, May 15, p. 16.

Bernard, P. (2001). Sciences-Po à l'heure de la "discrimination justifiée" *Le Monde*, April 27.

Blanchard, S. (1998a). Huitième manifestation des collèges et lycées en grève. *Le Monde*, April 25, p. 8.

Blanchard, S. (1998b). Les profs jugent le lycée. *Le Monde*, March 6, pp. 1, 13.

Bréchon, P. (Ed.). (1994). *Le discours politique en France. Evolution des idées partisanes.* Paris: La documentation Française.

Bruno, E. (1997). *La France et L'islam.* Paris: Hechette.

Césari, J. (1997a). *Etre musulman en France aujourd'hui.* Paris: Hachette.

Césari, J. (1997b). *Faut-il avoir peur de l'Islam?* Paris: Presse de Sciences Po.

Charlot, M., Lauran, A., and Ben Dhiab, A. (1978). *Mon avenir? Quel avenir? Témoignages de jeunes immigrés.* Paris: Casterman.

Chirac, J. (2001). *Provisional Verbatim Records. First Plenary Meeting, Monday, 15 October 2001* (vr/1 prov.) (pp. 16–21). 31st General Conference. Paris: UNESCO.

Citron, S. (1998). Et les collèges, monsieur Allègre? *Le Monde*, February 18, p. 14.

Coquillat, M., and Sellier, G. (1998). Et les filles? *Le Monde*, February 18, p. 14.

Debarbieux, E. (1996). *La Violence en milieu scolaire. 1. Etat des lieux.* Issy-les-Moulineaux: ESF éditeur.

De Certeau, M., Julia, D., and Revel, J. (1975). *Une politique de la langue. La Révolution française et les patois.* Paris: Gallimard.

Defrance, B. (1993). *Sanctions et discipline à l'école.* Paris: Syros.

De Queiroz, J.M. (1997). Ecole, laïcité, citoyenneté. *Cahiers français* (May–June) (Special issue: "Citoyenneté et société"), pp. 58–63.

Dubet, F., and Duru-Bellat, M. (2000). *L'hypocrisie scolaire. Pour un collège enfin démocratique.* Paris: Seuil.

Etienne, B. (1989). *La France et l'islam.* Paris: Hachette.

Fernoglio, J., and Herzberg, N. (1998). La Seine-Saint-Denis peine à émerger, après trente années d'abandon. And—Enquête sur la Seine-Saint-Denis, le département le plus défavorisé. Chômage, pauvreté, insécurité, etc.: Un concentré des maux de la société française. *Le Monde*, April 25, pp. 1, 8, 9.

Ferreol, G. (Ed.). (1994). *Intégration et Exclusion dans la société française contemporaine.* Lille: Presses Universitaires de Lille.

Furet, F. (1978). *Penser la Révolution française.* Paris: Gallimard.

Garcia, E. (2001). *Excellence for All: An Analysis of California's Recent Policies and Their Effects on Instructional Practices for Linguistically and Culturally Diverse Students.* Opening plenary in the Researching Literacy in Communities and Schools Conference of the International Association of Applied Linguistics Commission on Literacy, University of California, Santa Barbara, August 3.

Geisser, V. (1997). *Ethnicité républicaine. Les élites d'origine maghrébine dans le système politique français.* Paris: Presse de Sciences Po.

Granotier, B. (1970). *Les travailleurs immigrés en France.* Paris: Editions François Maspero.

Gruson, P. (1978). *L'Etat enseignant*. Paris: Mouton/Ecole des hautes Etudes en Sciences Sociales.

Guibert, N. (2001a). Jack Lang installe les langues régionales dans le service public de l'éducation. *Le Monde*, April 26, p. 10.

Guibert, N. (2001b). Les premiers étudiants issus des "conventions ZEP" font leur entrée à Sciences-Po. *Le Monde*, September 15, p. 12.

Gurrey, B. (1997). Introuvable éducation civique. *Le Monde*, December 2, pp. 1, 20.

Gurrey, B. (1998). Ecoles riches, écoles pauvres, les écarts ne cessent de s'aggraver. *Le Monde*, February 12, p. 8.

Hamoumou, M. (1994). Les harkis: Une double occultation. In G. Ferreol (Ed.), *Intégration et Exclusion dans la société française contemporaine* (pp. 79–104). Paris: Presses Universitaires de Lille.

Hervo, M., and Charras, M.A. (1971). *Bidonvilles*. Paris: Editions François Maspero.

Jencks, C., and Peterson, P.E. (1991). *The Urban Underclass*. Washington, DC: Brookings Institution.

Jencks, C., et al. (1972). *Inequality. A Reassessment of the Effect of Family and Schooling in America*. London: Allen Lane.

Kessler, D., and Bernard, P. (1997). Le Conseil d'Etat et le "foulard islamique." *Cahiers français* (May–June) (Special issue: "Citoyenneté et société") pp. 63–64.

Koubi, G., and Guglielmi, G.J. (Eds.). (2000). *L'égalité des chances. Analyses, évolutions, perspectives*. Paris: La Découverte.

Lamchichi, A. (1999). *Islam et musulmans de France. Pluralisme, laïcité et citoyenneté*. Paris: Harmattan.

Lequin, Y., Baubérot, J., Gauthier, G., Legrand, L., and Ognier, P. (1994). *Histoire de laïcité*. Besançon: Centre Régional de Documentation Pédagogique de Franche-Comté.

Limage, L. (1975). *Alphabétisation et culture. Cas d'études: L'Angleterre, le Brésil, la France et le Viet Nam*. Unpublished Ph.D. dissertation, Université Paris V–René Descartes.

Limage, L. (1979). *Education for Linguistic and Cultural Minorities. The Case of France*. Study prepared for the OECD-CERI project on the Financing, Organization and Governance of Education for Special Populations. Paris: OECD-CERI.

Limage, L. (1980). Illiteracy in Industrialized Countries: A Sociological Commentary. *Prospects* 11(2): 155–171.

Limage, L. (1984). Young Migrants of the Second Generation in Europe: Education and Labour Market Insertion Prospects. *International Migration* 22(4): 367–387.

Limage, L. (1985). Policy Aspects of Educational Provision for Children of Migrants in Western European Schools. *International Migration* 23(2): 251–261.

Limage, L. (1986). Adult Illiteracy Policy in Industrialized Countries. *Comparative Education Review* 30(1) (February): 50–72.

Limage, L. (1990). Illiteracy in Industrialized Countries. On Myth and Misunderstanding. In *Literacy Lessons*. Geneva: International Bureau of Education.

Limage, L. (2000). Education and Muslim Identity: The Case of France. *Comparative Education* 36(1): 73–94.

Limage, L. (Ed.). (2001). *Democratizing Education and Educating Democratic Citizens: International and Historic Perspectives.* New York: Routledge/Falmer.

Minces, J. (1973). *Les travailleurs étrangers en France.* Paris: Editions Seuil.

National Center of Educational Statistics. (1996). *Digest of Educational Statistics.* Washington, DC: U.S. Department of Education, table 203.

OECD-CERI. (1983). *The Education of Minority Groups. An Enquiry into Problems and Practices of Fifteen Countries.* Paris: OECD.

Ozouf, M. (1984). *L'école de la France. Essais sur la Révolution, l'utopie et l'enseignement.* Paris: Gallimard.

Robert, A. (1995). *Le syndicalisme des enseignants.* Series: Systèmes éducatifs. Paris: La documentation Française.

Salmi, J. (2001). Violence, Democracy and Education: An Analytic Framework. A manuscript from Salmi, J. (1993). *Violence and Democratic Society: New Approaches to Human Rights.* London: Zed Press.

Simon, J., and Solaux, G. (2000). L'ecole et L'egalite des chances. In G. Koubi and G.J. Gugliemi (Eds.), *L'egalite des chances: Analyses, évolutions, perspectives.* Paris: La Découverte.

Starkey, H. (2000a). Education for Citizenship: Reinventing the French Republic. Open University, unpublished manuscript.

Starkey, H. (2000b). Liberté, laïcité, identité. Is the Defence of Laïcité in Schools a Threat to the Fifth Republic? Open University, unpublished manuscript.

Starkey, H. (2001). *Education for Citizenship: Reinventing the French Republic.* Unpublished paper. London: British Open University.

Stasse, F. (1997). Egalité et discriminations positives. In *Regards sur l'actualité* (pp. 19–25). Paris: La documentation Francaise, Mensuel No. 232, June.

Tomasson, R.F., Crosby, F.J., and Herzberger, S.D. (2001). *Affirmative Action: The Pros and Cons of Policy and Practice.* Lanham, MD: Rowman and Littlefield.

U.S. Department of Commerce, Census Bureau. (1995). *1/1000 U.S. Census Sample, 1980, 1990; Current Population Survey (March).* Washington, DC: U.S. Department of Commerce, Census Bureau.

Vega, J. (1999). Language Minority Rights or the End of Bilingual Education in California. In L. Limage (Ed.), *Comparative Perspectives on Language and Literacy* (pp. 33–45). Dakar: UNESCO-BREDA.

Wieviorka, M. (1999). *La Violence en France.* Paris: Seuil.

CHAPTER 8

Recognizing and Educating Religious Minorities in England and Wales

LESLIE FRANCIS

HISTORICAL ROOTS

Contemporary educational provision in England and Wales rests on foundations that were put in place at the beginning of the nineteenth century. Understanding of these foundations needs to appreciate two key features of the religious and cultural context in which they were placed. At the beginning of the nineteenth century England and Wales were regarded and governed as one country. At the beginning of the nineteenth century the Church of England was the established church in Wales as well as in England.

The original initiative to provide a network of schools throughout England and Wales, which could do more than provide education for the children of those who could afford to pay significant fees, came not from the state but from voluntary initiatives. Moreover, these voluntary initiatives were inspired and shaped by the churches (Cruickshank, 1963; Murphy, 1971). Right from the outset, therefore, religious interests were involved in the provision of schools.

The crucial initiative was taken in 1808 when a group of Free Churchmen founded the Royal Lancasterian Society from which the British and Foreign School Society emerged in 1814, supported primarily by nonconformists and some liberal Anglicans. British schools were established to promote "the education of the labouring and manufacturing classes of society of every religious persuasion." Religious instruction in British schools was confined to scripture and "general Christian principles." It was one of the society's original rules that

[t]he lessons for reading shall consist of extracts from the holy scriptures; no catechism or peculiar religious tenets shall be taught in the schools, but every child shall be enjoined to attend regularly the place of worship to which its parents belong. (Francis, 1987: 12)

In a sense British schools were already established to serve the interests of religious minorities, in the form of individuals who had dissented from the established church.

The National Society was founded in 1811 by the established church as a direct response to the Royal Lancasterian Society and had the backing of the great body of Anglicans. National schools were established to promote "the education of the poor in the principles of the established church." Religious instruction in National schools was to include the doctrines, catechism, and liturgy of the established church. In its early days the National Society was willing to be liberal in its outlook and made allowances for children whose parents objected to the religious instruction given in the schools. The Royal Commission of 1818 made it clear that at this stage "[t]he church catechism is only taught and attendance at the established place of worship only required of those whose parents belong to the establishment" (Francis, 1987: 12). Later, however, National schools generally took a harder line and insisted on attendance for religious instruction and attendance at an Anglican church on Sunday as conditions of entry to the school. In this sense the National schools were already established to discriminate against religious minorities.

Very soon the greater resources of the National Society, in association with the parochial clergy, enabled it do draw ahead of the British and Foreign School Society. By 1830 the National Society had established 3,678 schools, educating approximately 346,000 children.

The state did not enter the field of public education until 1833, and then it did so not by establishing state schools but by distributing public funds to the National Society and the British and Foreign School Society. A government grant of £20,000 was distributed between the two societies to assist with school building. The government grant was essentially in "aid of private subscription," being available only to those voluntary bodies that could raise the first half of building costs and guarantee to meet all future running costs. Because of the greater voluntary resources available to the Church of England, by 1839 about 80 percent of the state grant went to Anglican schools. In this sense, state aid was already discriminating against religious minorities.

In 1839 a committee of the Privy Council was set up "to superintend the allocation of any sums voted by Parliament for the purpose of promoting education." Between 1833 and 1870 the state continued to contribute to public education solely through the administrative system provided by voluntary societies. In 1847 the state was spending £100,000 on education; a decade later it was spending £500,000. In 1847 it was spending public money only on school buildings; a decade later it was contributing toward teachers' salaries, toward the provision of apparatus, and by means of capitation grants, toward the annual income of the schools.

With the provision of state grants, the number of schools established under the sponsorship of the two societies continued to grow. By 1851 there were 17,015 Church of England schools with nearly 956,000 pupils and 1,500 nonconformist schools with 225,000 pupils.

The religious minority to lose out most significantly during these early days of state aid was the Roman Catholic Church. Originally state aid was only available to support schools that used the Authorized Version of the Bible, and Catholic teaching refused to approve this Protestant translation. Not until 1847 was state aid sanctioned for Catholic schools, and the Catholic Poor School Committee was established to handle this funding.

The overall consequence of leaving school building to voluntary initiative was threefold. In areas where denominational rivalry was strong and well financed, denominational schools were built to compete one with another. In such areas religious minorities were relatively well catered for, as Anglican, Catholic, and Free Church schools grew up side by side. In areas where the Church of England retained a monopoly on resources the Anglican school became the only option. In such areas religious minorities could either accept education at the hands of the Anglican church or go uneducated. In areas of rapid industrial expansion, where schools were most needed but where neither church nor chapel was well resourced, educational provision remained erratic. In such areas there were no religious winners.

When the 1870 Elementary Education Act established the machinery of school boards for building schools in areas where voluntary provision was inadequate, the intention was to supplement the work of the denominational societies, not to supplant them. By the end of the nineteenth century voluntary provision still accounted for 71 percent of the nation's schools.

LEGACY OF THE 1944 EDUCATION ACT

Although church schools came under increasing financial pressure during the first four decades of the twentieth century, by the time of the 1944 Education Act the churches still owned a sufficiently high proportion of the nation's schools to place them in a very strong position to influence the details of that act. The partnership between church and state in state-maintained education as we know it today is a direct result of the way in which the power of the churches was used (see, e.g., Butler, 1971).

The 1944 Education Act set out to reconstitute the educational system after World War II. At the heart of its thinking was provision of secondary education for all. To make this possible a large number of schools required extension, modernization, and reequipment; new senior schools were needed. On the one hand, the churches could not afford to maintain their voluntary schools and to bring them up to the new standards required. On the other hand, the state could not afford to buy up the church schools and was reluctant to annex them. In short, the denominational schools presented a major political problem.

The compromise achieved by the 1944 Education Act enabled the churches to give up some of their control over church schools in return for greater control over certain aspects of the rest of the state-maintained sector of schools. There were three components to this compromise. The first component established school worship as obligatory in all state-maintained schools. Although collective acts of worship had been a major feature of the English educational scene, they had never previously been made a statutory obligation. The second component made religious instruction obligatory in all county schools and specified that such instruction shall be in accordance with a locally agreed syllabus. Moreover, the churches, and the Church of England in particular, were guaranteed a key role in determining the content of the locally agreed syllabus. The third component extended to voluntary schools the choice between "aided" or "controlled" status. This choice enabled schools that could afford to retain a high level of independence to do so, while those that either could not afford or did not desire to retain such a high level of independence could nevertheless retain something of their church-related character.

The voluntary aided school approximated the status of the nonprovided school and involved the churches in continued financial liability. The managers or governors of a voluntary aided school were responsible for the capital expenditure on alterations required by the local education authority to keep the premises up to standard, for external repairs to the school building, improvements, and extensions to existing school buildings. Government grant aid was made available to meet 50 percent of these costs. In return for their continued financial involvement, the churches retained the right to appoint a majority of the school managers or governors and to provide denominational religious instruction and denominational worship. If the managers or governors of a voluntary aided school decide that they no longer wish or can afford to maintain voluntary aided status, the school may become voluntary controlled.

The voluntary controlled school gave the churches reduced rights but involved no ongoing financial liability. In this case, the churches retained the right to appoint a minority of the school managers or governors. Religious instruction is given according to the agreed syllabus, but parents may ask for denominational teaching "during not more than two periods each week." Provided the teaching staff of the voluntary controlled school exceeds two, up to one-fifth of the staff can be "selected for their fitness and competence to give such religious instruction." These are called "reserved teachers." The daily act of worship is in accordance with the trust deed and may, therefore, be denominational in character. Once a voluntary school had accepted controlled status, the act made no provision whereby the school could become aided.

The denominations responded differently to the compromise offered by the 1944 Education Act. Free Church opinion generally considered that the provisions for worship and religious education in county schools obviated the need for continued investment in church schools. The Roman Catholic Church rejected the greater state influence over voluntary controlled schools and opted for voluntary aided status. The Church of England remained divided on the issue. Some Anglicans, like Bishop Brook of St. Edmundsbury and Ipswich, adopted the view that the Christian presence in education could best be preserved through nondenominational religious education in county schools. He argued:

It is my conviction that so far as religious education is concerned it is neither buildings, syllabuses, nor timetables that matter most. What matters is that the teachers in all the schools whether voluntary or county shall be Christian men and women. (Francis, 1987: 18)

Others, like Bishop Kirk of Oxford, took a completely different line:

Undenominationalism is the first step on the road to complete irreligion, and . . . true religion is only possible by virtue of active and loyal membership in a worshipping community. Our church schools are essential means towards making our witness effective; we must not let them go. (Francis, 1987: 18)

In the absence of an agreed central policy on the comparable merits of voluntary aided and voluntary controlled status, each diocese formulated its own recommendations, which the school governors within its area could choose to follow or to ignore, at least as far as their independent sources of finance would permit. Some dioceses, like London, Southwark, and Blackburn, opted heavily for voluntary aided status; other dioceses, like Bristol, York, Coventry, and Lichfield, opted mainly for voluntary controlled status.

As a consequence of the different responses of the denominations to the opportunities and challenges of the 1944 Education Act, the contours of religious schooling in England and Wales were redrawn. Three features characterize this new picture. Schools operated by the Free Churches were closed or transferred to the local education authority. There are now very few Free Church schools remaining in England and Wales. The Roman Catholic Church initiated a policy of building new voluntary aided schools to meet the needs of the Catholic community. The provision of Anglican schools in England and Wales varied from one diocese to another.

As well as the Christian churches, one other religious group made good use of the opportunities offered by the 1944 Education Act. Like the Roman Catholic Church, the Jewish community sought state support for voluntary aided schools in areas where there were significant numbers of Jewish pupils.

In addition to the provision for religious schools within the state-maintained sector, the 1944 Education Act recognized the place of independent or fee-paying schools unsupported by state funding. A number of religious foundations continue to be associated with schools of this nature.

LEGISLATIVE CONTEXT

Following the 1944 Education Act, government initiatives and educational legislation left the church school issue relatively unaffected until the early 1980s, apart from three significant developments. The first of these developments had positive implications for church schools, while the other two developments had negative implications.

The first issue concerned the cost to the church of maintaining voluntary aided schools. According to the settlement of the 1944 Education Act, government grant aid was made available to meet 50 percent of the capital costs borne by the governors. Right from the outset the Catholic authorities argued the injustice of the financial burden carried by the church, in comparison with the much more favorable arrangement secured in Scotland under the 1918 Education Act (Scotland, 1969). During the years after the 1944 Education Act, the churches' inability to meet their financial commitment to church schools became increasingly clear. In subsequent legislation the government grant was raised in three stages: to 75 percent in 1959, 80 percent in 1967, and 85 percent in 1974. While these increases were generous in comparison with the expectations set in 1944, they may not have been sufficiently generous to compensate for the disparity between rising costs and dwindling church resources. The nature of the problem was well reflected in the title of a working party report prepared in 1972 by the Schools Committee of the General Synod Board of Education, *Crisis in Church Schools: A Report on Finance* (Schools Committee of the General Synod Board of Education, 1972).

The second issue concerned the structuring of secondary education proposed by the government circular 10/65. The reorganization of secondary education had one important implication for primary schools. In requesting local education authorities to submit plans for comprehensive reorganization, circular 10/65 listed a system of middle and upper schools, either of 9–13 and 13–18 or 8–12 and 12–18, as one legitimate way of implementing change (see, e.g., Hargreaves and Tickle, 1980). Local education authorities that opted for middle schools immediately placed two pressures on the Church of England dioceses to which they related. The first pressure concerned the decapitation of church primary schools. Given the fact that a high proportion of church schools are small rural schools, the removal of the upper classes of primary pupils reduced the total number of pupils below the level of viability. The second pressure concerned the financing of new middle schools deemed large enough to satisfy government criteria for secondary reorganization.

In a detailed analysis of the response of one rural diocese, St. Edmundsbury and Ipswich, to the challenge of circular 10/65, Francis documented the rapid closure of church schools in the villages and the inability of the church to develop a viable network of middle schools (Francis, 1986). One particular minute of the diocesan education committee summed up the situation: "The position of the Church of England was most uncertain, there being no money to implement proposals."

The third issue concerned the question of small schools. This debate was reestablished by the Plowden Report in 1967. Here the case against small schools was advanced in educational terms suggesting that small schools can restrict their pupils' social, emotional, and intellectual development, limit their social opportunities to mix with their peers, deprive them of the benefit of working within the range of teachers needed to offer different skills, and curtail their acquaintance with educational resources, curriculum materials, and extracurricular activities (Plowden Report, 1967). The case against small schools was bad news for the Church of England's large investment in small rural primary schools. This pressure on small schools was exacerbated during the 1980s by increasing financial concerns. For example, in 1981 the government circular *Falling Rolls and Surplus Places* advised a minimum primary school size of 100 pupils, while the White Paper, *Better Schools* in 1985 recommended that schools catering to 5- to 11-year-olds should have at least one form of entry (for further detail, see Francis, 1992). The continued importance of this issue for the Church of England is reflected in two booklets published by the National Society, *The Future of Small Schools* (Small Schools Working Party, 1991) and *Small Schools* (Lankshear, 1995).

From 1980 onward the impact of legislation on church schools accelerated considerably, including the 1980 Education Act, the 1981 Education Act, the 1986 Education (No. 2) Act, the 1988 Education Reform Act, the 1992 Education (Schools) Act, the 1993 Education Act, and the 1996 Nursery Education and Grant Maintained Schools Act.

The 1980 Education Act changed the constitution of governing bodies and strengthened the role and responsibilities of governors. The implications for church schools were enormous. First, in view of the autonomy of each school trust, the provision of new instruments and articles of government for Anglican schools took many years following this act, not least because of the complexity created by the need to ensure that the tradition of parochial involvement in the governing bodies was continued to the satisfaction of every parish. The response to this legislation was costly to the church. Second, the introduction of parents and teachers to the governing body began to shift the balance of power and range of opinion. While in voluntary aided schools the foundation governors continued to outnumber other governors, their majority was reduced from the two-thirds guaranteed by the 1944 Education Act. Third, governors were obliged to provide a range of information for parents, including a clear statement regarding admissions policy. From this stage onward, admissions policies needed to be explicitly stated, fairly operated, and subject to appeal procedures. This proved to be no simple task for church schools.

The 1986 Education (No. 2) Act carried three implications for church schools. First, a further revision was required for the instruments of government of voluntary controlled schools, despite the fact that in some areas the instruments created under the 1980 act had not yet been implemented. This involved further administrative effort. Second, the governors of all schools were required to meet once a year with the parents and to make a report to them. The third consequence of the act might have been beneficial to the church. Since 1944 it had been possible for voluntary aided schools to become voluntary controlled, but no mechanism existed for voluntary controlled schools to become voluntary aided. The 1986 act at last provided a route for voluntary controlled schools to gain or regain voluntary aided status. In view of the difficulty and costliness of this route, few schools have benefited from the change in law.

The most significant issue to face church schools as a consequence of the 1988 Education Reform Act concerned the option of grant-maintained status (see, e.g., Flude and Hammer, 1990). On the surface, there appeared to be many advantages to the church in opting for grant-maintained status. As far as the religious provision of the school is concerned, the same principles apply as to the status prior to opting out. In other words, grant-maintained schools that were formerly voluntary controlled can continue to provide denominational worship, while grant-maintained schools that were formerly voluntary aided can continue to provide denominational religious education as well as denominational worship. The advantage of opting out for the voluntary aided school is that governors cease to be responsible for 15 percent of capital expenditure. The advantage of opting out for the voluntary controlled school is that, having opted out, the foundation is responsible for appointing a majority of governors, rather than a minority as applied to voluntary controlled status.

The National Society and General Synod Board of Education greeted the opportunity for grant-maintained status with caution. A booklet published in 1988 included the following two warnings:

Governors of Church schools will need carefully to balance a proper self-interest with a Christian concern for the effects of their actions on the rest of the maintained system in their area. Going grant-maintained may be a means of escaping threats of closure or grudging ministrations from an unsympathetic local authority. It may also be a means of an already privileged, strong school gaining more privileges and becoming stronger at the expense of other schools (including church schools) in the area.... The absence of any continuing financial input from the church could strengthen the arm of any future government wishing to abolish church schools. (National Society, 1988: 6–7, 8–9)

The second challenge faced by church schools as a consequence of the 1988 Education Reform Act concerns the claims that the act has given to other schools much of the autonomy previously only enjoyed by church schools. As a consequence the church has needed to become clearer about the distinctive role of church schools within the state-maintained system in order to justify its continued involvement.

Third, the 1988 Education Reform Act made the provision of Standing Advisory Councils for Religious Education a statutory requirement on all local education authorities. The distinctive role of the Church of England within the structure of the Standing Advisory Councils for Religious Education has raised the wider expectations placed on diocesan education teams.

The 1992 Education (Schools) Act developed a whole new system of school inspection. According to this system, all schools became subject to a regular inspection conducted by the Office for Standards in Education at four-yearly intervals. Within the act this became known as section 9 inspection. Church schools also became subject to a separate denominational inspection, known as section 13 inspection. In voluntary controlled schools section 13 inspection concerned the school worship, while in voluntary aided schools section 13 inspection concerned the religious education as well as the worship. In addition, the governors could invite the section 13 inspectors to report on the wider school ethos. The National Society responded to the challenge of section 13 inspection by establishing a training program for inspectors and by developing appropriate guidelines and literature (Brown and Lankshear, 1995; Lankshear, 1993). Under the 1996 School Inspections Act, section 13 inspection became known as section 23 inspection, and section 9 inspection became known as section 10 inspection.

The 1993 Education Act strengthened the government's commitment to promoting grant-maintained status. As a result of this act, governing bodies of all county and voluntary schools were required to review annually the status of their school and decide whether or not to become grant maintained. Revising its guidelines on grant-maintained status, the General Synod Board of Education continued to remain cautious, although recognizing that the progressive weakening of local education authorities in some areas vitiated the old model of partnership:

Church school governors, in deciding whether or not to apply for grant-maintained status, will consider the gains and losses for their own school, but the decision will not rest there. *Every church school is a part of the church's total participation in the education system of the nation* and governing bodies need to reflect on the impact of their decision on other schools in the locality and on the churches' total contribution to the national system of education. (National Society, 1994: 7)

The 1996 Nursery and Grant Maintained Education Act promoted the development of nursery vouchers. This development has left church schools with an opportunity but raises a crucial question regarding the adequacy of resources with which to respond to this opportunity.

CHALLENGES TO CHURCH SCHOOLS

The continued involvement of religiously distinctive schools within the state-maintained sector of education is not without significant and formidable challenge. In particular, three main sources of challenge need to be recognized.

The first challenge to church schools is rooted in educational philosophy. The best-known proponent of this challenge is Paul Hirst, whose position is summarized in two key papers (Hirst, 1972: 6–11, 1981: 85–93). In the first paper, published in *Learning for Living* in 1972, Hirst argues that the concept of "Christian education" is a contradiction in terms. On this account, the theologian is precluded from making a distinctive contribution to *educational* theory. In the second paper, published in the *British Journal of Religious Education* in 1981, Hirst extends the argument to church schools. On this account, the church school is precluded from making a distinctive contribution to *educational* practice. The main strand in Hirst's argument rests on his understanding of what is to count as education; another strand rests on his analysis of the educational implications of secularization.

Hirst's first point is that "there has already emerged in our society" a concept of education, according to which education constitutes an area of discourse autonomous in its own right. Hirst illustrates what he means by this autonomy by developing the parallel between education and science. He argues:

Just as intelligent Christians have come to recognise that justifiable scientific claims are autonomous and do not, and logically cannot, rest on religious beliefs, so also, it seems to me, justifiable educational principles are autonomous. That is to say that any attempt to justify educational principles by an appeal to religious claims is invalid. I am anxious that the terrible story of the long battle which Christianity waged and lost over science and religion be no longer repeated in the area of education and religion. (Hirst, 1976: 155)

For Hirst, to speak of Christian education is a misleading anachronism.

Hirst's second point draws a distinction between a *primitive* and a *sophisticated* concept of education. The primitive concept is concerned with passing on to children what we believe, so that they in turn come to believe it to be true. The sophisticated concept is not determined by what any group simply believes but by what on publicly acknowledged rational grounds we can claim to know and understand. The goal of the sophisticated concept of education is to develop a rationally autonomous person whose life is self directed in the light of what reason determines.

Hirst argues that because of their religious beliefs Christians are involved in the primitive concept of education. It is, however, the sophisticated concept of education that has a place in schools and that excludes the possibility of a distinctively Christian contribution to the curriculum. Hirst argues that according to the sophisticated view of education,

[t]he character of education is not settled by any appeal to Christian, Humanist or Buddhist beliefs. Such an appeal is illegitimate, for the basis is logically more fundamental, being found in the canons of objectivity and reason, canons against which Christian, Humanist and Buddhist beliefs must, in their term and in the appropriate way, be assessed. When the domain of religious beliefs is so manifestly one in which there are at present no clearly recognisable objective grounds for judging claims, to base education on any such claims would be to forsake the pursuit of objectivity. (Hirst, 1972: 8–9)

Hirst's third point is to develop a distinction between *education* and *catechesis*: In catechesis, the aim is from the stance of faith, the development of faith. Hirst argues that when the churches are in business to educate, they need to play by the same rules as secular schools; when the churches are involved in catechesis, they cannot be said to be engaging in education. While theologians may contribute to the theory and practice of catechesis, they are firmly excluded from being allowed a contribution to the theory and practice of education.

Hirst's fourth point is that church schools need to take seriously the distinction between education and catechesis. According to this argument, the two activities obey different rules and are in fact logically incompatible. A school undertaking both activities would find itself at one and the same time committed to trying to develop commitment to reason and commitment to a particular faith. The consequence of attempting to combine these incompatible activities would be confusion for both pupils and teachers.

While Hirst does not pursue his case to its logical conclusion of arguing that church schools, like Christian education, are necessarily a contradiction in terms, he does wish to impose stringent limitations on the church school. According to Hirst, the important condition that can legitimate church schools being involved both in education and catechesis is that these two activities are sharply separated within the school, being self-consciously and deliberately presented to the pupils as clearly different in character and objectives. In practice, this means separating the two activities both in time and in place and by the use of quite different personnel to make out the differences between those involved in "teaching" and "preaching."

Thus, Hirst is not simply arguing that there are difficulties either in formulating a coherent theological understanding of education or in putting this understanding to work through church schools. He is arguing that the very *logic of education* outlaws the possibility of the churches having a distinctive contribution to make to educational theory and practice. Hirst's argument did so much to undermine the church's self-confidence in church schools before considered responses began to challenge this position (see, e.g., Francis, 1983; Thiessen, 1985).

The second challenge to church schools is rooted in an analysis of the implications of denominational schooling for social integration within a multicultural society. The sharpest presentation of this position was advanced by the committee of enquiry into the education of children from ethnic minority groups in the report *Education for All* (Swann Report, 1985). After reviewing the arguments for and against voluntary schools for other ethnic and religious groups, the majority voice of the committee stresses misgivings about the implications and consequences of separate provision of any kind. Having come to this view, the majority voice of the committee faces the consequence that

[o]ur conclusions about the desirability of denominational voluntary aided schools for Muslims or other groups, by extension seriously call into question the long established dual system of educational provision in this country and particularly the role of the churches in the provision of education. (Francis, 1987: 39)

Six members of the committee dissented from this conclusion and formulated a different minority recommendation, supporting the provisions of the 1944 Education Act concerning voluntary schools and wishing to enable other ethnic and religious groups to benefit from these provisions: "We believe that it is unjust at the present time not to recommend that positive assistance should be given to ethnic minority communities who wish to establish voluntary aided schools in accordance with the 1944 Education Act" (Francis, 1987: 40)

In an oral statement to the House of Commons of March 14, 1985, following the publication of the Swann Report, Sir Keith Joseph, secretary of state for education, gave an immediate assurance that the government did not wish in any way to call in question the present dual system of county and voluntary schools. The clear division of opinion within the committee of inquiry, together with the education secretary's immediate response, added a new sharpness and immediacy to the debate about the future of church schools within a multicultural society.

The year before the publication of *Education for All*, reports from both the Roman Catholic Church (Catholic Commission for Racial Justice, 1984) and the Church of England (General Synod of the Church of England Board of Education, 1984) had given consideration to this issue. The Anglican report *Schools and Multi-Cultural Education* specifically emphasized the view that church schools can function as important centers of reconciliation among people of different races and creeds.

The third challenge to church schools is rooted in an analysis of the implications of denominational schooling for equality of educational opportunity. The sharpest presentation of this position has been advanced in a series of papers from the Socialist Education Association. In their 1981 discussion document *The Dual System of Voluntary and County Schools*, a key appendix focuses on two primary objections to church schools (Socialist Education Association, 1981). The first objection concerns the problem of religious privilege in a pluralist society. This objection acknowledges that if certain churches are permitted to operate voluntary schools, every sect and faith should be allowed the same privilege. It is argued that this would lead to divisive sectarianism and some of the difficulties already evident in a place like Northern Ireland. The second objection concerns the political problem of privilege itself within a socialist educational system. This objection argues that the continuing existence of the segregated voluntary school sector will frustrate the achievement of the truly comprehensive system.

The Socialist Education Association's 1986 document *All Faiths in All Schools* reports that the majority of those who sent comments on the original document supported the view expressed in this appendix (Socialist Education Association, 1986). The new report proposes

[t]he eventual establishment of a new unified system of maintained schools, in which voluntary schools—without sacrificing their ethos and individual approach—could gradually develop the capacity to educate a greater diversity of intake from their own local communities, and where county schools—without sacrificing their unifying secular approach—could gradually develop the capacity to meet more widely the religious and cultural needs of their intakes. (Francis, 1987: 38–39)

In 1990 the Socialist Education Association again confirmed the policy on voluntary aided and voluntary controlled schools, demanding that no new such schools should be opened, and requested that the Labor front bench teams conduct talks with the churches regarding transferring voluntary schools to the county sector (see news report in *Education*, 1990: 370).

EDUCATIONAL POLICY

In light of these significant criticisms of the place of church schools within the state-maintained system of education in England and Wales, it is sensible to examine the way in which the two main stakeholders in church schools, the Anglican Church and the Roman Catholic Church, have presented their educational policies. This examination draws attention to the two very different perspectives on church schools promoted by the Anglican and Roman Catholic Churches.

The Roman Catholic Church, having been a religious minority movement within England and Wales since the days when the very first Catholic schools were built, has adopted a clear view that Catholic schools are there to serve as a clear alternative provision to members of the faith community. The Roman Catholic Church's original rationale for being involved in church schools has been expressed in the classic formula "Every Catholic child from a Catholic home to be taught by Catholic teachers in a Catholic school." Insistence on this basic view by religious leaders is now couched in far less assertive terms than earlier this century. In 1928 Pope Pius IX's encyclical letter "Divini Illius Magistri" confirmed "[t]he prescriptions of canon law which forbid Catholic children on any pretext whatsoever to attend . . . schools open indiscriminately to Catholics and non-Catholics alike."

By way of contrast, the "Declaration on Christian Education" issued from the second Vatican Council (Abbott, 1966) reminded parents of "their duty to entrust their children to Catholic schools, when and where this is possible, to support such schools to the extent of their ability, and to work along with them for the welfare of their children."

In the document *The Catholic School* (Catholic Information Office, 1977) the Sacred Congregation for Catholic Education replaces the note of command with that of reasoned argument in favor of the Catholic school.

The report to the Bishops of England and Wales, *Signposts and Homecomings* (Konstant, 1981), recognizes that Catholic education should be confined neither to the years of compulsory schooling nor to the Catholic school. At the same time, the report reaffirms the identity of the Catholic schools as "a believing and integrated Christian community." It argues:

Within a Catholic school the ultimate distinctive element is that its life is based on the vision of Christ in which all learning, growing, service, freedom and relationships are seen as part of a growth in the knowledge, love and experience of God. In other words there is a deliberate hope that the experience of belonging to this school will encourage personal commitment to Jesus Christ. (106)

The history of the Church of England's involvement in church schools is very different from that of the Roman Catholic Church. When the first Anglican schools were built, they were built to serve not the interests of a religious minority but the whole community. As the established church of the land, the Church of England could assume that everyone was a member unless they had deliberately become dissenters and affiliated to some minority denomination, like the Catholic Church or the Wesleyan Methodists. Church of England policy statements on church schools over the past 30 years demonstrate the tensions that exist for an established church that in principle represents the majority of the population but that in practice attracts a practicing membership no larger than that attracted by the Roman Catholic Church in England and Wales.

It is the Durham Report, published in 1970, that provides the coherent starting point for understanding the Church of England's policy regarding church schools during the latter part of the twentieth century (Durham Report, 1970). While the Durham commission was established as "an independent commission to inquire into religious education," the report devoted a whole chapter to the discussion of church schools. This chapter made two crucial points that have shaped the Church of England's self-understanding in education throughout the rest of the twentieth century.

First, the Durham Report developed and sharpened the distinction between the Church of England's two historic motives for involvement in education. The report styled these two motives as the Church of England's *domestic* and *general* functions in education. The domestic function characterizes the inward-looking concern to "equip the children of the church to take their place in the Christian community." The general function characterizes the outward-looking concern "to serve the nation through its children." The Durham Report recognizes that historically the two roles were "indistinguishable, for nation and church were, theoretically, one, and the domestic task was seen as including the general" (207).

Second, the Durham Report evaluated the contemporary relevance of these two distinct functions and came to the conclusion that emphasis should now be placed on the general function rather than on the domestic function. Recognizing that "nowadays no one would pretend to claim that nation and church are coextensive" (208), the Durham Report argues that the domestic task can no longer be seen as including the general task. Consequently:

The church should for the present see its continued involvement in the dual system principally as a way of expressing its concern for the general education of all children and young people rather than as a means for giving "denominational instruction." (Durham Report, 1970: 281)

The report underlines this point again by recommending that "religious education, even in a church aided school, should not be seen in domestic terms" (226). Elsewhere the report argues that many of the difficulties associated with church schools "would disappear if the aided school were looked on as a service provided by the church, rather than something provided for the church" (254).

Following the Durham Report in 1970, the Church of England's next major statement on church schools appeared in the Green Paper *A Future in Partnership* (Waddington, 1984). While the Durham Report was the result of a commission of inquiry, *A Future in Partnership* was a somewhat more personal document drafted by Robert Waddington, general secretary to the National Society. Two main pointers emerge from this Green Paper. Set starkly side by side, these two pointers may appear to be looking in somewhat different directions.

The first pointer builds on the Durham Report's commitment to the church's general function in education. The Green Paper argues that the idea of *partnership* should be stressed in preference to the *dual system* and that the *voluntary* aspects of church schools should be stressed in preference to *denominationalism*. The emphasis of this aspect of the Green Paper argues for a balance of power in state-maintained education over an increasing trend toward educational dominance by central government. The church is seen as one component, alongside other political, community, parental, and professional bodies, in an educational partnership that offsets the claims of central government in determining educational policy and practice. It is argued that the maintenance of church schools gives the church an institutional credibility in this context. On this account, the Church of England sees its rationale for involvement in education to be in terms of balance, partnership, and voluntarism, rather than in terms of denominationalism, religious distinctiveness, or the dual system.

The second pointer draws on the resources of theology to construct a model of church schools in the light of the doctrine of the Trinity. According to this model, church schools may be distinguished by 10 key characteristics. Waddington's 10 characteristics of the church school have been repeated in several subsequent National Society publications (see, e.g., Duncan, 1990). When pressed, these characteristics indicate a renewed commitment to the religious distinctiveness of church schools that goes beyond the aims of service to engage with the aim of nurture and formation.

For example, Waddington's first characteristic affirms that "Christian inferences are built into the ethos and teaching as signals for children to detect." The fifth characteristic defines church schools as a "house of the gospel in which, starting at governor and staff level, there is a deliberate attempt to link the concerns of Christ's gospel with the life of the school." The sixth characteristic sees church schools as "a place of revelation and disclosure in which the rigour of learning and the art of acquiring skill are seen as parables of the revelation of God and his continuous involvement in his creation." The eighth characteristic speaks of church schools as "a beacon signalling the transcendent by the development of awe, mystery and wonder through the curriculum, exemplified in acts of corporate worship including contact with the Christian calendar and sacraments" (71). Such a view of distinctiveness is reinforced by the final paragraph of the Green Paper, which begins:

Within that web of partnership, the Christian churches must provide a distinctive contribution, one that grows out of theological reflection on the nature and practice of education. The contribution must be educationally excellent, Christian in style and content, adventurous in its willingness to face change and to create new patterns of ministry in the education service. (Waddington, 1984: 105)

The sequel to the Green Paper, the General Synod paper *Positive Partnership*, returned to the analysis of the twin aims of the church's involvement in education (National Society, 1985). *Positive Partnership* paraphrases the Green Paper's strategy for church schools and makes the claim that the Green Paper argued "that in every church school even today both these aims should be consciously present—contributing to the provision of general education in the neighbourhood, and yet providing a specifically Christian form of education" (26).

Following the General Synod debate on *Positive Partnership* in 1985, the mind of the National Society on the nature and future of church schools is perhaps glimpsed most clearly through the writings of the deputy secretary and schools officer. Since 1985 two individuals have occupied this position, Geoffrey Duncan, followed by David Lankshear. Both have written with a distinctive voice.

Geoffrey Duncan's voice emerged clearly in his chapter in the collection of essays *Faith for the Future*, published in 1986 to mark 175 years of the National Society (Duncan, 1986). After reviewing a number of trends in church schools, Duncan concludes in this chapter, "For Church of England schools many of the tensions will cluster around the twin aims of fulfilling a general/community role and a domestic/nurture role, discussed in some depth by the Durham Report" (68). He recognizes that in an increasingly secular and multicultural society there are growing tendencies both to set up independent Christian schools and to emphasize the domestic or nurture role for voluntary aided schools. Against such trends Duncan clearly wishes to reemphasize the service role of church schools. In a second paper, two years later, Duncan writes explicitly to the theme "Church Schools in Service to the Community," arguing, "Difficult as it may be to hold the tension between a school's Christian foundation and the need to serve a population that is largely non-Christian, such a model still has much mileage in it" (Duncan, 1988: 148).

While Geoffrey Duncan chose the theme of service as the central notion underpinning his writings on church schools, his successor, David Lankshear, shifted the emphasis more to distinctiveness. This transition was facilitated by the new political climate initiated by the 1988 Education Reform Act and confirmed by subsequent educational legislation. In *A Shared Vision: Education in Church Schools*, the first question that Lankshear addresses to his readers is this: "What differences are observable in your local community between Anglican and county schools?" (Lankshear, 1992c: 19). Beginning from a perspective grounded in empirical observation of what is actually happening in church schools, rather than in doctrinaire prescription of what should be happening in church schools, Lankshear draws out and affirms the practical evidence of distinctiveness already there.

In a second publication in 1992, *Looking for Quality in a Church School*, Lankshear once again starts from the empirical reality of the different emphases in church schools.

Some schools serve a geographically defined community and offer education to all children within the area. Other church schools offer a Church of England education mainly to the children of parents who can claim membership of the Church of England. Most church schools fall somewhere in between these two different positions. (Lankshear, 1992b: 3)

Accepting this diversity, Lankshear argues:

The school itself should witness to the gospel both in its daily life and in the way in which it makes contact with the communities beyond its gate. It is part of the Body of Christ and as such will recognise a special relationship with the parish, the diocese and the wider church. (23)

Lankshear recognizes that such a view has implications for the weight given to Christian commitment in making staff appointments, participation in worship, prayers before and after meetings, and a pastoral and spiritual concern for all members of the school community.

In a third publication in 1992, *Governing Church Schools*, Lankshear makes the point that the lives of the two communities, local church and church school, should be "so interwoven that there is never an opportunity for people at the school to feel neglected, nor for members of the church to feel ignorant about the school" (Lankshear, 1992a: 26). In a fourth publication in 1996, *Churches Serving Schools* (Lankshear, 1996), Lankshear argues that church schools have a responsibility to ensure that "[n]o one can be in any doubt that they are church schools. Such schools will demonstrate that they have a clear understanding of what it means to be the church school in the location in which it is set" (81).

The renewed confidence in promoting the distinctiveness of church schools reached further heights in a report by the Board of Education presented to the General Synod in November 1998 under the title *Church of England Schools in the New Millennium*. The report speaks of "a moment of opportunity" created by the School Standards and Framework Act 1998. Four opportunities in particular are identified on the opening page of the report. Church schools will have the opportunity to develop their identity as a church school. Parishes will have the opportunity to see their church school as a significant part of their mission strategy. Dioceses will have the opportunity to deepen their service to church schools and to extend the provision of places on church schools in response to the needs of the church and community. The Church of England will have the opportunity to recover the energy and commitment to Christian education that founded so many schools in the first half of the nineteenth century and to couple it with planning for the next millennium.

Overall the report argues that church schools stand at "the centre of the church's mission to the nation." Church schools provide a "vital connection with the community" and with families "the church might not otherwise reach." Against this background the report made four recommendations. First, the report urged Diocesan Synods to make more resources available to Diocesan Boards of Education. Second, the report welcomed the opportunities for church schools to move to the voluntary aided category and encouraged dioceses to support governors in doing so. Third, the report drew attention to the fact that the Church of England owns 1 in 4 primary schools compared with only 1 in 20 secondary schools and, by implication, encouraged the development of more secondary schools. Fourth, the report invited the Archbishops' Council to establish a commission on church schools and church colleges.

According to the *Church Times* report of the Synod debate, the archbishop of Canterbury highlighted the change of tone reflected by the report *Church of England Schools in the New Millennium*.

It was not long ago that the clear trend was to minimise the religious character of church schools. . . . Now that trend is being reversed. We are more confident today about promoting the distinctiveness of our schools. . . . If people want more of what we can offer, then we must find ways . . . of providing it.

The archbishop of Canterbury issued a challenge to church schools to be unafraid and unambiguous about their Christian and Anglican identity.

In the Synod debate no one voted against the motion that welcomed more aided schools and urged greater resources for diocesan education teams, but the call for an Archbishops' Commission on Church Schools was lost through an amendment.

CONTEMPORARY MOVEMENTS

During the past two decades the contours of religious schooling in England and Wales have been influenced by four crucial ways in which religious groups have responded to the changing interface between education and religion. The first example concerns the case of the Muslim community, which developed an informal network of schools outside the state-maintained system and which has, after considerable campaigning, now received state funding for just two schools. The second example concerns the case of a significant segment of the Christian community that has developed a network of independent Christian schools outside the state-maintained sector in order to promote a distinctively Christian view of education. The third example concerns the way in which the Church of England rethought the provision of state-maintained schools in the area covered by the Diocese of Truro, in order to provide a more distinctive church-related environment. The fourth example concerns the initiatives to create ecumenical or shared church schools, involving cooperation between two or more Christian denominations.

Muslim Schools

The report of the committee of enquiry into the education of children from ethnic minority groups published in 1985 under the title *Education for All* (Swann Report, 1985) was divided on the issue of the provision of state-funded religious schools for the Muslim community. The majority report of the committee rejected such provisions, preferring to promote full integration of different faith communities within common schools. The minority report of the committee supported such provision as an appropriate right to be shared by religious minority groups.

In the absence of religious schools within the state-maintained system the Muslim community pioneered three courses of action during the 1980s and 1990s. The first course of action involved the creation and support of independent schools outside the state-funded system of education.

The second course of action concerned the development of a coherent and sustained educational perspective on the case for state funding for Muslim schools. The first fully developed statement of this case by Mark Halstead was published in 1986 by the Islamic Academy in Cambridge under the title *The Case for Muslim Voluntary-Aided Schools: Some Philosophical Reflections* (Halstead, 1986). A more recent statement of the case was provided by Akran Khan-Cheema in his contribution to the 1994 collection of essays published by the Islamic Academy under the title *Religion and Education: Islamic and Christian Approaches* (Khan-Cheema, 1994).

The third course of action concerned the continuing political pressure for the recognition of the rights of the Muslim community to the same privileges as already extended to the Christian churches and to the Jewish community. The case was voiced, for example, by Mohammed Ismail in the *Times Educational Supplement* during November 1990 in the following way:

"What I don't understand," says Mohammed Ismail, "is when people say, why should Muslims be given their own schools? Well, why not? Catholic and Jewish people have their own schools, so why not Muslims? We are taxpayers and ratepayers, too. And we're peaceful citizens." ("Forced to Take Part," 1990: 22)

Generally the Christian community has given public support for the case for Muslim voluntary aided schools. For example, a report in *Church Times* for January 1991 noted:

The Roman Catholic Church's education spokesman has backed the establishment of voluntary aided Muslim schools. He is the Rt Revd David Konstant, Bishop of Leeds and Chairman of the Bishops' Conference Education Committee; he expressed his support for the extension of voluntary aided status to schools for Muslims and children of other minority faiths during his presidential address to the North of England education conference last week. ("RC Backing for Aid," 1991)

In 1998 the Muslim community at last received state funding for two schools. The Islamic Primary School, Brent, in north London, and the Al

Farquan School, Birmingham, became grant-maintained schools in April 1998 and joined the voluntary aided sector in September 1999. The Sikh community also established its first voluntary aided school in 1999.

The Christian School Movement

The Islamic community has not been alone in England and Wales in seeking the development of a state-funded system of religiously distinctive schools. A parallel movement has emerged among a sector of the Christian community.

The Christian school movement in England and Wales has grown up among conservative Christian churches discontent both with the secular character of the state-maintained nondenominational schools and with the secular or liberal character of the Church of England schools within the state-maintained sector. A significant influence on this development has come from the Christian school movement in the United States (for a range of comment on the Christian school movement in the United States, see, e.g., Peshkin, 1986; Rose, 1988; Wagner, 1990).

In England and Wales the movement began with the opening of an independent school in Rochester in 1969. Between 1978 and 1988 between three and eight schools were founded each year. Initially the head teachers of these schools were brought together under the auspices of Christians in Education (CIE). Subsequently the Christian Schools Trust (CST) and the Christian Schools Campaigns (CSC) were established to promote the cause. In her summary of the reasons for the growth of the new Christian schools between 1978 and 1988, Ruth Deakin (1989) identifies five key factors.

First, Deakin points to the *secularization of schools*. She argues that Christian parents want to see Judeo-Christian values and principles and a Christian philosophical framework imparted to their children in schools as well as in the home. In the state sector a child from a Christian home might be influenced by a wide variety of values, as his or her teacher changes from year to year. She concludes that "at the moment our schools tend to reflect our society, where there is increasing secularisation, a rising materialism and excessive individualism" (5).

Second, Deakin points to *the failure of the multifaith approach*. She argues that a multifaith approach to religious education often permeates the whole curriculum and is associated with a phenomenological method that studies religion through observable external expressions. She concludes that "this focus on religious practice devalues religion's vital components—faith, belief and commitment. The result is a devaluation of all faiths" (6).

Third, Deakin points to the issue of *faith and epistemology*. She argues that all human beings and all schools have a faith position, whether it is clothed in religious language or not, which embraces all those values that are held to be important in life and determines our whole perspective on reality. She concludes that "a secularised curriculum is based on and therefore promotes a particular philosophy of life. Such a curriculum can never be religiously neutral" (7).

Fourth, Deakin points to what she describes as *a gap in the market*. She argues that in many ways the traditional churches have left a gap in the educational market and demonstrate a marked confusion about their role in education. She concludes that the new Christian schools "have been established by parents for particular religious, philosophical and pedagogical reasons because of the lack of any acceptable state provision" (8).

Fifth, Deakin points to what she describes as the positive development of *a Christian worldview*. She argues that many Christians today are rediscovering the fact that their faith has implications for the whole of their lives and not just for those areas like personal morality, private worship, and church meetings, which have traditionally been thought of as spiritual. Judeo-Christian values such as honesty, justice, right relationships, stewardship, and charity make demands on all spheres of life, including business, economics, science and technology, leisure, and the arts. She concludes:

Christians are therefore not merely interested in the relatively small part of the timetable devoted to religious education, or assemblies, but are deeply concerned about the whole constellation of values, attitudes and beliefs which consciously or unconsciously are continuously imparted to all children in all schools. (8)

Under Ruth Deakin's directorship the Christian Schools Campaign was formed as an educational pressure group to seek state funding for faith-based schools. At one level the pressure group was successful in influencing both the 1992 Education (Schools) Act on inspection criteria and the 1993 Education Act. At a more fundamental level, however, the campaign has not yet been successful in obtaining state funding for even one Christian school (Walford, 1995).

Further perspectives on the Christian school movement in England and Wales are provided in two essays by O'Keeffe (1992) and by Watson and MacKenzie (1996).

Ecumenical Schools

At the time of the 1944 Education Act it was clear that England and Wales remained denominationally structured societies. The real religious issue remained the differences between the denominations. In such a society it also remained highly appropriate for the competition between churches to be reflected in the competition between denominational schools. The Roman Catholic Church and the Church of England were the two key players in this denominational competition.

By the 1990s two important changes had undermined the stability and viability of such competition between the denominations in maintaining denominationally distinctive church schools. The lesser of the two changes concerned a growing awareness of England and Wales as multicultural and multifaith communities. The greater of the two changes concerned the growth of secularization and the declining membership of the denominations. In one sense these changes led to a decline in the proportion of pupils and teachers in church schools who would claim active commitment to the faith. In another sense, some Christians began to see strength in cooperation between the denominations rather than in competition between the denominations.

It is against this background that a small number of denominational schools have sought partnership with other denominations, leading either to joint schools or to more broadly based ecumenical schools. While such partnering has generally not been well documented, the story of one joint school, St. Bede's joint Anglican/Roman Catholic school, Redhill, has been most helpfully set out by Priscilla Chadwick (1994).

As the Christian community in England and Wales becomes more alert to the implications of becoming a minority group within an essentially post-Christian culture, the lessons of ecumenical cooperation in education will need to be extended to many more church schools.

REFERENCES

Abbott, W.M. (Ed.). (1966). *The Documents of Vatican II*. London: Geoffrey Chapman.

Brown, A., and Lankshear, D.W. (1995). *Inspection Handbook*. London: National Society.

Butler, R.A. (1971). *The Art of the Possible*. London: Hamish Hamilton.

Catholic Commission for Racial Justice. (1984). *Learning from Diversity*. London: Catholic Media Office.

Catholic Information Office. (1977). *The Catholic School*. Abbots Langley: Catholic Information Office.

Chadwick, P. (1994). *Schools of Reconciliation: Issues in Joint Roman Catholic–Anglican Education*. London: Cassell.

Cruickshank, M. (1963). *Church and State in English Education*. London: Macmillan.

Deakin, R. (1989). *The New Christian Schools*. Bristol: Regius Press.

Duncan, G. (1986). Church Schools: Present and Future. In G. Leonard (Ed.), *Faith for the Future* (pp. 67–68). London: National Society and Church House Publishing.

Duncan, G. (1988). Church Schools in Service to the Community. In B. O'Keeffe (Ed.), *Schools for Tomorrow: Building Walls or Building Bridges* (pp. 145–161). Barcombe: Falmer Press.

Duncan, G. (1990). *The Church School*. London: National Society and SPCK. *Education*, November 2, p. 370.

Durham Report. (1970). *The Fourth R: The Durham Report on Religious Education*. London: National Society and SPCK.

Flude, M., and Hammer, M. (Eds.). (1990). *Education Reform Act 1988*. Basingstoke: Falmer Press.

Forced to Take Part. (1990). *Times Educational Supplement*, November 9, p. 22.

Francis, L.J. (1983). The Logic of Education, Theology and the Church School. *Oxford Review of Education* 9: 147–162.

Francis, L.J. (1986). *Partnership in Rural Education*. London: Collins Liturgical Publications.

Francis, L.J. (1987). *Religion in the Primary School: Partnership between Church and State?* London: Collins Liturgical Publications.

Francis, L.J. (1992). Primary School Size and Pupil Attitudes: Small Is Happy? *Educational Management and Administration* 20: 100–104.

General Synod Board of Education. (1998). *Church of England Schools in the New Millennium*. London: General Synod Board of Education.

General Synod of the Church of England Board of Education. (1984). *Schools and Multi-Cultural Education*. London: Church House.

Halstead, M. (1986). *The Case for Muslim Voluntary-Aided Schools: Some Philosophical Reflections*. Cambridge: Islamic Academy.

Hargreaves, A., and Tickle, L. (Eds.). (1980). *Middle Schools: Origins, Ideology and Practice*. London: Harper and Row.

Hirst, P. (1972). Christian Education: A Contradiction in Terms. *Learning for Living* 11: 4.

Hirst, P. (1976). Religious Beliefs and Educational Principles. *Learning for Living* 15: 155–157.

Hirst, P. (1981). Education, Catechesis and the Church School. *British Journal of Religious Education* 3(3): 85–93.

Khan-Cheema, A. (1994). British Muslims and the Maintained Schools. In S.A. Ashraf and P.H. Hirst (Eds.), *Religion and Education: Islamic and Christian Approaches* (pp. 177–198). Cambridge: Islamic Academy.

Konstant, D. (Chairman). (1981). *Signposts and Homecomings: The Educative Task of the Catholic Community*. Middleton: St. Paul Publications.

Lankshear, D.W. (1992a). *Governing Church Schools*. London: National Society.

Lankshear, D.W. (1992b). *Looking for Quality in a Church School*. London: National Society and Church House Publishing.

Lankshear, D.W. (1992c). *A Shared Vision: Education in Church Schools*. London: National Society.

Lankshear, D.W. (1993). *Preparing for Inspection in a Church School*. London: National Society.

Lankshear, D.W. (1995). *Small Schools*. London: National Society.

Lankshear, D.W. (1996). *Churches Serving Schools*. London: National Society.

Murphy, J. (1971). *Church, State and Schools in Britain 1800–1970*. London: Routledge and Kegan Paul.

National Society. (1985). *Positive Partnership*. London: National Society.

National Society. (1988). *Grant-Maintained Status and the Church School*. London: National Society.

National Society. (1994). *Grant-Maintained Status and the Church School: After the 1993 Education Act*. London: National Society.

O'Keeffe, B. (1992). A Look at the Christian Schools Movement. In B. Watson (Ed.), *Priorities in Religious Education* (pp. 92–112). Barcombe: Falmer Press.

Peshkin, A. (1986). *God's Choice: The Total World of a Fundamentalist Christian School*. Chicago: University of Chicago Press.

Plowden Report. (1967). *Children and Their Primary Schools*. London: HMSO.

RC Backing for Aid to Muslim Schools. (1991). *Church Times*, January 11.

Rose, S.D. (1988). *Keeping Them Out of the Hands of Satan: Evangelical Schooling in America*. New York: Routledge.

Schools Committee of the General Synod Board of Education. (1972). *Crisis in Church Schools: A Report on Finance*. London: General Synod.

Scotland, J. (1969). *The History of Scottish Education*. London: University of London Press.

Small Schools Working Party. (1991). *The Future of Small Schools*. London: National Society.

Socialist Education Association. (1981). *The Dual System of Voluntary and County Schools*. London: Socialist Education Association.

Socialist Education Association. (1986). *All Faiths in All Schools*. London: Socialist Education Association.

Swann Report. (1985). *Education for All*. London: HMSO.

Thiessen, E.J.A. (1985). Defense of a Distinctively Christian Curriculum. *Religious Education* 80: 37–50.

Waddington, R. (1984). *A Future in Partnership*. London: National Society.

Wagner, M. (1990). *God's Schools: Choice and Compromise in American Society*. New Brunswick, NJ: Rutgers University Press.

Walford, G. (1995). The Christian Schools Campaign: A Successful Educational Pressure Group? *British Educational Research Journal* 21: 451–464.

Watson, K., and MacKenzie, P. (1996). The New Christian Schools in England and Wales: An Analysis of Current Issues and Controversies. *Journal of Research on Christian Education* 5: 179–208.

CHAPTER 9

Minority Education in the Palestinian Authority

AZIZ HAIDAR

The purpose of this chapter is to evaluate the Palestinian curricula in the context of minority education. It analyzes how the official Palestinian curriculum deals with the question of minority education in Palestinian society. We attempt to tackle this problem by addressing two primary issues: first, how the curriculum deals with the very existence of minorities in this society; and second, how minorities are presented, on the normative level, in the philosophy and policy of education and in textbooks.

Accordingly, our study refers to three relevant factors: (1) the Declaration of Palestinian Independence (DPI), which constitutes the normative framework for the education system; (2) the Palestinian curriculum plan, which articulates the philosophy and general objectives and principles of the Palestinian education system; and (3) a critical reading and review of the existing textbooks used in the subject framework of "national education."

Furthermore, in our analysis we will address the question of minority education and focus on the gap between the normative level, policy, and the reality regarding pluralistic education.

The case under study is a special one, resulting from the unique experience of the Palestinian people and the special conditions in which they lived and still live, which, in turn, affected their educational backgrounds as well as the features of their newly constructed education system. For the first time in their history, the Palestinians are now in a position to control their own education. The first necessary step to take is to formulate their own philosophy and objectives of education, in line with their needs and aspirations.

Our assumption is that the Palestinian curriculum planners and educators will demonstrate much awareness and sensitivity to the subject of
pluralism. This assumption is based on the fact that each minority group
in Palestinian society is numerically very small. On the one hand, Palestinian society is homogenous ethnically and nationally, with a Christian
minority that, while small, plays a very significant role in the national-
political struggle for independence. On the other hand, this society is
characterized by cultural diversity because of the experiences of its members in many host countries.

It is too early to provide a comprehensive and conclusive evaluation
of the Palestinian curricula; the textbooks are still in the stage of preparation, though a few are already being tested, theoretically and in the
classrooms. However, an analysis at the philosophical and policy levels
can yield valuable findings at this time.

HISTORICAL BACKGROUND

For the past 500 years, Palestinians have not enjoyed independence or
self-rule. They lived under the Ottoman rule and the British mandate.
Then the 1948 War resulted in the creation of the state of Israel on 79
percent of historic Palestine. The West Bank was annexed to Jordan in
1950, while the Gaza Strip came under Egyptian administration. Generally, the authorities under which the Palestinian citizenry and refugees
lived, in various Arab countries or under Israeli rule, provided the education of Palestinian children. Jordan bore most of that burden as more
than two-thirds of the Palestinian people found themselves in the Hashemite Kingdom, both east and west of the Jordan River. This meant that
during the period 1949–1967, most Palestinian children who pursued
regular schooling depended on the Jordanian educational curricula, including those in the UNRWA (United Nations Relief and Work Agency)
school system. Jordanian national education was geared to reinforcing
Arab and Islamic causes, Arab and Islamic unity, and solidarity, with
special emphasis on loyalty to the Hashemite crown and, like other Arab
schools, a clear circumvolution of the issue of Palestinian nationalism
(Graham-Brown, 1984: 34).

The geopolitical situation remained unchanged until 1967. The war
that year ended with the Israeli occupation of the rest of Palestine,
namely, the West Bank and Gaza Strip. From 1967 to 1994 the Palestinians followed the same (Jordanian and Egyptian) curricula used before
1967. However, Israel introduced modifications and censored these curricula; the texts "were subjected to complete censorship by the Israeli
military governor in charge of Palestinian education from 1967 until
1993. During this period, whole books were banned from school; words

and, sometimes, whole sections of textbooks were deleted" (Adwan, 2001: 57). High school examinations at the end of the twelfth grade—the *tawjihi* exams, or matriculation—were conducted by the Ministries of Education of the relevant country in each region. The Israeli administration frequently refused to permit improvements in the Jordanian and Egyptian systems to be adopted by Palestinian schools. This refusal sometimes went to ludicrous extremes (Rihan, 2001: 21). Rihan notes, "During the last decades of the twentieth century, education underwent significant transformations throughout the world including Israel, Jordan and other Arab states, while Palestinian education was forced to languish in a system rooted in the early decades of the twentieth century" (28).

Thus, the Palestinians could rarely exercise any control over the education they received or, indeed, over most other aspects of their lives.

On September 13, 1993, Israel and the Palestine Liberation Organization (PLO) signed the Declaration of Principles on Interim Self-government Arrangements (Oslo Accords). The subsequent Oslo Agreement established the PNA (Palestinian National Authority) whose responsibilities included local education. Under the PNA the education system in Palestine underwent significant change and progress: Principally, a Palestinian Ministry of Education was established. In addition, a Palestinian Ministry of Higher Education was instituted alongside the Council for Higher Education. This council was the only recognized functioning body for higher education under the Israeli occupation. For the first time ever the Palestinians were able to define their own curricula. Thus, the organization and hierarchy of the entire system of education underwent a process of restructuring and Palestinization.

According to the Palestinian Central Bureau of Statistics, the Palestinian population in the world by the end of the year 1999 was projected to reach approximately 8.6 million. Of this population, little more than 3 million live in the West Bank and Gaza Strip, consisting of the indigenous people of the territories and returnees from host countries after the establishment of the PNA (Palestinian Central Bureau of Statistics, 2000). Each of those varied groups had lived in different countries and thus were educated in different education systems. As a result, they possessed different cultural, social, and economic backgrounds. This diversity necessitates the establishment of a Palestinian education system with a philosophy that can help guide the reconstruction of a united society, characterized by common aspirations, goals, and objectives. One of the most decisive aims to achieve this end is the providing of a Palestinian curriculum reflecting the different intellectual, cultural, and geographical characteristics of the Palestinian people, on one hand, and its shared cultural elements and national identity, on the other.

GUIDING PRINCIPLES OF THE PALESTINIAN EDUCATION SYSTEM

A curriculum should be examined in the framework of the history, social context, and values of the past and present society that employs it.

Many sources and forces can be identified for selecting curriculum objectives and content. However, the function of the school and the type of curriculum followed tend to reflect the demands and expectations of the larger society. Sociopolitical forces exert a profound influence on the goals and functions of the school, and they also influence the direction, interpretation, and application of educational research.

The following analysis of the Palestinian curriculum refers to the three levels mentioned in our introduction.

The Normative Framework of the Curriculum

The First Palestinian Curriculum Plan, prepared by the Palestinian Ministry of Education, deems the Declaration of Palestinian Independence one of the main sources on which to base the Palestinian curriculum. This document, promulgated in Algiers on November 15, 1988, is perceived as the most important document expressing and explaining the Palestinian people's position, their ambitions, and commitments at this point of their transformation in the history of their struggle toward achieving self-determination (the document appears in full in Nasru, 1993: 89-95). The DPI describes the character of the future Palestinian state and draws the values and doctrines of its sociopolitical regime. Therefore, it is the primary document that articulates the normative and moral framework of the Palestinians, from which they can deduce their educational principles and premises. Other sources were taken into consideration (see below). Here we cite the relevant paragraph in the DPI that provides the normative framework for pluralistic education and relates to minorities specifically. This paragraph constitutes a basis for the Palestinian education system's philosophy:

The State of Palestine is the state of Palestinians wherever they may be. The state is for them to enjoy in it their collective national and cultural identity, theirs to pursue in it a complete equality of rights. In it will be safeguarded their political and religious convictions and their human dignity by means of a parliamentary democratic system of governance, itself based on freedom of expression and the freedom to form parties. *The rights of minorities will duly be respected by the majority, as minorities must abide by decisions of the majority.* Governance will be based on principles of social justice, equality and non-discrimination in public rights of men or women, on grounds of race, religion, color or sex under the aegis of constitution which ensures the rule of law and an independent judiciary. Thus shall these principles allow no departure from Palestine's age-old spiritual and civilizational heritage of tolerance and religious coexistence. (Nasru, 1993: 92–93)

It is proclaimed clearly here that the state is committed to providing education for all the Palestinian people. The Palestinians are all supposed to enjoy equal access to education at low cost, and educational institutions of proper quality and quantity should be set up to achieve this goal.

The paragraph also expresses a commitment to democracy, which implies that the education system should be administrated in a democratic way to achieve its human, egalitarian, national, and progressive goals. The realization of this principle in the sphere of education requires basing the education system on the right to seeking facts, ideas, and truth and developing or adapting ideologies in an educational climate that allows pluralism in curriculum structure and function.

Once the education system is based on democracy, it has to meet the various needs of society. This system has to allow the presentation of different programs of education, which help to reflect the individual differences among its beneficiaries. The Palestinian people, although relatively few in number (around 8 million), are rich in their diversity. This requires an educational plan with two important aims:

1. To provide programs that will unite all Palestinian people by virtue of their sharing the same national identity.
2. To provide programs that will satisfy the ambitions and needs of individuals and the various societal groups. The differences in previous experiences have to be considered and incorporated into the Palestinian education system. That is, awareness of these differences has to be translated into a functional educational plan that necessitates a trend of pluralism. In this case the curriculum will bring about "unity in diversity."

In a democratic system that guarantees minority rights, decision making in all the organizational structures of the education system should be based on the participation of all. Along with respect of the rights of the minorities by the majority, minorities must abide by the decisions of the majority.

The education system should function within a legislative structure based on principles of justice, equality, and nondiscrimination in dealing with the rights to admission and promotion of students and the rights to employment of educational personnel, promotion, job security, and professional development. According to the DPI, the Palestinian education system is supposed to emphasize the values of tolerance and religious coexistence and acceptance of the "other."

According to this analysis of the DPI, the education system is pluralistically oriented. It is committed to the value of pluralism in education and to providing sufficient and equal opportunities for all to fulfill their needs and aspirations and to express their individual and collective identities. Pluralism includes the right of persons belonging to minorities to establish and maintain their own institutions. It means also that the state is obliged to take measures to create favorable conditions to enable these persons to express their characteristics and to develop their culture, language, religious traditions, and customs.

We will now examine if and to what extent these guiding principles are translated into actual policy in the Palestinian curriculum plans.

Principles and Policy of the Two Palestinian Curriculum Plans

The first organized project devoted to the construction of Palestinian curricula was carried out by the Palestinian Curriculum Development Center, established in 1994 on the basis of a formal agreement between the United Nations Educational, Scientific, and Cultural Organization (UNESCO) and the newly established Ministry of Education of the Palestinian Authority (PA). The center submitted the comprehensive plan for the development of the first Palestinian curriculum for general education in 1996 (Palestinian Curriculum Development Center, 1996). The Ministry of Education and the Curriculum Development Center published the First Palestinian Curriculum Plan (FPCP) in 1998. The curriculum implementation was scheduled over a period of five years, starting from the 2000–2001 academic year.

These two sources are the focus of the following analysis, concentrating on their treatment of minority education issues. The first source, "The Comprehensive Plan," was produced by the Palestinian Curriculum Development Center and submitted to the PA Ministry of Education and UNESCO in September 1996. It provides a comprehensive assessment and evaluation of the existing curricula in use in the Palestinian school system in the West Bank and Gaza Strip. It also outlines new aims:

The aim of the curriculum is to enable every Palestinian who successfully completes twelve years of schooling to have adequate broad knowledge, positive values of participation, modernity, equal coexistence of societies, democracy and technical skills either to join the labor force or to pursue his/her education, or both. (Palestinian Curriculum Development Center, 1996: 7)

It is clear from this paragraph that the comprehensive plan is committed to the normative codes expressed in the DPI (see above). The basic philosophy of the proposed curriculum that intends to transmit relevant knowledge, values, and skills is "rooted in the Palestinian consciousness of its national heritage, its long and significant history and its national affiliation with the land of Palestine and with Arab culture" (7).

The comprehensive plan lays down the principles, which are derived from the basic belief that the Palestinian people have an authentic distinctive identity, on the one hand, and vast cultural diversity, on the other (6).

The divergence of culture resulted from several developments mentioned in the historical background. These developments, especially after 1948, produced different values, traditions, and patterns of thinking and lifestyles. They have tremendous impact on the human dimensions of the Palestinian people. The authors of the comprehensive plan believe:

The awareness of this dimension of the Palestinian identity constitutes a basis which strengthens pluralism and variety of lifestyles, and at the same time it demonstrates the ability and liability of the Palestinians to live together and to cement the solidity and persistence of [national] affiliation and self consciousness. (61–62)

The cultural divergence is emphasized more strongly when the authors refer to the Arab and universal dimensions of the Palestinian identity. The former, which is the most salient, in the Palestinian cultural and national identity is their Arab affiliation. The latter dimension brought about the adoption of significant cultural elements while living in the diaspora for about five decades (63).

Based on the above, the comprehensive plan establishes that, at this stage, the goal of the Palestinians should be the reconstruction of Palestinian society, by means of achieving a high level of national integration. The role of the education system is crucial because it constitutes one of the most essential and effective mechanisms to reach this end. Thus, "[t]he Palestinian curricula is supposed to contribute to achieve national integration as a solid basis for the reconstruction of a people, which is united in its affiliation and its behavioral codes and destiny" (63).

The authors of the comprehensive plan proposed by the Palestinian Curriculum Center demonstrate much sensitivity regarding the religious issue, particularly religious diversity. They also show awareness of the necessity for pluralistic education. Accordingly, the comprehensive plan suggests offering religious education in all stages of schooling. It is worth mentioning that the plan emphasizes the importance of the comparative study of religion.

The second source, "The First Palestinian Curriculum Plan," was produced by the Ministry of Education (1998) and ratified by the Palestinian Legislative Council. It lays down the principles on which Palestinian education must be based and derive its contents and includes a projection for the full implementation of the curriculum reform plan until 2004. The ministry also prepared a broader document covering all aspects of educational reform under the title the "Five-Year Education Development Plan 2000/2001–2004/2005." It provides a clear presentation of priorities of Palestinian education. The following are paragraphs cited from the general and basic Principles of the Palestinian Curriculum, which are relevant to our study:

Sources of the Palestinian curriculum:

The Palestinian curriculum is based on the general educational philosophy of the Palestinian Arab society. Its principles have been derived from our heritage and religion, from our Declaration of Independence, and from our ambitions for the future of our people, and our understanding of the role of the education in developing this society.

Features of the political system:

Palestine is a democratic State, ruled by a democratic parliamentary system.

Universal values:

. . . Palestine is a peace-loving state, working towards international understanding and cooperation based on equality, liberty, dignity, peace and human rights. . . .
    . . . Social justice, equality and the provisions of equal learning opportunities for all Palestinians, to the limits of their individual capacity must be ensured without discrimination on grounds of race, religion, color, or sex. . . .

The official plan focuses on four dimensions of the Palestinian identity:

The national Palestinian dimension

. . . Palestinian national and cultural identity must be fostered and developed. . . . Never has the identity of a people been exposed to dangers of vanquish or demolition as the Palestinian one has. The preservation of this identity from dissolution remains the basic indication of the existence of this people and a guarantee for its survival at the present and in the future. . . .

The pan-Arab dimension

. . . The Palestinian people are an integral part of the Arab nation, working toward unity, liberty, development and prosperity of the nation. . . . The Palestinian people are part of the Arab nation and Palestine is also part of the Arab Homeland. As a result, commitment to using the Arabic Language as a means of communication and transmitting thoughts remains a basic principle of the Palestinian curriculum, [as does] encouraging students to use it with full competence in speaking, reading and writing. . . . Palestinians are also deeply rooted in Arab Nationalism. The Palestinian Charter and the document of the Declaration of Independence emphasize this affiliation. . . .

Islamic faith and culture

... The intellectual basis of the Palestinian curriculum stems from faith in Allah, the Almighty, concentrating on the Arab-Islamic cultures. Palestine is the land of Divine messages and Palestinians are known for their ability to adapt and acquaint themselves with various models of life throughout history as well as their ability to respect others while preserving one's own affiliation and originality....

... The Palestinian curriculum is based on the essence of the Islamic culture, doctrine and affiliation to Islam. This actually deepens the rooting of the establishment of the Palestinian society.

The international dimension

... Mastering foreign languages is one of the gateways to other nations' cultures and keeping in touch with them. The Palestinian curriculum does not neglect this and emphasizes the teaching of foreign languages.

Diversity

The plan emphasizes the cultural and social impact of the host societies on the Palestinians:

A great proportion of the Palestinian people lives outside Palestine in the Diaspora assimilating with other societies. Providing a Palestinian curriculum will be a great help to the PNA (Palestinian National Authority) to rebuild and reestablish a unified society in aspiration, loyalty, culture, behavior and goals or objectives. This can be achieved through producing a Palestinian curriculum reflecting the intellectual, cultural and geographical characteristics of the Palestinian people.

A careful study of the First Palestinian Curriculum Plan reveals the following:

First, in comparison with the former plan, the current one adds religion to the Palestinian curriculum's principles, even before the PDI. It does not clarify what religion it means, but the succeeding paragraphs reveal that it points to Islam.

Second, the Palestinian political system as declared in the political agenda of the PNA and as stated in the DPI is to safeguard the Palestinians' political and religious convictions, and their human dignity, by means of a parliamentary democratic system of governance. It is based on the freedom of expression and the freedom to form political parties. Governance is based on principles of social justice, equality, and non-discrimination of men and women on grounds of race, religion, color, or sex; and the rights of minorities are respected.

Accordingly, decision making in all the organizational structures of the education system has to be based on the participation of all with the respect of the rights of the minorities by the majority, as long as minorities comply with the decisions of the majority.

In a sharp contradiction to the democratic character of the system, declared above, this proposed curriculum is highly centralized. It determines in detail the ideological and educational goals, tasks, and materials of teaching, the teaching subjects, and the number of lessons as well as pedagogical activities, right through to school types and structures. The Palestinian education system is administrated officially on central, regional, and district levels, yet the power of policymaking, curriculum development, textbook production, examinations, teacher certification, recruitment, promotion, and all the important educational matters are given to the central government, which exercises this power through the Ministry of Education. The ministry also prepares the educational budget, and once approved, the ministry makes the final determination as to who gets what, when, and how.

In fact, as mentioned earlier the power of decision making is given to the central government. No real participation in decision making at the lower ranks is yet allowed.

Third, implementing these principles in the education system means practicing equal and just treatment of students of different religions. It implies, accordingly, granting all of them the opportunity to learn their religion within the public system of education—or at least the option not to learn the subject at all.

One can argue that it is normal and acceptable to determine that Islamic culture is a basis of the Palestinian curriculum, as the religion of the overwhelming majority of the students is Islam. Nevertheless, the question arising from this principle pertains to the opportunities given to non-Muslims to learn and express their faith, within the public education system.

Fourth, the four dimensions of identity mentioned above—the Palestinian, the pan-Arab, the Islamic, and the international—are translated into content by concentration on the teaching of history, values, morals, and national heritage, as well as the study of foreign cultures and languages. Whereas this focus is represented in the plan's intensive introduction of the social sciences and national education subjects, Islamic education, Arabic language, history, and geography, it does not include any practical suggestions for applying these ideas and values, as referred to by the PDI.

Fifth, because of the different experiences of the Palestinians, and as a result of their different cultural and social characteristics, the role of the curriculum must be to integrate the different groups into a harmonious society. Actually, the plan refers to the Palestinian society as ultimately becoming a homogeneous one. In practice, pluralism is used in a political sense only. It means that people have the right to affiliate with the political party they desire and enjoy freedom of expression of their thoughts and ideologies. Yet they all function within the perspective of the well-being of the Arab nation, to which they belong. The operational definition of pluralism in the education system means the right to a choice of interest in the educational endeavor to subjects other than cultural and civil subjects:

1. The right to choose a foreign language in addition to the national language. English as a second language is to be taught from the first grade rather than from the fifth grade, as was the case in the old system.
2. The right to be introduced to a wide variety of elective courses in the various fields. (Rihan, 2001: 27)

However, with respect to minority education, despite the emphasis on universal values, the plan does not take into account the fact that the Palestinian people are not united in their religious affiliation. Instead, it emphasizes that the curriculum must reflect the Islamic content of the Palestinian identity and culture. This trend is clear also in the following:

To sum up, the Palestinian curriculum must reflect the dimensions of the Palestinian identity and its special features. It should also reflect the Islamic affiliation, endeavor to achieve the unity of the Arab and Islamic worlds, work for its freedom, realize its independence, act constructively with other nations, and participate in the development of human ideas, and in humanitarian, political, economic, and cognitive issues. (Palestine National Authority, Ministry of Education, 1998: 8)

Pluralism and the Status of the Minority in Education

The comparison between "the first comprehensive plan" of the Palestinian Curriculum Development Center and "the official curriculum plan" produced by the Ministry of Education reveals a basic contradiction. The latter did not take into consideration the religious and cultural divergence within Palestinian society. It could thus be concluded that this plan denies the principle of pluralistic education. The following analysis consolidates this conclusion.

According to the ministry's First Palestinian Curriculum Plan, Islamic religion is obligatory for all Muslim students at all stages. The emphasis on the absolute necessity of Islamic content in education is reiterated five times, while the plan ignores the fact that Palestinian society is composed of different religious and cultural groups. Instead of offering the subject of *religious education*, as does the Comprehensive Plan for the Development of the First Palestinian Curriculum for General Education (1996), the system makes Islamic education a compulsory subject, worth 100 out of the 1,000 points (10 percent) in the *tawjihi* (matriculation) certificate

Table 9.1
Allocation of Class Hours According to the Plan of the First Palestinian Curriculum of the Palestinian Ministry of Education (in percent)

Subject/grade	1–4	5–9	10	11	12
Islamic education	10.0	8.4	8.3	8.5	9.3
Arabic language	26.7	19.7	13.9	14.3	15.6
National education	6.7	8.4	5.9	—	—

(see Table 9A.4 in the appendix). Non-Muslim students, meanwhile, are allowed to study any of the elective subjects instead of Islamic education.

In other words, the system does not recognize the very existence of the non-Muslims or the necessity to acknowledge their right to study different texts in line with their religious faith. The allocation of class hours toward the general *tawjihi* exams makes evident the emphasis on Islamic education (see Table 9.1). Christian students, on the other hand, are not required to sit for the Islamic education exam, but the plan does not state this fact explicitly. Indeed, the plan does not refer to Christian minority students' right to choose to study their own religion within the public education system and whether they are free to study Islamic education or not in public schools. Christian children, who represent a very small minority (1.5 percent), usually enroll in private and missionary schools where they do study their own religion.

This fact leads to the two-pronged conclusion that the system is not a secular one and that it does not refer to the basic right of non-Muslim students for separate religious education within the public system. The result is that all Christian students must study in private schools; it should be added, however, that this is not only because of their insistence to study their religion but also because of the public schools' low level, which means that the principle of "access to education at low cost" is not implemented completely.

Nevertheless, most significant in our findings is that despite the ignoring of minorities in the curriculum plan (at the policy level), the facts are different in practice. First, all Christian communities maintain their own educational institutions. They also accept Muslim pupils, and it is a fact that the overwhelming majority of the Muslim elite attend these private schools. It is a voluntary separation that the state (Palestinian Authority) allows within its education system, which means that the minority chooses or has access to an appropriate form of schooling for its children. Second, on the level of subjects and texts, among the 29 completed textbooks for grades 1 and 6, 2 are designed for teaching Christian pupils their Christian religion (Attalah, 2000; El-Hayek, 2000).

An Analysis of the New Textbooks

The content of each textbook is determined by a detailed curriculum outline that was developed under the supervision of the Ministry of Education for all subjects and all grades. This outline served as a guide to the groups of authors selected to write the various textbooks. The ministry followed a rigorous process of review and evaluation before each textbook was approved.

According to Adwan (2001: 60),

[T]he new Palestinian textbooks describe Palestinians through various examples of daily activities. There is much emphasis on the way the Palestinians live in their cities, towns and refugee camps, and on their culture and heritage. . . . Palestinians are also described as religious people and the texts portray the significant role religion plays in their daily life. At the same time, Palestinian pupils learn to look positively at others. . . . Jews are even presented in a favorable light.

Rihan (2001: 29) adds that

illustrations—whether drawings or photographs . . . reveal a healthy diversity of local scenes. Both urban and rural backgrounds are used, men are shown in Western and traditional dress, and women are shown in Western, village and Islamic dress. Gender roles are not stereotyped: women are shown as doctors and teachers as well as wives and mothers, and men are shown in many different roles. A drawing in the first grade Islamic education textbook shows the mother washing the dishes, while the son—significantly, not the daughter—is drying them. Although Palestinians are overwhelmingly Muslim, churches are shown as well as mosques. These examples reveal a serious effort to develop attitudes of tolerance towards diversity and acceptance of pluralism within Palestinian society.

The Palestinian Ministry of Education published a clarification regarding the contents of the new textbooks that states:

The Palestinian textbooks produced do not include any racist remarks against any people. . . . Palestinians are Muslim and Christian, so our textbooks teach tolerance between them. This is part of civic education. Our textbooks focus on Palestinian society at this stage. . . . this teaching is part of our efforts to build a civil society and a modern democratic state. In the textbooks we have produced so far, we have not dealt with any people, religion or country outside of Palestine. But the intention of the Ministry is to avoid all forms of stereotyping on the basis of race, gender, religion, or disability. Additionally, we expect [the textbooks] to encourage the development of positive images of people who are different from ourselves. (Ministry of Education—Palestine 2001: 117)

According to Rihan (2001: 29), the curriculum "concentrates on Palestinian, Arab and Islamic social studies in the lower grades. Whether a healthy attitude of openness to other societies is maintained cannot be determined until the textbooks for the higher grades with their broader worldwide scope are published."

Actually, the share of Islamic education is much bigger than it appears in Table 9.1 because a great deal of its texts are included in other subjects. It is significant, in particular, in Arabic-language courses: The Islamic texts taught represent the major source for studying Arabic grammar and literature.

But most striking is the share of Islamic texts in the National Education textbooks. The texts are supposed to be targeted to all Palestinian students and to demonstrate the shared values, irrespective of religious affiliation.

The introduction of civic education as a new subject and the inclusion of national education in social studies are important innovations in the curriculum. These two subjects will be taught in grades 1–10. They complement the already existing Islamic education (which is taught throughout the 12 grades) and are supposed to "provide a broader and more balanced foundation for the formation of individual and group identities" (Rihan, 2001: 27). Another innovation in the curriculum is that despite the declared policy in the ministry's curriculum plan new textbooks were designed for teaching Christian religion.

Finally, we provide a brief analysis of textbooks assigned for teaching the subject National Education. Our analysis is based on a survey of six textbooks for elementary schools (grades 1–6). The examination of this subject is of great significance: The new textbooks were produced by the Palestinian Authority, and in this regard they reflect its official educational policy and its implementation.

The content of the textbooks is the most important indication of the attitude toward the minority. The title "National Education" indicates the intention of the Ministry of Education to teach all the Palestinian pupils the same shared national values, despite their different religious affiliations or cultural backgrounds. Accordingly, we expect that the texts will manifest the common values and emphasize the shared interests. These texts are inconsistent with the goal to foster and develop the Palestinian national and cultural identity and to "rebuild and reestablish a unified society in aspiration, loyalty, culture, behavior and goals or objectives" (see the paragraph on diversity above). Each of the first four textbooks (grades 1–4) includes a separate unit of Islamic education. In the other two, this part is embedded in different units. In all units devoted to the study of society, values and morals, traditions, or institutions, the examples and prototypes are taken from Islamic history and instructions. The major sources quoted are the Qur'an, Muslim personalities, and Muslim texts. The Christian minority, or others, are mentioned incidentally in the course of texts about archeological sites, religious holidays, tourism, or Palestinian cities. However, in "National Education" there are very few hints of religious or cultural divergence; for example, a picture presented in a grade 6 textbook (Palestinian National Authority, 1996f: 70) shows two clerics—a Muslim and a Christian—shaking hands to symbolize tolerance. The Palestinian society and people were defined on several occasions, but minorities were never referred to. Furthermore, in all of these definitions it was emphasized that the Palestinian society and people are coterminous with Muslims (e.g., "the Palestinian Muslim society," "the Palestinian Muslim nation," "united in its culture and religion").

CONCLUSION

Until the establishment of the Palestinian Authority, foreign political regimes determined the nature and quality of the education systems and curricula that the Palestinians followed. The Palestinians never had any kind of control over their own education, being obliged to follow education systems designed by others inside and outside Palestine. This in turn affected their educational background, knowledge, skills, experience, qualifications, and affiliation.

The establishment of the Palestinian National Authority in 1993 gave the Palestinian people the opportunity for the first time in history to rule themselves and to control their own education at all levels. The development of a Palestinian philosophy of education that takes into account the reality, needs, diversity in educational backgrounds, and even the different cultural elements, which affected the Palestinians in their different countries of residence, is necessary for establishing a unified society.

This chapter analyzed how the Palestinian curriculum deals with the existence of minorities in this society and how they are presented on the normative level in the philosophy and policy of education and in textbooks. While the examination of the first two levels is possible, that of the textbooks is only partial because few of them have to date been completed and some are still in the testing stage.

Our study reveals that according to the Declaration of Palestinian Independence the education system is pluralistically oriented. It is committed to provide sufficient and equal opportunities for all to fulfill their needs and aspirations and to express their individual and collective identities. Pluralism includes the right of minorities to establish and maintain their own institutions, which means also that the state enables these persons to express their characteristics and to develop their culture, language, religious traditions, and customs.

An analysis of the philosophy and planning (policy) levels, the practical level, and the public school textbooks, however, reveals contradictory results: On the level of policy we found that the education system and the First Palestinian Curriculum Plan emphasize theoretically and practically the Palestinian national identity and commitments to the Arab unity. Palestinian history is studied as an integral part of the Arab, Islamic heritage and civilization. The curriculum for the preliminary stage concentrates on Palestinian, Arab, and Islamic social studies. Moreover, the allocated share of Islamic education is bigger than it appears in the plan, because a number of Islamic-related texts are included in other subjects. This is particularly significant in Arabic-language courses, where Islamic texts serve as the major source for teaching Arabic grammar and literature.

Based on the historical experience of the Palestinian people and the role of the small Christian minority in the Palestinian national struggle for independence, our assumption was that the Palestinian curriculum planners and educators would show much awareness and sensitivity to the subject of pluralism. This assumption has been partially validated; We found that the consequences of the social, cultural, and political reality and the needs of the Palestinian society are not adequately reflected in the philosophy and practical manifestation of the education system. On the policy level this system is completely centralized and not at all pluralistic. The allocation of resources, especially teaching hours, is not committed to the universal values clearly stated in the DPI, especially regarding minority education in public schools. The system is not a secular one; the emphasis on the absolute necessity of Islamic content within it is salient, and the curriculum plan ignores the fact that Palestinian society is composed of different religious and cultural groups.

This trend is very clear in the National Education textbooks for public schools: Each one of the textbooks for grades 1–4 includes a separate unit of Islamic education. In the grades 5–6 textbooks this part is embedded in different units. In all units devoted to the study of society, values and morals, traditions, or institutions, the examples and prototypes are taken from Islamic history and instruction. The Christians and other minorities are mentioned incidentally in texts about archeological sites, religious holidays, tourism, and Palestinian cities. The Palestinian society and people are defined on several occasions, but minorities are never mentioned. Furthermore, in all these definitions, it was emphasized that the Palestinian society and people are coterminous with Muslims.

Nevertheless, most significant in our findings is that despite the ignorance of minorities in the curriculum plan (at the policy level), the facts are different in practice as Christian communities maintain their own educational institutions. This marks a voluntary separation that the state (Palestinian Authority) allows within its education system, and thus two textbooks of Christian religion (for grades 1 and 6) were also newly written for this sector.

APPENDIX

Table 9A.1
Number and Percentage of Subject Classes for Each Grade in the
Preparatory Stage (Grades 1–4) in the Palestinian Curriculum

Subjects	1st Grade	2nd Grade	3rd Grade	4th Grade	Total	Percentage
Islamic Education	3	3	3	3	12	10.00
Arabic Language	8	8	8	8	32	26.70
English Language	3	3	3	3	12	10.00
General Science	3	3	3	3	12	10.00
Mathematics	5	5	5	5	20	16.66
Social Sciences and National Education	2	2	2	2	8	6.66
Arts and Crafts	2	2	2	2	8	6.66
Physical Education	2	2	2	2	8	6.66
Free Activity	1	1	1	1	4	3.33
Civics	1	1	1	1	4	3.33
Total	30	30	30	30	120	100.00

Source: Palestinian National Authority, Ministry of Education–Curriculum Administration
(1998).

Table 9A.2
Number of Subject Classes for Grades 5–9 in the Palestinian Curriculum Plan

Subjects	5th Grade	6th Grade	7th Grade	8th Grade	9th Grade	Total	Percentage
Islamic Education	3	3	3	3	3	15	8.43
Arabic Language	7	7	7	7	7	35	19.66
English Language	4	4	4	4	4	20	11.24
General Science	5	5	5	5	5	25	14.04
Mathematics	5	5	5	5	5	25	14.04
Social Sciences and National Education	3	3	3	3	3	15	8.43
Arts and Crafts	2	2	2	2	2	10	5.62
Physical Education	2	2	1	1	1	7	3.93
Free Activity	1	1	1	1	1	5	2.81
Civics	1	1	1	1	1	5	2.81
Technology and Applied Science (2)	2	2	2	2	2	10	5.62
Elective Subject (3)	—	—	2	2	2	6	3.37
Total	35	35	36	36	36	178	100.00

Source: Palestinian National Authority, Ministry of Education–Curriculum Administration
(1998).

Table 9A.3
Number and Percentage of Classes for Subjects Taught in the Tenth Grade in the Palestinian Curriculum Plan

Subjects	Number of Classes	Percentage	Technical Subjects	Number of Classes
Islamic Education	3	8.33	Agriculture	3
Arabic Language	5	13.88	Industry	3
English Language	4	11.10	Commerce and Administration	3
Science (Physics, Chemistry, Biology)	4	11.10		
Mathematics	5	13.88		
Social Science and National Education	2	5.55		
Arts and Crafts	1	2.80		
Physical Education	1	2.80		
Technology and Applied Sciences	2	5.55		
Elective Subjects	2	5.55		
Vocational Literacy	1	2.80		
Technical Subjects	6	16.66		
Total	36	100.00		

Source: Palestinian National Authority, Ministry of Education–Curriculum Administration (1998).

Table 9A.4
Distribution of Points for Subjects in *Tawjihi* System

Subject	Maximum Points
Islamic Education	100
Arabic Language	200
English Language	150
Mathematics	150
Two scientific subjects	200 (100 for each subject)
Two literary subjects	200 (100 for each subject)
Total	1,000

Source: Palestinian National Authority, Ministry of Education–Curriculum Administration (1998).

REFERENCES

Adwan, S. (2001). Schoolbooks in the Making: From Conflict to Peace: A Critical Analysis of the New Palestinian Textbooks for Grades One and Six. *Palestine-Israel Journal* 8(2): 57–69.

Attalah, H. (2000). *Christian Religious Education, Grade Six.* Ramallah: Ministry of Education, Palestinian National Authority.

El-Hayek, N. (2000). *Christian Religious Education, Grade One.* Ramallah: Ministry of Education, Palestinian National Authority.

Graham-Brown, S. (1984). *Education, Repression and Liberation.* London: World University Service.

Ministry of Education—Palestine. (2001). The Palestinian Curriculum and Textbooks: Clarification from the Ministry of Education–Palestine. *Palestine-Israel Journal* 8(2): 115–118.

Nasru, F. (1993). *Preliminary Vision of a Palestinian Education System.* Ramallah: Birzeit University, Center for Research and Documentation of Palestinian Society.

Palestinian Central Bureau of Statistics. (2000). *Projected Palestinian Population in the World End Year 1999.* Ramallah: Author.

Palestinian Curriculum Development Center. (1996). *A Comprehensive Plan for the Development of the First Palestinian Curriculum for General Education.* Ramallah: Author.

Palestinian National Authority, Ministry of Education. (1996a). *Palestinian National Education, Grade 1.* Ramallah: Author.

Palestinian National Authority, Ministry of Education. (1996b). *Palestinian National Education, Grade 2.* Ramallah: Author.

Palestinian National Authority, Ministry of Education. (1996c). *Palestinian National Education, Grade 3.* Ramallah: Author.

Palestinian National Authority, Ministry of Education (1996d). *Palestinian National Education, Grade 4.* Ramallah: Author.

Palestinian National Authority, Ministry of Education. (1996e). *Palestinian National Education, Grade 5.* Ramallah: Author.

Palestinian National Authority, Ministry of Education. (1996f). *Palestinian National Education, Grade 6.* Ramallah: Author.

Palestinian National Authority, Ministry of Education–Curriculum Administration. (1998). *First Palestinian Curriculum Plan.* Ramallah: Curriculum Development Center.

Rihan, R. (2001). The Palestinian Educational Development Plan: Promise for the Future. *Palestine-Israel Journal* 8(2): 19–33.

CHAPTER 10

Promoting Intergroup Attitudes in Israel Through Internet Technology

YAACOV KATZ AND YAACOV YABLON

INTRODUCTION

Israeli society is split into a number of national, ethnic, and religious sectors and groups, each of which has a different social, economic, and political agenda. Because of the heterogeneity of Israeli society, the agendas of the different sectors often clash with conflict resulting between some or all of the sectors. One of the major conflicts in Israeli society focuses on the Jewish-Arab axis. Israeli Jews and Arabs are wary of each other and latent hostility that is directly related to the Israeli-Arab conflict. As time passes, the gap between the two populations grows wider, and the two sectors have become increasingly more polarized (Tessler and Grant, 1998).

The Israeli educational authorities are aware of the problems inherent in Jewish-Arab conflict and have invested educational and budgetary resources in the development of numerous intervention programs designed to mitigate the negative aspects of the conflict within the school system (Winer, Bar-On, and Weiner, 1992). Bar and Askalah (1988) specifically indicated the importance of joint Jewish-Arab projects as the major medium for fostering improved Jewish-Arab relations. These projects provide an information base as well as a meeting place that lead to a reduction of ethnic stereotypes, anxieties, and misconceptions. They promote dialogue for conflict resolution and understanding of own and other's ethnic identity through a positive interethnic experience.

The tension between the Israeli Jewish and Bedouin sectors is very much rooted in the differential level of governmental, municipal, and public services available to both populations. This leads to the widening of educational, cultural, and socioeconomic gaps between the two groups, resulting in tensions and frustrations (Glaubman and Katz, 1998).

CHARACTERISTICS OF THE BEDOUIN POPULATION IN ISRAEL

The Bedouin Arab population is largely nomadic in its tradition of moving about the Negev desert areas in search of grazing fields for cattle, sheep, and goats, fertile land for wheat and barley, and temporary shelter from the elements. The nomadic tradition is deeply ingrained in the Bedouin way of life and is perhaps the most vital characteristic in Bedouin culture (Abu-Saad, 1997). However, since the establishment of the State of Israel in 1948, the Bedouin population in Israel has undergone radical change and has been transformed from a traditionally nomadic population to one that is now largely urbanized (Ben-David, 1988). The successive governments of Israel since 1948 and up until the present embarked on a policy of urbanization of the Bedouin population for two main reasons: (1) to provide the Bedouins with efficient governmental services such as education, health, and welfare in towns and villages and (2) to use the large tracts of land traditionally used by the nomadic Bedouins for the establishment of cities, towns, and villages for the ever-increasing Israeli population. The process of urbanization of the Bedouins continues to the present day. Latest figures indicate a Bedouin population of 130,000 residents in the southern Negev region; approximately two-thirds are now resident in urban cities, towns, and villages, with one-third resident in temporary nomadic tent settlements (Melitz, 1995).

The Bedouin population has been loathe to accept the process of urbanization, and as time passes, the Bedouins are increasingly more active in their attempts to reject government attempts to settle them in cities, towns, and villages (Glaubman and Katz, 1998). As time passes, the urbanization policies of the successive Israeli governments are perceived by the Bedouin population to be discriminatory and designed to move them from their tribal lands without consideration of their traditional, cultural, social, and economic needs (Abu-Rabia, 1986). In addition to the problem of urbanization the Bedouin population has other acute problems such as a lower standard of living than the national average and unemployment is higher than the national average. All these problems contribute to a feeling of alienation and desperation on the part of the Bedouins as well as a feeling of hostility toward the Jewish authorities and population at large.

BEDOUIN EDUCATION IN ISRAEL

The Bedouin educational system is administered by the Department of Arab Education within the framework of the Israeli Ministry of Education. Since the establishment of the State of Israel the number of Bedouin children in the school system has grown from only 150 in 1948 to 27,500 in 1998 (Katz, 1998). However, despite this numerical progress, Katz indicated that the Israeli educational authorities have not been able to close the vast quality gap between the Jewish and the Bedouin educational system.

Katz (1998) indicated that the Bedouin educational system is characterized by a number of serious limitations that mitigate against educational achievements and success. Bedouin schools are typified by a significant lack of physical facilities, such as classrooms, libraries, laboratories; a significant lack of qualified teachers; a significantly high student dropout rate; a remarkably low rate of success in the Israeli matriculation examinations, which serve as a major criterion for entry into education at the tertiary level; an almost total lack of extracurricular activities offered to students by school authorities; and an almost total lack of parental interest in their children's educational future.

According to Katz, these limitations are perceived by the Bedouin population to be part of a planned governmental policy of neglect and are viewed as an extension of grievances held against the Israeli government. Thus the Bedouin community feels grossly discriminated against and especially in education because of the inferiority of the Bedouin school system in comparison to schools attended by Jewish students in Israel. All this has compounded the Bedouins' feelings of frustration, anger, and even hostility against the majority Jewish population and against the successive Israeli governments that have consistently failed to contribute to an improvement of their educational system as well as to their social and economic status. The feelings of inequality and bitterness have given rise to the fomentation of anti-Israeli Islamic fundamentalism and a general wariness of the Israeli authorities and Jewish population (Ben-David, 1993).

JEWISH EDUCATION IN ISRAEL

The Jewish educational system in Israel is highly developed and enjoys a large budget that allows for dynamic development of facilities, school-based technology, advanced teaching and learning methodologies, and varied extracurricular programs for students at all levels in the school system (Gaziel, 1999). The level of teachers is good, with almost all teachers in the educational system in possession of a college degree and a teaching diploma. School facilities, such as classrooms, libraries, laboratories, computer rooms, and sports facilities, are well developed; achievement of Jewish students in matriculation examinations is on a par with achievement in the average Western country; the dropout rate of students is fairly low, and in general, Jewish parents are involved in their children's education.

In marked contrast to the Bedouin population, the Jewish population in Israel can be described as generally satisfied with the educational outputs of the schools, which cater to Jewish students. Jewish parents cooperate with their children's schools and provide assistance and support when necessary and are at ease with the generally successful Jewish educational system (Gaziel, 1999).

THE INTERNET AS A MEDIUM FOR THE PROMOTION OF INTERPERSONAL RELATIONSHIPS

As we examine the virtual world of the Internet and the cyber relationship established by users, it appears that during recent years interpersonal communications and relationships have radically changed owing to the universality of the Internet. Social relations that were traditionally almost exclusively maintained in the community by face-to-face interaction are now formed and conducted in cyberspace through the medium of Internet communications. Thus, in addition to whatever else it may be, the Internet communication system has become a fundamentally social medium (Kraut et al., 1998; Parks and Roberts, 1998).

Therefore, it appears that there is now no doubt that the Internet serves as a social meeting place, and as such it provides new opportunities for the development of interpersonal relationships (Parks and Floyd, 1996). It may be said that in modern society the Internet might have greater social influence than any other medium known. This is because nowadays the Internet is used to widen one's social network, to form online virtual communities, to find a marriage partner, to become involved in successful business relationships, and even to fulfill sexual fantasies (Wysocki, 1998). Walther (1992) and Walther, Anderson, and Park (1994) added that Internet-based relationships are characteristically more intimate and intensive than those maintained in a face-to-face setting. Thus for Internet users the face-to-face relationship has been complemented by a social technology that creates a completely new type of interpersonal relationship.

Research conducted by Wysocki (1996, 1998) also indicates that Internet users form more intimate relations with their peers in less time than that taken to create traditional face-to-face connections. This finding may be explained by the seeming disadvantage of the online relationship, namely, the use of anonymity that allows for self-disclosure without taking any risks. This serves as a springboard for the forming of intensive, pleasurable, deep, and rich interpersonal connections. An added advantage of the online relationship is the ability of the participant to "disconnect" easily from a distasteful or unsuitable connection as well as the opportunity provided by the medium to enter into simultaneous relationships with a number of people (Schnarch, 1997). Thus, it appears that online relationships do not differ in terms of the breadth and depth achieved in offline relationships but may also lead to greater self-disclosure and feelings of intimacy.

The main purpose of this project was to bridge the gap between Jewish and Bedouin high school students, using mediation workshops, face-to-face meetings, and intensive Internet-based chatroom and e-mail correspondence. Most especially, the study investigated the potential contribution of ICT (Information and Communication Technology) to the improvement of intergroup attitudes through the medium of the Internet. These strategies used in the project were designed to foster activities between Jewish and Bedouin Arab students that conceivably lead to a greater feeling of equality and understanding between the students as well as to greater tolerance and coexistence between the two population groups.

METHOD

Sample

The research sample comprised four eleventh-grade high school classes, two attending a Jewish high school, and two from a Bedouin Arab high school. In each class there were approximately 25 students with a total of 93 students, evenly spread between the two genders, participating in the project.

Instruments

An 80-item questionnaire was specially designed to examine Bedouin and Jewish eleventh-grade high school students' perceptions of the other ethnic group as well as their perceptions about their own ethnic identity. The questionnaire was administered twice to the project participants in a yearlong "before-and-after" research paradigm.

Procedure

In the first phase of the project six teachers (three from each high school) participated in an intensive two-day workshop designed to train them as moderators of student workshops in both the Jewish and Bedouin Arab high schools. The topics discussed by the teachers during the workshop were as follows: dealing with ethnic stereotypes, perception of interethnic inequality, interethnic democracy and equality, interethnic understanding, interethnic tolerance, and the importance of interethnic peace.

In the second phase of the project the Jewish and Bedouin Arab students met in a daylong face-to-face gathering, during which they participated in three activities:

1. All students responded to the research questionnaire that examined their perceptions of the other ethnic group as well as their perceptions about their own ethnic identity.

2. Students attended two lectures given by experts on interethnic mediation in order to prepare them for their participation in the yearlong project.

3. Students participated in informal face-to-face interethnic small-group meetings in which they were encouraged to get to know each other and to form acquaintances that would be the basis of intensive interactions in an Internet-based chatroom as well as through the medium of e-mail.

In the third phase of the project, students from both Jewish and Bedouin Arab high schools participated in weekly workshops, moderated by the six teachers initially trained in phase one of the project, on the following topics: understanding of interethnic stereotypes, perceptions of inequality, understanding of democracy and equality, student needs for interethnic understanding, importance of tolerance, and peace. In addition, students from both schools participated in weekly intensive Internet-based chatrooms in which they discussed their perceptions of each other and problems related to interethnic understanding, equality, tolerance, and peace. The six teachers responsible for the weekly workshops moderated the chatrooms. The students also corresponded through e-mail on topics that arose from the weekly workshops and chatroom discussions.

In a second face-to-face daylong meeting that summed up the yearlong project and was similar in its structure to the first face-to-face meeting, the Bedouin and Jewish students again responded to the research questionnaire, which examined their perceptions of the other ethnic group as well as their perceptions about their own ethnic identity. The students attended a lecture by a well-known Arab Israeli TV sportscaster who is well respected by all sectors in the Israeli population. They also met in small groups for intergroup activities and discussions about their impressions of the project and how they could plan for further intergroup social contact in the future.

Table 10.1

Means and Standard Deviations on Social Feelings and Psychological Attitudes for Jewish and Bedouin Arab Students in Pre- and Postexperimental Configuration

Ethnic Group	Factor	Mean (Before)	S.D. (Before)	Mean (After)	S.D. (After)
Jewish Students	Social Feelings	2.56	0.53	2.89	0.70
Jewish Students	Psychological Attitudes	3.31	0.63	3.63	0.91
Bedouin Students	Social Feelings	3.94	0.55	3.81	0.72
Bedouin Students	Psychological Attitudes	3.77	0.54	3.83	0.47

RESULTS

In order to examine the influence of the interethnic contacts, the Jewish and Bedouin Arab students were compared in a pre- and postexperimental design on the factors deriving from the research questionnaire. Two significant factors, labeled "social feelings" and "psychological attitudes," each of which had an eigenvalue greater than unity and explained 10 percent of the variance, were computed from the data in a primary components factor analysis with varimax rotation. The first factor, social feelings, included 11 significant items that demonstrated social affinity (such as understanding, closeness, warmth) in the interethnic situation. This factor had a reliability level of 0.79 as computed by the Cronbach Alpha method. The second factor, psychological attitudes, included eight significant items that indicated psychological feelings (such as anxiety, anger, fear, tension) toward members of the other ethnic group. This factor has a Cronbach Alpha coefficient of reliability that reached 0.71. The mean scores and standard deviations on the two factors in the pre- and postparadigm are presented in Table 10.1.

In order to establish possible intergroup and intragroup differences, a number of t-tests were conducted. For possible intergroup differences both before and after the project, independent sample t-tests were carried out for Jewish and Bedouin Arab eleventh graders. For the intragroup pre- and postexaminations, paired sample t-tests were conducted for both Jewish and Bedouin Arab students.

From the results of the t-test conducted to examine possible intergroup differences before the beginning of the project, it is apparent that the Bedouin Arab students had a more intensive level of social feelings toward the Jewish students than the latter had toward their Bedouin Arab counterparts ($t = -12.18$, d.f. = 91, $p < 0.001$). Similar t-test results were evident for the psychological attitudes factor ($t = -3.6$, d.f. = 91, $p < 0.001$). Regarding possible intergroup differences between Jewish and

Bedouin Arab students after participation in the yearlong project, the Bedouin Arabs remained significantly higher on the social feelings factor than the Jewish students (t = −6.17, d.f. = 90, p < 0.001). However, for the psychological attitudes factor, after participation in the project, the gap between the two groups was narrowed, with no significant difference between the levels of the Bedouin Arab and Jewish students.

In the paired sample t-test that examined possible changes in the Bedouin Arab students as a result of their participation in the project, results indicated that no significant changes occurred. On the other hand, the paired sample t-tests that examined possible changes among the Jewish students as a result of their participation in the project indicate a significant increment in social feelings (t = −2.62, d.f. = 95, p < 0.001) as well as in psychological attitudes (t = −1.97, d.f. = 95, p < 0.005) of these students toward their Bedouin Arab counterparts.

Additional analyses of research data not directly connected to the main research factors, namely, social feelings and psychological attitudes, but nevertheless important for understanding the effects of the yearlong project on the Bedouin Arab-Jewish relationship, indicate that the Jewish students perceived Bedouin Arabs as being more democratic than they did before participation in the project (t = −1.96, d.f. = 95, p < 0.005) and more flexible as well (t = −3.34, d.f. = 90, p < 0.001).

Another result emerging from data not directly connected to the research factors indicates that regarding the value of their participation in the project, the Jewish students indicated that after participating in the project they better understood the situation of Bedouin Arabs in Israel (t = 2.93, d.f. = 95, p < 0.005), and their opinions about Bedouin Arabs in Israel became more crystallized (t = 2.61, d.f. = 95, p < 0.005).

DISCUSSION

One of the major goals of a developed society is to do its utmost to bridge intergroup, interethnic, and intercultural gaps between different sectors in the general population. Many societal interventions have traditionally been employed in order to close these gaps in different societies. However, with the advent of the rapid development of ICT, the major aim of the project was to investigate whether a sophisticated Internet-based socioeducational experience is capable of promoting attitudinal change between different and sometimes socially hostile population groups. Thus the research examined the promotion of feelings of equality, understanding, tolerance, and peace between Jewish and Bedouin Arab eleventh grade high school students. It is apparent that despite the deep social gap that exists between the Jewish and Bedouin populations in Israeli society, a rationally constructed technology-based intervention project has the ability to contribute to development of a greater affinity and closeness between the two groups.

The major contribution of the project was to bring about a positive significant change in the perceptions held by Jewish students about their Bedouin Arab counterparts and to shore up positive Bedouin Arab attitudes maintained toward the Jewish students throughout the project with new and important knowledge not available to the Bedouin Arab students before participation in the project. Thus the project contributed significantly to the creation of realistic intergroup perceptions and relations in a complicated societal situation and led to an improvement of intergroup attitudes as indicated in the research findings.

The positive change as a result of participation in the project was more emphasized in the group of Jewish students who adopted more positive social feelings and psychological attitudes toward the Bedouin Arabs. They also perceived the Bedouin Arabs as being more democratic and flexible after participating in the project and declared that their attitudes to the Bedouin Arabs became more clear, and they became more aware of Bedouin Arab traditions, culture, and way of life.

The Bedouin Arabs maintained a positive level of social feelings and psychological attitudes toward their Jewish counterparts throughout the project. The fact that there was no significant increment in the Bedouin Arab attitudes toward the Jewish students can be explained as an artifact of a "ceiling effect" (Anastasi, 1988) regarding their perceptions of the Jewish students. As the attitudinal level at the onset of the project was highly positive the "ceiling effect" left little room for measuring improvement as the initial Bedouin Arab attitudes were very positive toward the Jewish population.

The positive effect of the project on the Bedouin Arab and Jewish participants is also evident in the results that do not have a direct connection to the research factors. These results indicate that the participants learned much about each other resulting from the frank and open opportunity the project provided both Bedouin Arab and Jewish students to significantly discuss contentious and sensitive issues. In addition, the project provided the participants with the opportunity to clear up their misconceptions on their own ethnic groups in intragroup workshops before establishing contact in intergroup meetings in which deeper and more thorough discussions that touched the most sensitive and telling issues affecting both Bedouin Arab and Jewish students were conducted. This openness is vital for effective intergroup contact that leads to intergroup understanding, acceptance, and attitudinal change (Amir et al., 1982).

The positive results of this project indicate that the use of technology such as Internet-based chatrooms and e-mail correspondence suggests that technological methodologies are similarly suitable for the promotion of intensive interpersonal contacts and attitudinal change as are face-to-face meetings and contacts. It is apparent that the technology used in the project provided the participants with additional motivation and incentive (following Levine and Donitse-Schmidt, 1996) and added significantly to the intergroup contact.

In summary, one can point to many research projects that have attempted to bridge social gaps between different ethnic, cultural, and religious groups. The present study can serve as a model for the further development of the use of technology in social research based on interpersonal and intergroup contact.

NOTE

This chapter was sponsored by the Institute for Community Education and Research, School of Education, Bar-Ilan University.

REFERENCES

Abu-Rabia, A. (1986). *Educational Development among Bedouin Tribes of the Negev Desert*. Paper presented at the Bi-National Conference on Education in Holland and Israel, Yeroham, Israel.

Abu-Saad, I. (1997). The Education of Israel's Negev Bedouin: Background and Prospects. *Israel Studies* 2(2): 21–39.

Amir, Y., Ben-Ari, R., Bizman, A., and Rivner, M. (1982). Objective versus Subjective Aspects of Interpersonal Relations between Jews and Arabs. *Journal of Conflict Resolution* 26(3): 485–506.

Anastasi, A. (1988). *Psychological Testing*. New York: Macmillan.

Bar, H., and Askalah, J. (1988). *Jewish and Arab Youth Meetings at "Givat Haviva."* Givat Haviva: Institute for Arabs Studies. (Hebrew)

Ben-David, Y. (1988). *Negev Bedouin Agriculture: Suggestions for the Adoption of Governmental Policy*. Jerusalem: Jerusalem Institute for the Study of Israel. (Hebrew)

Ben-David, Y. (1993). *The Settlement of Bedouins in the Negev: Reality and the Need for Improvement*. Jerusalem: Florsheimer Institute for Policy Research. (Hebrew)

Gaziel, H. (1999). Educational Policy in Israel: Structures and Processes. In E. Peled (Ed.), *Fifty Years of Israeli Education* (pp. 67–84). Tel-Aviv: Ministry of Defence Publishing. (Hebrew)

Glaubman, R., and Katz, Y.J. (1998). *The Negev Bedouin Community: Educational and Community Characteristics* (Research Report Number 11). Ramat Gan: Institute for Community Education and Research, School of Education, Bar-Ilan University. (Hebrew)

Katz, Y.J. (1998). *Report of the Commission of Inquiry into Negev Bedouin Education*. Jerusalem: Ministry of Education, Culture and Sport. (Hebrew)

Kraut, R., Patterson, M., Lundmark, V., Kiesler, S., Mukophadhyay, T., and Scherlis, W. (1998). Internet Paradox: A Social Technology That Reduces Social

Involvement and Psychological Well Being? *American Psychologist* 53(9): 1017–1031.

Levine, T., and Donitse-Schimdt, S. (1996). Classroom Environment in Computer Integrated Science Classes: Effects of Gender and Computer Ownership. *Research in Science and Technological Education* 14(2): 163–178.

Melitz, A. (1995). *Changes in Negev Bedouin Education.* Beer-Sheva: Ministry of Education and Culture. (Hebrew)

Parks, M.R., and Floyd, K. (1996). Making Friends in Cyberspace. *Journal of Communication* 46(1): 80–97.

Parks, M.R., and Roberts, L.D. (1998). "Making MOOsic": The Development of Personal Relationships On Line and a Comparison to Their Off Line Counterparts. *Journal of Social and Personal Relationships* 15(4): 517–537.

Schnarch, D. (1997). Sex, Intimacy, and the Internet. *Journal of Sex Education and Therapy* 22(1): 15–20.

Talmi, E., and Talmi, M. (1977). *Lexicon of Zionism.* Tel-Aviv: Maariv Library.

Tessler, M., and Grant, A.K. (1998). Israel's Arab Citizens: The Continuing Struggle. *Annals of the American Academy of Political and Social Science* 555: 97–113.

Walther, J.B. (1992). Interpersonal Effects in Computer Mediated Interaction: A Relational Perspective. *Communication Research* 19(1): 52–90.

Walther, J.B., Anderson, J.F., and Park, D.W. (1994). Interpersonal Effects in Computer Mediated Interaction: A Meta Analysis of Social and Antisocial Communication. *Communication Research* 21(4): 460–487.

Winer, A., Bar-On, A., and Weiner, E. (Eds.). (1992). *Directory of Institutions and Organizations Fostering Coexistence between Jews and Arabs in Israel.* New York: Abraham Fund.

Wysocki, D.K. (1996). *Somewhere over the Modem: Relationships over Computer Bulletin Boards.* Unpublished Ph.D. dissertation, University of California, Santa Barbara.

Wysocki, D.K. (1998). Let Your Fingers Do the Talking: Sex on an Adult Chatline. *Sexualities* 1: 425–452.

CHAPTER 11

The Bedouin Community in the Israeli Negev: Educational and Community Characteristics

RIVKA GLAUBMAN AND YAACOV KATZ

INTRODUCTION

The Bedouin community has traditionally existed as a nomadic tribal society roaming in the Negev desert regions of Israel and the Sinai Peninsula. In recent years the Bedouin community in the Negev has undergone a far-reaching change from a traditional nomadic society to one that is semiurban (Ben-David, 1988). This change occurred significantly due to the policy of the various Israeli governments, and today more than 150,000 Bedouin are living in the Negev (Abu-Saad, 1997). Approximately half of them have settled in permanent cities, such as Tel-Sheva, established in 1976, and Rahat, founded in 1978 (Alfenish, 1987). Some still follow the traditional customs of their society, which is in a transition stage—about one-third live in huts part of the year and wander from place to place the rest of the year, and one-sixth continue to live a completely nomadic life (Abu-Rabia, 1986; Melitz, 1995). Ben-David (1988) noted the conflict between the policy of urbanization and modernization adopted by Israeli governments and the Bedouin's demands to set up agricultural settlements and their desire to retain the traditional agricultural lifestyle and to reduce the impact of modernization on their society. Over the years the government has attempted to attract the Bedouin to newly built cities, where services such as electricity, running water, telephones, roads, public transport, schools, and clinics are provided. However, thus far only about 48 percent of the Bedouin in the Negev have moved to the new cities planned by the government authorities (Ben-David, 1993; Glaubman and Katz, 1998).

This status of the Bedouin community, as a society in transition, creates a number of problems (Kressel, 1976), such as changes in the economic situation as well as the redevelopment of social, community, and educational institutions (Kressel, 1981; Shohat, 1990, 1991). These processes have occurred under the influence of modern Israeli society, characterized by its Western trait. This fact increases the Bedouin's difficulties in transition from a traditional nomadic society to a modern urbanized community, integrated into general Israeli society, while at the same time aspiring to retain Bedouin uniqueness in culture and tribal family identity. This need is particularly noticeable in light of the changes that have occurred in the family structure and marriage behavior among urbanized Bedouin (Kressel, 1976). As a result of these processes, the relationship between the Bedouin community and the governing authorities is constantly changing (Kressel, 1981), and so are educational frameworks and needs.

Characteristics of the Negev Bedouin Community

Alfenish (1987) mentioned three interconnected processes that are relevant to the phenomena observed among the Bedouin community in transition: kinship systems and their connection with Islamic ideology; state control of kinship systems; and the role of family relationships and ideologies. Kressel, Ben-David, and Abu-Rabia (1991) listed the strengthening of the economy, political effects, and military forces in the Southern Negev and the Sinai Peninsula as being the major factors in the change in the Bedouin's sources of income. In the past, state control of Bedouin urbanization was expressed by determining the urban settlement's composition while ignoring the tribal makeup (Alfenish, 1987) and disregarding demographic processes in urban planning (Meir, 1984). Members of Bedouin tribes were forced to resettle or emigrate, and the resettlement of the tribe affected the individual's decision as to whether to settle or emigrate. Kinship and their legal ramifications had more impact than any other factor on the individual's decisions with respect to the Bedouin's future (Kressel, Ben-David, and Abu-Rabia, 1991). The result of the settlement processes conducted in this format was the breakup of the tribal system and damage to the social-cultural background, leading to intertribal conflicts and social disruption (Alfenish, 1987). In addition, these special settlement processes also had implications for the social self-image of the various Bedouin groups (Ibrahim, 1982) and the processes connected with the composition of the population (e.g., fertility rate, population growth, and death rate) in the past three decades (Meir, 1984). At the beginning of the urbanization process, the birthrate rose and the death rate declined, and the economic situation of the Bedouin community improved. After some time, as modernization increased, the birthrate declined, a phenomenon similar to the demographic processes characterizing modern society (Jakubowska, 1986).

The economic changes deriving from the necessity to change from income available to a nomad society (sheep breeding, camel herding) to patterns of living related to more permanent settlements (modernized agriculture, field crops, semiskilled work, and construction-related jobs) affected changes in social values. Thus, the social change that occurred in dealing with needy people that is presently being implemented by the public authorities replaces the assistance and support that had been provided in the past within the traditional tribal framework (Meir, Ben-David, and El-Assam, 1990; Sebba, 1991).

These complex processes that affected Bedouin society in transition had a significant affect on tribal leadership and its status in the community. Chatty (1977) and Lavie (1989) emphasized that the effect of these changes has been felt among Bedouin communities in the entire Middle East, not only in Israel. The status of the sheikh (the tribal leader) has been weakened under governments, and instead of his previous leadership status that depended on property and landownership, the sheikh's leadership has become more dependent on his charismatic ability to serve as a spiritual, political, and religious leader. The new settlement constellation, which brought various tribes together, has increased the problem of leadership authority. Due to these changes in the Bedouin community, changes have taken place in the society's institutions in general and the educational system in particular.

There is an inclination on the part of the educational authorities to empower Bedouin schools as community schools. However, the development of the community school is possible only in a situation where both the community and the school display a distinct number of characteristics and features on the basis of which the community school can grow. These characteristics include parental involvement, cooperation between parents and teachers, social and community activities on the part of the students, teachers, and educational staff, development of a child-based society with democratic characteristics, and school management designed to integrate the community into the school.

The purpose of this chapter is, therefore, to characterize the Bedouin community as it is today, based on variables relevant to education in general and the trend of fostering community schools in particular, to understand the extent of the existence of the relevant variables and the steps necessary to promote the conditions required for community development.

The Educational System in the Negev Bedouin Community

The educational system in the Bedouin sector has undergone a profound change since the 1950s, both through the initiatives of successive governments and the involvement of the Bedouin themselves. Abu-Rabia (1986) and Shohat (1990) noted that upon the establishment of the state there were only 150 Negev Bedouin children in schools, while in 1995 there were 27,100 Bedouin children in formal educational frameworks—kindergartens, primary and secondary schools (Melitz, 1995). According to Melitz (1995), only about 8 percent to 10 percent of the children are not integrated in the educational system from first grade onward. The number of Bedouin students projected for 2000–2001 was approximately 33,000, constituting a one-third increase in the student population, with the growth being anticipated mainly in the secondary schools. The percentage of girls grew from 27 percent of the overall student population in 1977 to 44 percent in 1998 (Glaubman and Katz, 1998). The number of classes grew significantly, as did the number of students. In addition, the number of students participating in matriculation exams has increased considerably over the past 10 years. The number of Bedouin teachers has grown, as well as the percentage of Bedouin teachers among the general population of teachers in the Bedouin schools. In 1978 only a third of the teachers were Bedouin, while in 1997 they constituted about 65 percent of the total number of teachers. As of 1998, all school principals at the various levels are Bedouin. Furthermore, the psychological counseling services have developed, as well as the educational welfare services. The awareness of the need for formal education has increased, and the importance of its role and value in the Bedouin community has risen with it (Abu-Rabia 1986; Glaubman and Katz, 1998; Meir and Barnea, 1987).

The growth in numbers has been accompanied by structural changes: The number of kindergartens adjacent to primary schools has risen. This increase accelerated, mainly at the beginning of the 1990s, when the number of children in the kindergartens almost doubled. Six-year comprehensive schools were built in the majority of the Bedouin towns, permanent school buildings were erected, transportation was organized for students from points closer to their residential locations, and a "Negev Bedouin School Authority" headed by a number of Bedouin sheikhs was established (Glaubman and Katz, 1998).

Despite these impressive changes, Abu-Saad (1991) contends that Negev Bedouin education requires urgent reform. Abu-Saad indicates three central areas where, in his opinion, Bedouin education suffers from discrimination compared with Jewish education. The first area concerns equipment and facilities that are lacking or not suitable for teaching and education; the second issue is the need to improve the qualification and training of Bedouin teachers and school principals; the third is the ratio of students to teachers in classes that are usually overpopulated. Bedouin schools follow the curriculum prevailing in Israeli state schools, with the addition of subjects such as Arabic and Islam. In recent years, the Bedouin have become aware of the need to teach Bedouin culture and tradition to the younger generation and to train teachers who will be able to teach their culture in addition to regular subjects (Melitz, 1995). With the rise in Islamic religious extremism in recent years, a trend has been noticed among the sheikhs and public figures to prefer religiously oriented local Bedouin teachers to better academically trained teachers resident in the north of Israel (Melitz, 1995).

Girls in the Bedouin Community—Education and Status

The concepts relating to the education and status of girls in the Bedouin community are affected by opposing trends of social-secular and traditional-religious, developing in Bedouin society. The percentage of girls who go to school is continuously increasing. In 1965 only 9.1 percent of the students in the Bedouin sector were girls; 23 years later, in 1988, this figure had risen to 37.3 percent, and in 1998, 44 percent of the total number of Bedouin students were girls. Despite this increase in general, it should be noted that the percentage of girls in each cohort declines with the rise in the level of the class. Forty-seven percent of all kindergarten children are girls, but in eleventh and twelfth grades they constitute only 35 percent of the total number of students (Melitz, 1995; Shohat, 1991).

Melitz (1995) explains the relatively low proportion of Bedouin girls in school on the basis of traditional and economic parental outlooks. Economically, so long as part of the Bedouin's living is based on shepherding, the girls and women are employed as cheap labor, and therefore the girl shepherd is absent from school. Traditionally, coeducational schools cause many families to avoid sending their daughters to school, particularly if the father's status in the tribe might be endangered by his daughter's studying together with boys. On the other hand, young people, including girls, are interested, more than ever before, in acquiring a formal education in order to adapt to the modern way of life, both socially and economically. The greater their exposure to the modern way of life, the greater the girls' awareness of the importance of education. According to Kressel (1986, 1992), the social structure and conventions of group dynamics, connected to the perception of shame and honor surrounding the issue of gender and sex in the Bedouin community, affect the status of women, which continues to be inferior due to the unremitting use of the symbols of shame and honor when determining the community's policy. In addition, Kressel points out the family interest in enhancing its status in the community by restricting its women to the home so that they can fully devote their time to raising the family, an important social drive in Bedouin community life.

In contrast to the trends of restricting women to the home, perpetuating their inferiority, and restricting their education, Jakubowska (1986),

Laish (1989) and Meir (1984) point to the opposing trend of the decline in fertility of Muslim women in Israel, Bedouin women included, due to the effects of modernization. Marx (1987) also indicated contradictory changes in the status of women, emphasizing that under certain conditions the status of women improves, while men's status declines over the years. The reason for that, according to Marx, is due to the development of a close relationship developing between women and their children, often directed against the father-husband. This contention of change in women's status in the Bedouin sector is reinforced by Abu-Lughod (1989), who studied the Bedouin in the Egyptian Western Desert. Abu-Lughod specifically mentioned Bedouin women and youth, who have become trapped between the conservative and traditional demands of the Islamic movement, on the one hand, and the options offered by modern and popular culture, on the other.

These contradicting trends in economics, tradition, and culture affect the status of women and also have an effect on sheikhs and on school principals. Some are not interested in girls' education, others are interested in encouraging girls, although some want this to happen in the framework of separate education for boys and girls, while a third group is interested in continuing the coeducational model. This phenomenon adds to intertribal tensions. We have not found a study in which the girls themselves express their position, nor are any findings available dealing with the status of educated girls in the community.

OBJECTIVES OF THE STUDY AND METHODOLOGY

Objectives of the Study

This study examines a number of communal and educational aspects of the life of the Negev Bedouin, in light of their being characterized as "a society in transition." The specific objectives of the study are as follows:

1. To define the Negev Bedouin community within the sequence of changes it is undergoing, from the recent past to the present and into the foreseeable future. The characteristics of the community will focus on those aspects relevant to the trends of cultivating community schools.

2. To describe all stages and frameworks of the Bedouin educational system and to examine the relationship between them and the Bedouin community and its present and future objectives and frameworks.

3. To describe the status of girls in the Bedouin community and to examine the possibilities of their development as educated women within the community at large.

4. To characterize the community components of the Bedouin school, the public's position on the matter, and the possibilities of developing it as a community school.

Sample

The research population consisted of a representative sample of all types of Negev Bedouin groups: those that have undergone urbanization, those still living in the traditional nomadic framework, and those in transition. The sample included representatives of Bedouin families, public leaders, educational personnel, and government officials involved with the Bedouin sector, most particularly in the educational system.

Public and Community Officials

A representative sample of 33 government officials, public leaders, and community and education personnel, national and local, were interviewed in the study.

Students

A representative sample of 726 students, 86.5 percent (N = 628) of whom lived in seven permanent towns and also studied in 11 schools located there, together with another 13.5 percent (N = 98) of students who came from scattered rural locations, served as the respondees in the study. The students were selected according to age; that is, from eighth grade (in the junior high schools) and tenth grade (secondary schools), in which there is representation of all types of the Bedouin population, including boys and girls from all types of urban and rural settlements. The majority of schools were six-year schools, a few define themselves as junior high schools, and one school defines itself as a community school. More than half of their population required special additional educational assistance (according to the testimony of principals), and only a small minority was defined as coming from well-established families socioeconomically. All schools in the sample were coed and catered to both boys and girls. According to the breakdown of the sample, it can be determined that the respondees quite extensively represented the students in the Negev Bedouin sector according to all relevant criteria.

Parents

A representative sample of 130 parents participated in the study, broken down pro rata to the Bedouin population according to their place of residence, type of settlement, and schools in which their children studied. About two-thirds of the parents in the sample had families of five or more children, about one-quarter had families of two or three children, and less than one-tenth came from families with only one or two children. Approximately one-third of the fathers, and the great majority of the mothers, had not even a primary school education. About one-quarter of the fathers (and around 16 percent of the mothers) completed primary school, and another quarter (and one-tenth of the mothers) completed high school. Only some 10 percent of the fathers and 3 percent of the mothers achieved postsecondary education. A large proportion (40 percent) of these parents were unskilled and were never trained to work in any particular field. About one-tenth were trained as semiskilled workers, around 16 percent were engaged in skilled employment, and only 3.5 percent acquired an academic profession. Another third of the parents did not actually define their occupations, about one-fifth were independent operators, around half were salaried workers, and over one-third were unemployed. The dwelling places of the parents were distributed over all types of Bedouin residential locations in the Negev: Half lived in permanent homes, some in huts or sheds, about one-tenth in tents, and the others were distributed over other types of residential dwellings and agricultural villages. According to these figures, it may be said that the parents constituted a representative sample of the general parent body of students in the Negev Bedouin educational sector.

Teachers

A representative sample of 101 teachers employed in various types of schools and living in various types of settlements in the Negev participated in the study. About two-thirds of the teachers were native Negev Bedouin, and about one-third came from other locations in the north of the country (Nazareth, Taibe, Sakhnin, and 10 other locations). Half of them lived in the settlement where the school was located, and the other half lived elsewhere. The majority lived in permanent homes, and a very few were scattered in other types of residences.

Principals

This representative sample included 17 school principals serving in various types of schools and settlements in the Negev. There was only one woman among them (9 percent), while among the teachers 20 percent are women. Teachers were much younger than the principals, and the academic education of about 14 percent of the teachers exceeded that of the principals, 70 percent of whom held a bachelor's degree. About one-third of the teachers and principals lacked an academic degree. The age ratio between principals and teachers also explained the seniority differences between them: Almost 80 percent of the principals had seniority of 13 years or more and had been working for a significant number of years in the school, compared with more than half of the teachers who were just beginners, with up to three years seniority. Less than 10 percent of teachers were working in the school for more than nine years. With respect to living quarters, the majority of the principals lived in the settlement where the school was located, while half the teachers lived in settlements other than where the school was. The majority of the educational personnel, both principals and teachers, lived in permanent homes, but some lived in huts, tents, and sheds.

Instruments

In order to collect information on the situation of the settlement, living conditions, educational institutions, occupations, and livelihood according to age, gender, and public status of the members of the community, a review was made of maps and plans of the Bedouin settlements in the Negev and of statistical data from official reports; interviews were conducted with government officials responsible for the Bedouin sector, and with public leaders and community and educational personnel at both national and local levels; a survey was made of documents and studies relevant to the subject; and observations were conducted within the Bedouin community.

In order to describe the educational system and the complex relationships within it, a review was made of all educational frameworks in which children studied in all types of Bedouin settlements in the Negev; interviews were conducted with supervisors and principals; and questionnaires that examined educational expectations and levels of satisfaction with the educational system were distributed to the research sample.

To describe the status of Bedouin girls, community and social attitudes and expectations vis-à-vis their education, questionnaires were distributed and interviews were conducted with public figures, community personnel, students, and parents, and information was also collected from existing statistical databases.

To clarify specific needs, attitudes, and expectations of the population and educational personnel (supervisors, school principals and teachers, and local educational authority personnel) with respect to community schools, structured questionnaires were distributed and semiopen interviews were conducted concerning the self-definition of the interviewees, their relationships within the community, and their educational and community expectations.

All data collected in the study were statistically analyzed in order to describe the existing situation, to understand the processes that led to it, and to present coordinated recommendations and proposals with respect to further educational-community action among the Negev Bedouin. The plethora of information was broken down into components, each of which encompassed various aspects of one particular issue.

Procedure

During the first stage, information was collected on the present situation of the State of Israel's policy vis-à-vis the Bedouin, the Education Authority of the Negev Bedouin, the school in the urbanization process, and the breakdown of the students in the regional schools.

During the second stage, the information was classified, and the principal variables were formulated in relation to the characteristics of the educational system of the Bedouin community. These variables served as the basis for constructing and validating the tools and collecting the specific data according to each of the objectives of the study as set forth above.

During the third stage, the data were collected within the Bedouin community itself, using customary scientific methods in order to obtain a comprehensive survey that provides a reliable picture of the developments up to now and makes it possible to present a forecast and recommendations for the future in the field of community education.

RESULTS

The Negev Bedouin Community—Characteristics and Positions

The Negev Bedouin community was examined from two aspects: characteristics concerning population distribution and urbanization processes; and declarations by Bedouin public leaders and their positions with respect to the urbanization process and local education.

Characteristics of the Negev Bedouin Community

Statistical data from the official reports (Ministry of Education, Culture and Sport, 1996) generate important information on the Negev Bedouin community in two principal demographic spheres:

- There has been a consistent population increase in the Negev Bedouin community since the establishment of the state in 1948 to date. A sevenfold increase occurred between 1948 (13,000) and 1995 (91,490), and 93,000 were counted in 1996 (28,000 scattered about and 64,400 in permanent locations), and this trend is continuing.

- The urbanization process has been spreading since 1992, the year in which the ratio between Bedouin living in towns and those living elsewhere was 1:1.32, compared with 1995, when the ratio shrank to 1:1.06, testifying to a clear and significant urbanization trend. Parallel data of the Bedouin population in the towns and permanent settlements between 1992 (total 33,377 inhabitants) and 1995 (44,406), show a consistent and ongoing growth of 33.04 percent, and in

1996 there were already 64,400 Bedouin in towns, a further increase of 31.04 percent.

The Positions of Public Leaders on the Urbanization and Education Processes

The interviews showed that in the opinion of public leaders and community personnel the urbanization process is vital and could contribute to solving the problems of the individual, society, and the community. Ninety percent of them believed that this process would lead to a rise in the standard of living, increased involvement of inhabitants in community activities, development of welfare projects, increased planning and construction in the permanent settlements, and the erection of public centers such as local youth cultural centers. Public leaders understand that the move to permanent towns will cause a significant change in lifestyle compared to what prevailed in the temporary villages or nomads' tents. However, most of them expressed concern about the younger generation who are undergoing, in their opinion, a process of alienation from the Bedouin tradition as a result of the transition to permanent residences. In addition, they are worried that the urbanization will lead to integration into the modern Israeli labor market, which they feel will have a negative effect on Bedouin youth. However, despite their concerns, 65 percent of them believe that the urbanization process has positive implications for the development of democratic processes within the Bedouin community. On the other hand, 35 percent expressed their objection to democratic processes that, in their opinion, clash with Bedouin tradition, and they would rather have the institutions and authorities appointed, not elected. Most (85 percent) agree with the need for self-administration, that is, election or appointment of local people to official positions in the Bedouin community, and reject the election or appointment of external officials. Ninety percent of the public leaders and community personnel define themselves as Israeli Bedouin, and the remaining minority as Arabs or Palestinians. The interviewees' personal pride in their identity as Bedouin was particularly noticeable.

Almost all public leaders who participated in the study believe that the educational system in the Bedouin sector has failed. In their opinion, the schools are functioning on a very poor level. They do not provide students with the possibility to attain satisfactory educational achievement, they do not teach them the values important to the Bedouin community, and they do not make any significant contribution to the community. The majority believes that there is almost no cooperation between the educational system and the municipal authorities with respect to allocating resources to the schools. Among the reasons they gave for this phenomenon are the difficulties in establishing and maintaining schools due to the remote locations where the children come from. Seventy percent of them believe that cooperation will increase in the future, when the urbanization process is completed, and the teachers will understand that there is no choice but to generate cooperation between the school and the parents and to act in a community mode acceptable to parents, community leaders, and educators. In their opinion, parental involvement in formal educational activities is quite marginal, and there is no desire on the part of local educational authorities to have parents join in the educational activities. On the other hand, they also pointed to reasonable cooperation between school managements and parents, in order to promote the educational system and enhance links between schools and the community. In the opinion of 75 percent of the leaders, the community school could provide a reasonable response to the educational needs of the Bedouin community, and more than 80 percent believe that this is the desirable model for the Bedouin sector. Sixty-five percent support increased involvement of parents in decision making in the school, together with the need to reinforce the status of principals and teachers in Bedouin schools. An internal conflict can be seen surrounding the belief that the Bedouin have the strength to solve their education-related problems by themselves without assistance from sources outside the community. Some of them (35 percent) object to getting outside help, while 40 percent believe in their own power to solve problems.

Improving the status of women and girls in the Bedouin community as well as integration of Bedouin into the Israeli labor market seem to be most important. Therefore, many of the leaders (about 70 percent) justify the inclination of the students to complete high school, and some of them (55 percent) support the idea that Bedouin youth should do their national duty by volunteering to serve in the Israel Defense Force.

Satisfaction with School

Satisfaction with school was expressed under about 10 different headings, such as satisfaction with the quality and standard of school, atmosphere, social activities, physical and general conditions, the desire to go to school (by students), the choice of school (by parents), teachers' satisfaction, and principals' satisfaction with the standard of teachers. The results indicate that the majority of Bedouin are quite satisfied with the school in all aspects. The principals were most pleased (77 percent) compared with all other interviewees (74 percent of teachers; 70 percent of parents; 64 percent of students). Among the parents (7 percent), and mainly among the students (9 percent), there were also some who were not at all satisfied or satisfied only to a certain extent (27 percent of students, 22 percent of parents, and 21 percent of teachers).

There are two phenomena worthy of noting: one, the differences in attitudes toward school between public leaders and those directly connected with the school; and the other, the phenomenon of the principals who stand out in their one-sided positive view of school, as opposed to students and parents, who are relatively more critical regarding what is happening. This phenomenon shall repeat itself with respect to the other findings.

Girls' Status in the Bedouin Community

There are two aspects to this issue: the level of expectations with respect to girls' status and education and their actual status in the Bedouin community.

Expectations with Respect to Girls in the Bedouin Community

These expectations include equal rights for women and men among Bedouin; the expectation of seeing more women in central positions in the community; the preference for female teachers as educators; expectations with respect to age of marriage and the manner in which girls dress; and the expectation of a higher education for the girls in the family, in the context of livelihood and children's education. The results show that parents and students have rather similar levels of expectations concerning the status of girls in the Bedouin community, which can be characterized as low (31 percent) to medium (55 percent, parents; 49 percent, students). Only a small minority of parents (9 percent) may be said to have a high level of expectation. It should also be stated that among the parents who participated in the sample there are hardly any whose expectations of the girls were very low (less than 4 percent), compared with 11 percent of the students whose expectations were very low.

Not all interviewees agree with granting positions of responsibility to women in the community. Students (61 percent), and their parents even more so (68 percent), expressed greater consent than teachers (60 percent) and principals (50 percent). The latter even totally avoided expressing full consent (0 percent) to granting positions of responsibility to women. In each group there were some who did not agree with the granting of positions of responsibility to women. On this point as well, students are more conservative than their elders.

The Status of Girls in the Bedouin Community

The perception of the actual status of girls in the Bedouin community included the attribution of importance, teaching competence, learning skills, and role of society and family; reference to gender equality; mixed society and coeducation of boys and girls in schools; the extent of girls' attendance at school; their representation on student committees; girls' learning skills; their participation in extracurricular activities; the extent to which boys and girls are assisted in order to progress in their studies and succeed in exams; equal status for male and female teachers; granting positions of authority and responsibility to women in general and to women teachers in particular; the importance of their presence in teaching; the capabilities of women teachers; the nature of relationships and respect between students and teachers; the ability of women at home to assist students with their studies. The results show that the majority of the interviewees (approximately 84 percent or more) agreed that the status of girls in Bedouin society is high to very high. Only a very small proportion believed that on certain issues their status declines to medium. Here also, all (100 percent) of the principals contended that the status of girls in the Bedouin community is high to very high with respect to all areas, while only among the parents are there a few (4 percent) who believed that girls' status is very low. However, when they express their opinions regarding equal status in teaching for both male and female teachers, and that it is even desirable that this should be the case in the future, the majority (74 percent) did not agree that it is necessary to grant equal rights to women in teaching. Nevertheless, as we have seen, many of them agreed to the granting of positions of authority and responsibility to women in the community. Women are apparently stricter in their approach to education compared with their general functioning in the community, where they are more progressive in their opinions. On the other hand, principals were certain that women teachers enjoy equality and that the present situation is how it should be (100 percent), although this position does not correlate with their unenthusiastic opinion about granting positions of responsibility to women. Teachers agreed to a more significant extent (74 percent), but students agreed less (56 percent), that it is necessary and right for women teachers to enjoy equality at school, although each group has quite a minority (14 percent of teachers; 20 percent of students) who did not agree that women teachers should enjoy equality at school.

In summary, it may be said that although the opinions expressed by the interviewees showed inconsistencies, and they were not uniform with respect to existing rights or those they are prepared to grant the girls, there was a considerable measure of support for equality and consent to granting positions of authority and responsibility to women in the community in general and in education in particular. That is to say, opinions on the issue of Bedouin women's status are progressing regarding the status of girls in Bedouin society, but much improvement needs to be made before true equality is achieved.

Community Schools

Being the central objective of the work, this field is the most extensive and comprehensive in the study and includes three subthemes: factors in the work and policy of the school in the context of developing and encouraging collaborative and mutual relationships between all those participating in the educational effort—students, parents, teachers, and principals; the school and the parents' home—kinship systems and mutual expectations; and the Bedouin community—social aspects within and beyond the school and its community.

Factors Dealing with Policy Planning of the School

Each group of subjects in the study has its own specific point of view, but for the purpose of the chapter, we combined all questions on the same subject, while presenting findings for each specific group. This subject is broken down as follows:

1. Nature of the relationship between class teachers, teachers, and principal vis-à-vis the students. All research subjects tended to perceive the relationship between teachers and students in school in a positive light, as teachers, both in their individual capacity and as members of the school's pedagogic council, are concerned with and are interested in students and their problems; they are available and willing to become involved in activities with the students and their families both in the school and on home visits; teachers established school student councils and offered students optional activities according to their interests; students generally respected teachers and expressed an interest in the curriculum. All principals (100 percent) tend to see school life in a more positive light than teachers, while it is the parents who are the most critical (only half believe that the situation is good, and 16 percent contend that the situation is bad). Teachers also tend to hold more positive opinions (73 percent) and are somewhat similar to the principals in this respect, while students hold attitudes similar to those of their parents, although they are relatively more positive than their parents (66 percent positive). The majority of the students (about 80 percent) were very pleased with the principal's attitude toward them. However, there was a group of students (more than 10 percent) that was not at all happy and another group of students (12 percent) that believed that the principals' attitudes were not particularly positive toward the students.

2. Attitudes toward school policy regarding the preparation of parents and students for educational involvement. In order to shed light on the extent to which both school authorities and parents are prepared to invest efforts to bring the parties closer on the issue of establishing community schools, we examined their expectations regarding school policy concerning the involvement of parents and students in decision making,

traditionally considered the sole responsibility of the management and teachers. The findings indicate the extent to which principals and teachers are in favor of taking the action required to instruct the parties on how to become involved in school life and activities. The majority of parents, on their part, expressed their willingness to accept such directions (71 percent), and to a greater extent the principals (94 percent) and the teachers (85 percent) expressed willingness to provide the necessary directions.

3. School policy regarding the encouraging of parental involvement, in reality. Data were also collected on the actual existence of activities aimed at increasing parents' involvement in school life, for instance: organization of parents' evenings and workshops to increase involvement; involving parents by means of getting them to volunteer for activities; involving parents in problem solving and decision making; requesting parents' support of joint curricular aims; maintaining of regular communication; establishing of parents' committees; the school's function in the community; teachers' willingness to specialize in issues dealing with parental involvement in school; and principals' personal involvement in the promotion of parental involvement in school matters. In this area, significant disagreement was apparent between parents and school personnel, particularly principals. The latter, as usual (94 percent), believed that in their school many activities take place testifying to the existence of a policy aimed at encouraging parents' involvement in school. Teachers largely support this contention about the existence of parental activities (90 percent). The majority of parents, on the other hand, do not agree that there are many such activities. Only one-third (31 percent) agreed with the principals, compared with almost one-half (46 percent) who argued that few or very few of these types of activities took place.

4. Principals' policy with respect to the development of teachers and administrative work:

• The institution's policy on the development of teachers. This policy is purported to promote the development of teachers and their participation in all fields of school policy: participation in decision making regarding the school's objectives and selecting the subject matter to be studied; coordination and collaboration among teachers; encouragement of self-realization activities; giving useful and clear information about curriculum and methods of relating to students; providing teachers with sufficient teaching equipment; the existence of a positive relationship with the principal, who is then willing to listen to teachers' opinions without any apprehension; and principals' ability to deliver constructive criticism of teachers. The results showed that the teachers are usually very satisfied (70 percent) with the institution's policy on teacher development and with the atmosphere in the school. About one-third are quite satisfied, and very few (1 percent) believe that there is no teacher development in the institution.

- Principals' policy on organizing administrative work—collaborating with executives in the school on problem solving, preferring local teachers over external teachers, holding meetings with the teachers, visiting their classrooms, and monitoring their work. Almost all principals (88 percent) are very satisfied with themselves, and absolutely none (0 percent) are dissatisfied with the way their administrative work is organized. Although they admit that there is room for improvement, and while in some areas the standard is not yet satisfactory, they believe that their organizational policy complies well with all requirements.

- Principals' policy on regional cooperation, both in declarations of intent and in reality: holding planned meetings with the local authority, maintaining contacts with principals at all levels of education—primary schools, junior high, and high schools. In this field the difference among the principals is noticeable: Some (41 percent) maintain great or very great involvement, some (24 percent) medium, while the involvement of others (35 percent) is low. That is to say, according to their own testimony, the level of the school's policy concerning regional educational cooperation is not uniform, and the difference among principals is extensive.

School and Parents—Relationships and Expectations

This issue of the relationship between the school and the parents has six different aspects. It is one of the most complex areas of the study, and it has great significance regarding the community school that is the focus of the present study.

1. Expectations regarding children's education. Because of the importance of higher education for their children's future, parents have expectations regarding the school's contribution in this regard. The findings clearly indicate the gap between parents and students. According to almost all students (85 percent), their parents expect them to continue their studies, to which they attribute great importance. In comparison, the expectations expressed by the parents themselves are low. Over one-half of them (58 percent) have high to very high expectations that their children will continue their studies in institutions of higher education. Regarding expectations of the students themselves, about two-thirds (68 percent) of the students expect to complete school with a matriculation certificate and believe that it is expected of them to adopt the behavioral norms of high school students in the Jewish sector, that is, to continue to a higher education. At the same time, about one-third of them are not sure of continuing in higher education, and a very small minority (3 percent) has no expectations regarding higher education at all.

2. Parents' relationships with the school. The examination of the relationship between the school and the home environment includes the following: the extent of the importance attributed by the parents to the school and their involvement for the benefit of the future of their children and their favorable attitude toward studies; the level of familiarity of the

teachers and principals with the parents; reciprocal meetings and clarification of regulations between school faculty and parents; the extent to which the parents are respected by the school; the extent to which the school is respected by the parents; and the extent to which parents are willing to allow their children to continue with their studies at the expense of helping them in agricultural and other chores. All interviewees held a positive opinion about the relationship between the school and the home environment.

In each group, particularly the parents and principals, there was a small minority who viewed the relationship between the school and the home environment in a rather gloomy light. The opinion of students (67 percent positive, 5 percent negative) and teachers (63 percent positive, 4 percent negative) was relatively positive, believing that the relationship between the school and the parents is rather positive. On the other hand, parents (58 percent positive) and principals (51 percent positive) were less happy with the home-school relationship. It is interesting that the principals held the most critical attitudes about the home-school partnership, believing that this relationship needs to be improved.

3. Expectations of parents' involvement in the school. The expectations of parents' involvement in school life are important with regard to the question of establishing community schools in the Bedouin community. Expectations concern increased involvement of parents in the school; benefit from involvement in the community school's contribution to the efficiency of teaching and to the success of the students; and the extent to which parents should be encouraged to become involved in the school. In general, it may be said that the majority of the interviewees (about 85 percent) expressed high-level expectations concerning involvement of parents in the school, and almost none of them have low expectations. The distribution of expectations at the high end of the scale is interesting. The expectations of teachers were most positive (87 percent), and the expectations of the majority of principals were high (65 percent). It is interesting that students (71 percent) and their parents (65 percent) were also positively inclined toward parental involvement in school.

4. The actual level of parents' involvement in the school. This aspect of the study deals with the actual extent of parental participation in the specific activities of the school—parents' meetings, school trips, committees, social activities, determining programs, financial assistance—and to what extent students wish their parents to be involved in these activities. Unlike the expectations that everyone expressed for more parental involvement in school life, in the case of actual involvement, the lack of agreement among the interviewees was noticeable. Students (81 percent) and teachers (76 percent) testified that parental involvement was high, compared with only a minority of principals (35 percent), and especially very few parents (18 percent), who believe that this was so. Both

students and teachers seem satisfied with the present situation. On the other hand, principals, and particularly parents, are critical of the present situation and want to improve it. If we compare the reality of the situation to the level of expectations, principals and parents appear to be disappointed with the situation and want to see more parents involved in school activities, since they believe that such involvement will improve the quality of the school and that it is of great importance for students' success in their studies.

A different picture is obtained from another angle, which is evidence of the existence of joint activities between teachers, parents, and students. Here the opinions of parents and students are closer, although they do not see eye to eye with principals and teachers. Here, again, it is the parents who were the most critical. About half the students believed that the level of activity is good to high, while only about 40 percent of the parents believed this. One-third or more of the parents and a similar number of students stated that the activity is slight or that there is no joint activity of teachers, parents, and students, while the principals, at the other extreme, perceived the situation of activities as relatively good. Less than one-quarter of principals believed that the level of activities is low, but there were none who felt that there was a total dearth of joint activity between teachers, parents, and students. The opinions of teachers were similar to those of the principals. Up to one-third of them believed that the level of activity was good, and only 10 percent believed that joint activity was nonexistent.

The parents depicted a similar picture, when they were asked to give specific details of the activities in which they are involved in the schools. About half (48 percent) were somewhat involved in activities in schools, and only a minority of parents (13 percent) were involved to a very great extent. Almost half of them (43 percent) were involved at a medium level, and a small group (about 10 percent) admitted to no activity at all.

5. The nature of relationships between parents and children, in the context of the school. This aspect examined the interaction between parents and their children in the context of the school and the contribution of each to this relationship. On the part of the parents, examined were the extent of their information on their children's activities throughout the day; the extent to which they show interest and talk to their children about what happens at school and about their grades; and the extent to which they assist their children in their homework and in preparation for examinations, read what their children have written and listen to them, and discuss TV programs with their children and important events in their lives. On the part of the students, examined were the extent to which they contribute to a closer relationship between the home and the school and the extent to which they request assistance from their parents in the preparation of homework and revision for examinations, share

with their parents what they have learned, and discuss with them personal and general events. A significant group of students (72 percent), and a slightly smaller group of parents (62 percent), were satisfied with the relationship between parents and students. However, there are relatively more parents (38 percent) who were not satisfied with their level of interaction with their children. In their opinion, parents are not sufficiently involved in the daily issues that concern their children and do not communicate with them sufficiently on matters that interest them; a proportion of children (28 percent) testified that they do not share with their parents everything that concerns their school and social lives.

6. Teachers' perception of their status and function:

- Teachers' attitudes about their willingness to invest effort in their work. A large group of teachers (69 percent) was willing to make a large to very large investment in raising the standard of studies. However, there is also quite a significant group of teachers (48 percent) who admitted that the extent of their willingness to invest in these efforts is medium to low. That is to say, they are prepared to fulfill their formal duties and are not willing to make any additional efforts.

- Teachers' perception of their status. Teachers seem to be rather pessimistic with respect to their status as perceived by others in the community. Only a few of them (less than 15 percent) believe that their status is perceived as very high. The vast majority (86 percent) believed that teachers' status is perceived as no higher than medium, and the rest believe that teachers' status is perceived by the public as low. This may explain why there is a significant proportion of teachers who are not willing to invest any efforts in order to promote the standard of studies in the classrooms, their thinking being that if their input is not appreciated, why should they invest efforts over and above the minimum required?

- Teachers on expectations from them with respect to parents' involvement. The majority of teachers (80 percent) understood that the expectations of them in this field are high. About one-fifth (20 percent) believed that the level of expectations from them is medium, and none believed that there are no such expectations from teachers. Accordingly, in the teachers' opinion, they can benefit to a great extent from cooperation with parents and their children; at the same time, they felt that they are in need of special training on how to encourage parental involvement. In the final analysis, it is important that they be trained, because this involvement might be useful for students studying in their classes.

In conclusion, it seems that parents do not agree with school personnel (students, teachers, and principals) as to the nature of the relationship between the school and the home. Concerning the level of their expectations and attitudes, they feel that they are close to school personnel and show quite a significant desire to increase their involvement in the school. However, in their view of the actual state of affairs, some disagreement becomes apparent. Principals are inclined to see the picture in a more positive way than the others, while the parents are the most critical, contrary to the expectation common to all, regarding the importance of the parent-school relationship. Perhaps, if actual parental involvement had been more intensive, it would have been possible to elicit greater agreement with respect to the perception of the actualities of the parent-school partnership.

The Bedouin Community—Social Aspects

The social aspects characterizing the Bedouin community are perceived as important within the context of the community school. Therefore, we considered it important to examine this issue, in addition to the various social and community aspects.

1. Self-definition and self-reference—among the reference groups. Bedouin, Arab, Palestinian, Israeli, Bedouin-Israeli, or other, the parents, students, and principals have a similar sense of belonging. Approximately half identify themselves as Bedouin-Israeli or Bedouin. Very few identify themselves as Palestinian, about 12 percent identify themselves as Arabs, and even less as Israelis. The students, to a lesser extent, consider themselves, relative to their parents, more Bedouin and more Israeli. Only a tiny group does not feel that it belongs to any of these groups. In contrast, about 50 percent of the teachers identify themselves mainly as Arabs, about 12 percent among them identify themselves as Bedouin, and very few as belonging to another group (Bedouin, 5 percent; Palestinian, 5 percent; Israeli, 10 percent).

To summarize the issue of identity, we can say that the parents and students are similar to each other, although there is somewhat of a generation gap. There are few differences between students and parents in their sense of national identity. In contrast, the teachers display somewhat different and varying positions on the issue of identity from those of students and their parents.

2. Social and community aspects of the Bedouin community. This area is divided into five aspects:

• The extent of the Bedouin community's social involvement in Israel. This includes the social atmosphere in the community; the situation and status of Bedouin in Israel; the extent of the maintenance of relationships with Jewish schools in the vicinity; economic conditions, crime, and violence in the Bedouin sector; Bedouin attitudes toward democracy, the peace process, and the activities of the resistance organizations.

   Principals, as well as parents, perceive the level of the Bedouin's involvement in Israeli society as high. Students and teachers are split in their opinions; the majority of teachers believe that the involvement of Bedouin in Israeli society is more or less average, and one-third state that the involvement of the Bedouin community in Israeli society is quite low. The majority of principals (82 percent) felt that Bedouin schools indeed emphasize democracy and the peace process to a very great extent. A minority of principals believed that they do it only on an average level, but none of them say that these issues are not dealt with in schools.

• Social satisfaction with the community, the atmosphere, and the relationships and ties within the community, such as human rights in the Bedouin community and the extent of family-related clashes among students in the schools. Students and parents appeared to be quite pleased with the situation (about three-quarters of the students and 70 percent of the parents). In contrast, principals, and particularly teachers, are less satisfied with the atmosphere and relationships within the community. This issue may be described as testifying to the major difference between teachers and principals, on the one hand, and parents and students, on the other.

• Expectations of improvement in the social-community situation in the school. This question is important when examining the expectations of the community school and its contribution to the social situation of the community. The expectation of improvement in the social-community situation in the school is correlated with satisfaction with the community and not correlated with satisfaction at school, as expressed above. Students' (80 percent), and parents' (79 percent) expectations for improvement in the social-community situation were high in contrast with expectations of teachers (57 percent) and principals (79 percent), which were rather low. The clients—students and parents—had higher expectations for the community school than the service providers in the school—teachers and principals. The educational staff was more pessimistic and had low expectations regarding the possibility of an improvement in the social-community situation in the school.

• Importance of volunteering for military service. To what extent is it important for Bedouin boys and girls, who according to Israeli law are exempt from military service, to voluntarily join the Israel Defense Force? The opinions of both students and teachers were quite similar in their breakdown, with a majority opposed to military service. About 50 percent of the students and the teachers contend that military service is not very important or not at all important. Only one-third say that military service is important or very important, and the rest take no clear position or give only a lukewarm response.

• Parents' perception of community and public education affairs. Due to the importance of parents' opinions and positions when it comes to community education, some questions were addressed to parents only, as follows:

The majority of the parents (about 60 percent) had almost no faith in public leaders or school personnel when it comes to dealing with public affairs and politics, mainly concerning the education of their children. A quarter of parents expressed some measure of faith in public and educational personnel, and only about 16 percent had a great measure of faith in local Bedouin leadership.

Close to 60 percent of parents viewed the urbanization process as promoting the Negev Bedouin community in general and their children's education in particular. Another quarter of them viewed this process with reservation, as contributing little to their advancement, and a group of around 16 percent were pessimistic on this issue, contending that the contribution of the process to their advancement or the education of their children is totally insignificant.

It is noticeable that the majority of parents (around 72 percent) considered it important that their children should become familiar with Israeli society. Another 20 percent attributed some importance to this issue, and only a minority of less than 10 percent objected to it, contending that it is completely unimportant and will not contribute in any manner to the Bedouin community. Regarding the issue of the necessity of adaptation to Israeli society, a minority of about 25 percent believed that it is important for Bedouin society to adapt itself to modern life in Israel, whether by adapting religious rulings or by young people volunteering to serve in the Israel Defense Force. Around half took an intermediate position, thereby indicating that although they recognize the importance of adapting to some extent, they have reservations about the issue. About one-third of the parents did not attribute any importance to this point; that is, in their opinion, Bedouin society does not have to adapt itself to modern life in Israel.

DISCUSSION

In light of the responses of public leaders, students, parents, teachers, and principals to the research questionnaire, a somewhat complex picture of the situation of the Negev Bedouin community and its educational and community characteristics emerges. Although there is consensus on certain issues among the various sectors, in many fields there are different approaches and even disagreement among them. In reviewing the various educational and community aspects, it is interesting to see which characteristics are acknowledged by all and, in contrast, which characteristics are viewed differently by each group in the community.

The Urbanization Process

The conflict noted by Ben-David (1988) is reflected in the statements made by public leaders and parents. On the one hand, they recognize the fact that the urbanization process will lead to a general rise in the Bedouin's standard of living and will accelerate development of democratic processes within the community. At the same time, they are concerned that the process will lead to alienation from Bedouin tradition, as well as to greater integration into Israeli society, pointed out by Shohat (1990, 1991) and Kressel (1976, 1981). Indeed, the urbanization process is not agreed upon by all equally. Public leaders have accepted the urbanization process as a necessity of life in view of the fact that the Bedouin community lives in the State of Israel and Israeli society is significantly urbanized and inclined toward Western standards. Only one-quarter of the parents agree with them and view the urbanization process positively, since it will lead to growing integration of the Bedouin into Israeli society and the labor force and will develop democracy and modernization in the community. They are also in favor of the Bedouin youth serving in the military as a lever for better and fuller integration into Israeli society. In contrast, significant proportions of parents object to and are even afraid of Bedouin integration into Israeli society, and about one-quarter of the parents are totally opposed to such integration.

Three aspects can be observed in the relationship with Israeli society: integration into Israeli society, adaptation to Israeli lifestyle, and serving in the Israeli army. As shown by the findings, there is no uniform approach to all aspects. A majority of public leaders are concerned about the Bedouin community's integration into Israeli society but believe that it is important for Bedouin young people to adopt democratic and egalitarian social processes such as those typical in Israeli society. Furthermore, the public leaders are in favor of the Bedouin youth joining the Israel Defense Force, so as to enable them to penetrate the Israeli labor market more easily and to assure Bedouin civil rights and social equality in the state. Bedouin public leaders are better acquainted with the social and economic problems affecting Bedouin society in Israel (Alfenish, 1987; Avinoam, Ben-David, and El-Assam, 1990; Meir, 1984), resulting from the urbanization process. The parents, students, teachers, and principals are in favor of the Bedouin community's social integration in Israel to a growing extent, in order to maintain the status and rights of the Bedouin community within Israeli society. On the other hand, when matters touch upon Bedouin lifestyle and its compatibility with life in Israel, although the majority of parents are interested in their children becoming familiar with Israeli society, they object more than public leaders to the adoption of Israeli social norms by Bedouin youth. Apparently, the problematic changes occurring in tribal and family composition and lifestyle due to urbanization (Alfenish, 1987; Ibrahim, 1982; Jakubowska, 1986; Sebba, 1991) led to the concerns and reservations they expressed. Parents are also in favor of Bedouin youth joining the Israel Defense Force, for the same reasons—penetrating the Israeli labor market and assuring their rights and social equality. It is interesting that they do not connect the service in the Israel Defense Force with their concern about adopting Israeli social norms. Students, as well as the teachers and principals, are divided in their opinions on the need for Bedouin youth to integrate into Israeli society. Furthermore, significantly less than half are in favor of their serving in the Israel Defense Force, while a majority are against military service. Maybe they are not yet aware of the problems of integrating into the labor market, or perhaps this can be explained in the context of their concept of tradition and identity.

Tradition, Identity, and Affiliation

In this area there is a definite distinction between schoolteachers and members of the Bedouin community, public leaders, principals, parents, and students regarding self-identity. The majority of the public leaders express concern for the young people becoming alienated from Bedouin tradition. Both parents and principals are in favor of Bedouin youth continuing to preserve traditions. Contrary to the fears expressed by the adults in the community, the majority of students are in favor of continuing to preserve Bedouin traditions. The majority of students, parents, and principals also emphasize their self-identity mainly as Israeli Bedouin or just Bedouin.

In contrast, a significant group of teachers emphasized their Arab identity rather than Bedouin identity. With respect to students, teachers expressed the position that young people should be allowed more flexibility to decide whether or not to continue preserving Bedouin tradition. Apparently, the differences stem from the fact that the majority of the teachers come from Arab villages in the north of the country and do not belong to the Bedouin community in Israel. According to Melitz (1995), in 1992 the proportion of Bedouin teachers out of the total teacher population was 65 percent. However, in our study, only 17 percent defined themselves as Bedouin, and half defined themselves as Arabs. Abu-Saad (1991) concluded that there is still a need to expand the qualification and education of the Bedouin teachers, mainly for the purpose of teaching the Bedouin culture and tradition (Melitz, 1995). The gap in identity between teachers and the Bedouin community may also contribute to the distance between teachers and students. Teachers expressed negative opinions about the behavior of Bedouin youth; students felt that teachers were responsible for disciplinary problems and the students' declared unwillingness to volunteer for activities organized by teachers and school.

Perception of the Educational System in General and the Community School in Particular

Public leaders agree that the Bedouin educational system does not fulfill the needs of the community. They believe that the level of the students' achievements is low, and there is no teaching about values important to the Bedouin community. In their opinion, parental involvement in what is happening in the educational system is marginal, and the local education authorities are not even interested in having the parents participate in making decisions concerning the educational system. At the same time, public leaders point to cooperation at the school level between principals and teachers, on the one hand, and parents, on the other. Public leaders believe that if run efficiently and effectively, the community school could make an important contribution to the educational system in the Bedouin sector.

Parents, students, teachers, and principals all state that Bedouin show medium to high involvement in the community. According to the principals, the school deals intensively with social issues. Compared with the positions taken by public leaders on the subject, the students, parents, teachers, and particularly the principals express overall satisfaction with the educational system and the general social situation among the Bedouin, contrary to Abu-Saad's (1989) and Reichel, Neumann, and Abu-Saad's (1986) findings. However, teachers are more pessimistic on this issue, and the majority state that the general social situation can be described as only marginally satisfactory and in need of improvement. The awareness of the need for formal education continues to grow (Abu-Rabia, 1986; Meir and Barnea, 1987), and teachers have high expectations of the level of education provided for Bedouin students. They contend that the Bedouin educational system does indeed generally fulfill their expectations and that there is reasonable cooperation among all parties who are supposed to contribute their share to educational success. Teachers and principals emphasize the importance of parental participation in decision making in the educational system, and in line with the suggestions proposed by Abu-Saad (1991) with respect to equipment, teachers' level of qualification, and larger staff, parents now make greater demands such as the provision of short further education courses for both parents and teachers to enable them to cooperate usefully and pertinently. They also perceive an understanding between teachers and principals as important, and a community school that encourages cooperation between the community and education personnel can contribute significantly to improving educational and community services in the Bedouin sector.

Public leaders, as well as students, teachers, and principals, are all in favor of community schools in the Bedouin sector. This type of school seems a solution for many of the educational problems the Bedouin community encounters. Parents and students believe that the community school will make a significant contribution to promoting education for both students and the community, mainly due to parental participation in school activities. They also expect the community to contribute to the improvement of the relationships between parents and students. Everyone believes that it is necessary to increase investment in the community school so as to achieve more intensive community building. They are all in favor of joint activity between school and parents, so that the latter can participate in educational decision making. At the same time, the expectations of both teachers and principals are higher than those of parents with respect to the latter's involvement in school. In actual fact, the gap between them is even greater when they relate to training available concerning involvement in the school. Teachers and principals believe that the level of training available to teachers and parents in this field is good. However, parents do not think so. Parents are divided in their opinions, and many of them contend that the existing parental training is not commensurate with the needs. Students and parents believe that the present situation can be improved; however, teachers and principals express doubts as to whether any improvement can be expected in this field. It appears that their doubts arise from their negative opinions concerning the Bedouin social-community situation.

A community school requires teacher training and maintaining extensive connections between the school and community sources. When asked, teachers and principals expressed satisfaction with the level of teacher development and the organization of the school. However, the level of principals' involvement is fluctuating and very different from one school to the next. In addition, public leaders complained of the lack of contact between the local and municipal educational authorities, on the one hand, and school and parents, on the other.

Status of Women in the Bedouin Community

The study's findings indicate a positive attitude toward change in women's status in Bedouin society, thereby confirming the findings of recent studies (Abu-Lughod, 1989; Jakubowska, 1986; Kressel, 1986, 1992; Laish, 1989; Meir, 1984). However, it appears that the desired actual change has not yet occurred, and there are many internal contradictions in this field. On the one hand, all interviewees contend that the present situation is satisfactory since there is reasonable equality in the educational system with respect to girls' rights. The students, parents, teachers, and principals all agree that women and girls should be treated fairly, they have high expectations with respect to their status, and they recommend the provision of equality to women in order to enable them to achieve central positions in the society, in community, and in education. On the other hand, we found in the sample only one woman principal, and female teachers are relatively few. Furthermore, the parents also explicitly expressed great reservations with respect to women's functioning as teachers. Indeed, public leaders admit that the present situation in the Bedouin community regarding the status of women and girls still requires improvement, compared with desirable and customary levels of gender equality in a democratic society.

SUMMARY AND CONCLUSIONS

Bedouin leaders contend that the Bedouin education system is unsatisfactory, while students, parents, teachers, and principals express reasonable satisfaction with the standard of education and schools in the Bedouin sector. It is generally agreed by all of them that the community school and parents' participation in making educational decisions could contribute to the improvement of the standard of education and culture within the Bedouin community. However, in order to reap maximum benefit from such cooperation, both parents and teachers must be trained to participate in the school's educational program. Therefore, it appears that it is necessary to promote the opening of community schools based on discussion with the participation of public leaders, educational personnel, parent representatives, and school officials. This community group can then decide on the nature of the programs needed to train those participating in school-community processes. Intensified discussion of issues of common interest can promote cooperation and lead to a reduction in the gaps found among the parties. Discussion can promote real feedback that will enable education personnel to draw more reliable conclusions and to execute required changes that will benefit the Bedouin educational system. Conceivably it would also be worthwhile to have experts on community schools from the Ministry of Education participate in these discussions in order to enrich the encounters with their experience.

A significant proportion of the teachers in the Bedouin sector are Israeli Arabs from the north of the country. These teachers come from different cultural backgrounds that lead to potential value-based conflicts between themselves and their students. Therefore, it appears necessary to train more teachers from the Bedouin community in order to increase identification and coordination of expectations between the clients (students and parents) and teachers.

The issue of the integration of the Bedouin into Israeli society and the development of democratic processes constitute difficult dilemmas for the Bedouin community. Thought must be given to these dilemmas, and there should be more dialogue between leaders and families, in order to set up communication channels through which solutions to common problems may be found without the Bedouin compromising on the issue of tradition. For that purpose it is also necessary to examine the real needs of the Bedouin youth with respect to serving in the Israel Defense Force and to clarify the advantages and disadvantages for the young people entailed in such service before they make a decision.

The perception of the status of women and girls is not realistic. The fact that there is one woman school principal and a small number of female teachers indicates, in the interviewees' opinion, that there is equality, although in a more open society the same fact would indicate obvious inequality and even discrimination against women. Mention should be made of the fact that there is a certain measure of social desirability in the responses to questions concerning the equality of girls, since it is clear that the status of women and girls is an important issue in Israeli society in general and was a sensitive issue for all interviewees. Accordingly, it appears that it is necessary to develop educational programs designed to promote gender equality and to discuss how such equality can be improved.

In general, much still needs to be done in order to close the quality gap between Bedouin education and that enjoyed by the general Israeli population. It is important to take the responses of students, parents, teachers, principals, and public leaders into consideration when suggesting measures designed to improve the Bedouin educational system. Bedouin identity, tradition, and culture need to be maintained when introducing changes into Bedouin education, and all measures should be undertaken on the basis of community consensus and unity.

REFERENCES

Abu-Lughod, L. (1989). Bedouins, Cassettes, and Technologies of Public Culture. *Middle East Report* 19(4): 7–111.

Abu-Rabia, A. (1986). *Education Development among Bedouin Tribes of the Negev Desert*. Paper presented at the Bi-National Conference on Education of Holland and Israel, Yeroham, Israel.

Abu-Saad, I. (1989). *Organizational Climate and Teachers' Job Satisfaction in the Bedouin Elementary Schools of the Negev in Southern Israel*. Unpubished Ph.D. dissertation, University of Minnesota, Minneapolis.

Abu-Saad, I. (1991). Towards an Understanding of Minority Education in Israel: The Case of the Bedouin Arabs of the Negev. *Comparative Education* 27(2): 235–242.

Abu-Saad, I. (1997). The Education of Israel's Negev Bedouin: Background and Prospects. *Israel Studies* 2(2): 21–39.

Alfenish, S. (1987). Processes of Change in Kinship System and Family Ideology in Bedouin Society. *Sociologia Pluralis* 27(4): 323–340.

Avinoam, M., Ben-David, J., and El-Assam, S. (1990). *Vicissitudes of the Elder's Status in the Urbanizing Bedouin Society and Their Public Implications: Research Report 1988–1990*. Beer-Sheva: Ben-Gurion University. (Hebrew)

Ben-David, J. (1988). *The Bedouin Agriculture in the Negev—Suggestions for Policy Formation*. Jerusalem: Jerusalem Institute for the Study of Israel. (Hebrew)

Ben-David, J. (1993). *Reality and the Need for Its Advancement*. Jerusalem: Florsheim Institute for Studies of Policy.

Boyd, J. (1977). *Community Education and Urban Schools*. London: Longman.

Carspecken, P.F. (1991). *Community Schooling and the Nature of Power*. London: Routledge.

Chatty, D. (1977). Leaders, Land and Limousines: Emir versus Sheikh. *Ethnology* 16(4): 385–397.

Glaubman, R., and Katz, Y.J. (1998). *The Negev Bedouin Community: Educational-Communal Characteristics*. Research Report Number 11. Ramat Gan: Institute for Community and Education Research, Bar-Ilan University.

Ibrahim, S.E. (1982). Images of the New Social Order. *International Review of Modern Sociology* 12(1): 105–131.

Jakubowska, L.A. (1986). Urban Bedouin: Social Change in a Settled Environment. *Dissertation Abstracts International* 47(4): 1384A.

Kressel, G. (1976). *Privacy Compared with Tribalism: Dynamics of the Bedouin Community in the Urbanization Process*. Tel-Aviv: Hakibutz Hame'uchad. (Hebrew)

Kressel, G. (1981). The Ecological and Cultural Adjustments of Urbanized Bedouin in Central Israel. In A. Laish (Ed.), *The Israeli Arabs: Continuity and Change* (pp. 140–167). Jerusalem: Magnes Press. (Hebrew)

Kressel, G. (1986). Latent Payments and Gains Implied in the Confinement of Women to the Household Setting: The Case of Reproduction among the Negev Bedouin. *Israel Social Science Research* 4(1): 51–64.

Kressel, G. (1992). Shame and Gender. *Anthropological Quarterly* 65(10): 34–46.

Kressel, G., Ben-David, J., and Abu-Rabia, K. (1991). Changes in Land Usage by the Negev Bedouin since the Mid-19th Century. *Nomadic Peoples* 28: 28–55.

Laish, A. (1989). The Israeli Arabs: Between Religious Revival and National Awakening. *New East* 32: 1–9. (Hebrew)

Lavie, S. (1989). When Leadership Becomes Allegory: Mzeinas Sheikhs and the Experience of Military Occupation. *Cultural Anthropology* 4(2): 99–136.

Marx, E. (1987). Relations between Spouses among the Negev Bedouin. *Ethnos* 52(1–2): 156–179.

Meir, A. (1984). Demographic Transition among the Negev Bedouin in Israel and Its Planning Implications. *Socioeconomic Planning Sciences* 18(6): 399–409.

Meir, A., and Barnea, D. (1987). The Educational System of the Israeli Negev Bedouin. *Nomadic Peoples* 24: 23–35.

Meir, A., Ben-David, J., and El-Assam, S. (1990). *Changes in the Elder's Status in Urbanized Bedouin Society: Public Implications*. Beer-Sheva: Ben-Gurion University. (Hebrew)

Melitz, A. (1995). *Changes in the Education of the Negev Bedouin*. Beer-Sheva: Ministry of Education and Culture, Office of the Southern District. (Hebrew)

Ministry of Education, Culture and Sport. (1996). *Facts and Figures*. Jerusalem: Department of Educational Statistics.

Poster, C., and Kruger, A. (1990). *Community Education in the Western World*. London: Routledge.

Reichel, A., Neumann, Y., and Abu-Saad, I. (1986). Organizational Climate and Work Satisfaction of Male and Female Teachers in Bedouin Elementary Schools. *Israel Social Sciences Research* 4(2): 34–48.

Sebba, R. (1991). The Role of the Home Environment in Cultural Transmission. *Arch. and Comport* 7(3): 205–222.

Shohat, M. (1990). *The Growth of the Bedouin Section's Education System, South District*. Beer-Sheva: Ministry of Education and Culture, South District Office. (Hebrew)

Shohat, M. (1991). *Changes in the Bedouin Section's Education System 1992*. Beer-Sheva: Ministry of Education and Culture, South District Office. (Hebrew)

CHAPTER 12

Jewish-Arab Relations and the Education System in Israel

MAJID AL-HAJ

THEORETICAL FRAMEWORK

Since the 1970s we have been witnessing an increased interest in multiculturalism, both as a concept and as a strategy for legitimizing diversity, empowering minorities and disadvantaged groups, and dealing with problems of equality and equity (see, e.g., Banks, 1981, 1997; Giroux, 1997; Kymlicka, 1995; Lynch, 1986; McLaren, 1995; Sleeter, 1996; Wieviorka, 1998). However, despite the large body of research on issues of multiculturalism and multicultural education, there are still no comprehensive criteria for defining the parameters of cultural communities (Belay, 1992: 296). These parameters usually include nationality, ethnicity, race, gender, class, and other visible divisions (Belay, 1992: 296). But this does not resolve the confusion in defining the borders of these communities and the meaning of multiculturalism as a basis for organizing the relationships between and within these groups.

The different approaches toward multiculturalism may be classified under two main headings: mainstream and critical multiculturalism. Mainstream multiculturalism emphasizes the right to be different and the importance of recognizing cultural diversity (Goodstein, 1994: 107). However, this approach adopts the literal definition of diversity as reflecting the existence of numerous cultures that contribute to the richness of the national or global community (Goodstein, 1994: 107). Mainstream multiculturalism, which merely highlights "otherness," does not question the basic issue of the ideological hegemony of the dominant culture (Giroux, 1992: 18; cited by Schwartz, 1995). Furthermore, in this type of multiculturalism, the term *diversity* and its content are defined by those who hold power. Thus disadvantaged groups, minorities, and women who are engaged in such discourse are generally forced to use a language not of their own making (Estrada and McLaren, 1993).

Unlike mainstream multiculturalism, critical multiculturalism does not view "diversity" per se as a goal. It argues, instead, that diversity should be framed "within a politics of cultural criticism and commitment to social justice" (Estrada and McLaren, 1993: 31). Hence "multiculturalism without a transformative political agenda can just be another form of accommodation to the larger society" (31).

On the same footing, studies indicate that in highly stratified societies in which the subordinate groups have no control over the school system, diversity in curriculum and school objectives is used to "marginalize rather than empower subordinate groups" (Clark, 1993: 64).

According to the critical approach of multiculturalism, students should be given the context for analyzing and interpreting the information provided by the formal curriculum (Goodstein, 1994). Supporting the important role of students, Roads emphasizes that "critical multiculturalism relates not only to what gets taught, and what gets defined as relevant knowledge, but also to the very nature of the teaching itself." Thus, unlike traditional education, critical multiculturalism is aimed at encouraging students to be active and critical and to be democratic participants in both education and social life (Roads, 1995: 269–270).

Israel may be an ideal case for dealing with multiculturalism in a complex set of social, cultural, and political factors. Israel was established as a nation–state by Jews and for Jews. It is heavily based on Jewish immigration from all over the world to Israel. This has created a pluralistic society that is deeply divided across national, ethnic, religious, and social cleavages. At the same time, the establishment of Israel and the 1948 Israel-Arab war turned the indigenous Palestinian Arab population from a majority into an involuntary minority. In what follows we will present the Jewish-Arab encounter as the central cleavage of the social structure in Israel; then we will describe the formal policy toward Arab education and its reflection in the curriculum prescribed for Arab schools as compared to Hebrew schools, mainly in subjects that aim to shape pupils' orientation and identity.

MULTICULTURALISM IN ISRAEL

The Social Structure

In terms of its social structure and relative to its population, Israel is probably one of the most pluralistic and multicultural societies in the world. The 1998 population of nearly 6 million includes a Jewish majority that originated in about 100 countries, and about a million Palestinians (*Statistical Abstract of Israel*, 2000: 2–48). There is also a large population of over 200,000 foreign workers, who constitute 9 percent of the labor force in Israel and about 50 percent of the workers in agriculture and construction (Fisher, 1999: 15). As elsewhere, this group, which arrived as temporary workers, is becoming an integral part of the local population, affecting not only the economic structure of Israel but also the social and cultural spheres (Nathanson and Achdut, 1999).

The Jewish population is divided by ethnicity and religious orientation and by length of time in Israel. There are Ashkenazim (European and American origin) and Mizrahim or Sephardim (North African and Asian origin); religious and nonreligious; and recent immigrants and veteran Israelis (especially against the background of the influx from the former Soviet Union since 1989) (see Kimmerling, 1998). The Arab population, too, is not homogenous but, rather, divided by religion (Muslims, Christians, Druze) and other social categories.

The Jewish-Zionist character of Israel and the continuing Israel-Arab conflict, with the Palestinian issue at its center, have made the Jewish-Arab division the most salient and most problematic in Israel. The two groups differ in nationality, religion, language, national aspirations, social lifestyles, and many cultural components. The very definition of Israel as a Jewish-Zionist state has deeply affected its structure, priorities, and borders of legitimacy (Rouhana and Ghanem, 1998; Yiftachel, 1999). Not only are Arabs situated outside the Jewish national consensus in Israel; they are also outside the legitimate borders of the Israeli political culture (Al-Haj, 1997). In addition, security has been placed at the very center of the political, social, and cultural experience and legitimized the militaristic nature of Israel, at the expense of its civilian character (Ben-Eliezer, 1999). The sociodemographic segregation of the two groups merely deepens the Jewish-Arab divide. Some 90 percent of Arabs live in segregated Arab towns and villages. Even the other 10 percent, who live in mixed cities, tend to reside in segregated Arab-majority neighborhoods (Al-Haj, 1997).

This analysis raises some major questions: What relationship has developed in Israel between the social structure, the political culture, and the educational system? Has the multicultural social structure of Israel resulted in the development of multicultural education? If so, what kind of multiculturalism exists in Israel? To deal with these questions, we shall first sketch the Arab educational system in Israel, followed by a comparative analysis of the curricula in Arab and Hebrew schools, as reflected in the subjects of history, language, and civics.

Education

Since the establishment of Israel, there has been a contradiction between the expectations of the Palestinian population in Israel and of the Israeli establishment regarding the Arab educational system. While Palestinians sought to use education as a catalyst for empowerment and social change, the Israeli establishment used education as a mechanism of control. Its policy is composed of various interconnected components: the expansion of the educational system among the Arab while placing "security considerations" at the center, purging Arab education of any Arab national content, and introducing contents that legitimize the state's ideology (for a detailed analysis of the Arab educational system in Israel, see Al-Haj, 1995).

There was, however, a dispute among Israeli policymakers regarding the best way to achieve these goals. Two central approaches are worth mentioning: the assimilation and the controlled-segregation models. The assimilation model held that the Arabs who remained in Israel should be seen not as a national minority but as a collection of religious groups and minorities of various types who should be assimilated into Israeli society and detached from their Arab national identity (Al-Haj, 1996: 98). The advocates of this approach, chiefly Arabists in the Ministry of Religious Affairs and the Office of the Prime Minister, wanted Arab schools to use the same curriculum mandated for Jewish schools and teach it in Hebrew (98).

The assimilationists were in the minority; the controlled-segregation approach, advocated by senior officials in the Ministry of Education, prevailed. This approach held that it would be difficult to assimilate the Arabs into Israeli society for a number of reasons: The Arabs could be expected to oppose it; assimilation would require the allocation of equal resources to Arab schools, but resources were limited and the formal scale of priorities was incompatible with this; Jewish society itself had not agreed as to the definition of the Israeli culture that should be adopted and fostered, and assimilation of the Arabs would only complicate the debate. On the other hand, the advocates of controlled separation believed that Arab education should not be allowed any form of autonomy, because this was contrary to the Jewish-Zionist character of the state and a threat to its security.

As a result, the model that came to guide policy toward Arab education was based on administrative and sectarian separation, with Jewish control of the administration, staffing, resources, and most important of all, the content of the educational system. This approach led to the separate development of multiple Jewish educational systems (the state stream and the state religious stream, and the independent ultra-orthodox school system) and an Arab system (including both state and confessional schools). In the context of the policy of control, the educational system in the Arab sector became "education for Arabs" controlled by Jews through the state and a channel through which the ideology and narrative of the dominant Jewish majority is conveyed. This situation is conspicuous in the administrative structure of education, in the staffing system, and in the material taught in various subjects (see Al-Haj, 1996; Amara and Mari, 1999; Mari, 1978; Mazawi, 1994; Nakhleh, 1977).

The main aim of the educational system among Arabs has been, therefore, to legitimize the ideology of the state (as a Jewish-Zionist state), to enhance loyalty to the state, to maintain order and stability, and to educate for Jewish-Arab coexistence in which Arabs rationalize their inferior status (Al-Haj, 1996; Mari, 1978; Peres, Ehrlich, and Yuval-Davis, 1968).

While Arab education has been emptied of any Palestinian-Arab national content, Hebrew education has been focused on a national Zionist content. Only in 1975 were the goals of Arab and Hebrew education reformulated. The reformulated goals for Arab schools included a call to educate Arab students "to love the country shared by all its citizens." This was considered a revolutionary goal by many Arab and Jewish educators and was welcomed by the Arab leadership. Later, however, the word *shared* was omitted, and the goal was stated as "to love the country"—with no word about whose country and how Arab pupils are connected to it (Al-Haj, 1996).

The goals of Arab and Hebrew education are also reflected in the curriculum, mainly in subjects that are supposed to affect students' identity and orientation, as will be demonstrated in the following analysis.

History Curriculum

A comparison of the history curricula in Jewish and Arab schools reveals that whereas the emphasis in Jewish schools is on the Jewish national theme, the curriculum for Arab students ignores the Arab national theme. Arab students learn "that human culture is the fruit of the combined endeavors of all peoples of the world," whereas Jewish students learn that the Jewish people played a central role in shaping human culture. Values of Arab-Jewish coexistence, with the accent on the superiority of the Jews, are inculcated in Arab students by the repeated emphasis on the shared role played by Jews and Arabs in history and the shared destiny of the two peoples. Values of coexistence are not conveyed to Jewish students, for whom the Arabs as a people are included in the term "other nations." What is more, Arab students are expected to understand the importance of the State of Israel to the Jewish people and not to Jews and Arabs in the same degree (Farah, 1991).

The asymmetry between Arab schools and Jewish schools is also reflected in the allocation of teaching hours in the two streams for world history, Arab history, and Jewish history. In both systems, world history occupies about 60 percent of the curriculum. Other historical topics are divided quite asymmetrically. Whereas Jewish schools devote about 40 percent of their teaching hours in history to Jewish history, Arab schools devote only half this proportion to Arab history. What is more, whereas Arab students devote about 20 percent of their history classes to Jewish and Zionist history, Jewish students are exposed to parallel Arab topics in less than 2 percent of their history studies (based on Al-Haj, 1996: 104–106).

The history curriculum for both Jewish and Arab schools was revised in the mid-1970s according to the objectives proposed by the Peled Committee.[1] Even after that revision, however, Jewish students were educated to love Israel as their homeland and the state of the Jewish people, while Arab students were taught to internalize the message that they are not full citizens but partial partners in Israeli society and must obey the rules that are set by the Jewish majority and are consistent with the basic ideology of the state (Al-Haj, 1996).

The imbalance and asymmetry in the official objectives proposed for Arabs and Jews was criticized (Mari, 1978; Nakhleh, 1977; Sarsour, 1981). The core of this criticism was that the proposed objectives included no recognition, overt or indirect, of the fact that the Arabs in Israel constitute a national minority and are an inseparable part of the Palestinian people. What is more, the goals emphasized the aspiration for peace only in Arab schools. The goals drafted for Jewish schools made no mention of the aspiration for peace or of Jewish-Arab coexistence (Sarsour, 1981).

A third version of history curriculum was drafted by the Ministry of Education in the 1990s. An analysis of the goals and history textbooks in Jewish and Arab schools reveals some changes in the values presented to students. The declared aims refer to very important educational values, such as fostering judgment of historical events on the basis of humane and ethical values and fostering understanding and tolerance of the feelings, traditions, and ways of life of other peoples and nations (Ministry of Education, 1998: 10). But after stating these liberal generalities the curriculum in practice fails to relate to a cardinal point—the form in which the Arab-Israeli and Israel-Palestinian conflict and the various and contradictory narratives about this conflict are to be considered.

In addition, because the history curriculum was drafted after the beginning of the peace process in the region, and especially the Oslo Accords with the Palestinians, the peace treaty with Jordan, and the first steps toward a comprehensive peace in the Middle East, one might have expected that it would relate to the central question: What is the role of the history curriculum in a transition from conflict to peace? What new themes, both informative and value, should reflect the historic change taking place in the region?

These questions are also left unanswered in the enumeration of the general goals, which relate to information, the acquisition of skills, types of historical concepts, analysis of social phenomena, development of historical thinking, fostering judgment of historical events, enhancing understanding and tolerance, and strengthening an identification with the people and the state (Ministry of Education, 1998, 1999).

In fact, the only innovation with regard to values is in the goals for Arab schools: "Fostering a sense of affiliation with the Palestinian Arab people and the Arab people on one hand, and with the State of Israel and its citizens on the other" (Ministry of Education, 1999: 8–9). This statement about fostering a sense of affiliation with the Palestinian Arab people appears for the first time as a central objective of the history curriculum in Arab schools. In the previous curriculum the goals related, as stated, to developing "a feeling of identification with the Arab nation and its culture" with no specific reference to the Palestinian people (Al-Haj, 1996).

However, that "fostering a sense of affiliation with the Palestinian Arab people" is accompanied by fostering a sense of affiliation "with the State of Israel and its citizens," with no reference to the nature of the State of Israel and the status of its Arab citizens (Ministry of Education, 1999: 8-9). Consciously or unconsciously, then, Arab students are called on to "enhance the sense of belonging to the state of Israel and its Israeli citizens" as a Jewish state and not as a binational state, a state of all its citizens, or a multicultural democracy.

What is more, one of the key goals in the curriculum for Jewish schools is "recognition of the role of the state in the life of society and fostering a desire for active participation in shaping its destiny" (Ministry of Education, 1998: 12). This section, which is missing from the curriculum for Arab schools, aims at perpetuating the status quo that internalizes Jewish students' perception that Israel is a Jewish state, not a civil state shared by Jews and Arabs. Unlike Jewish students, Arab students are not called on to participate actively in shaping the destiny of the state and to feel full members thereof.

A comparison of the goals prescribed for Arab schools and for Jewish schools reveals that the principle of fostering an ability to understand the other's position and to get to know other views of the same events and national problems is applied in Arab schools. In Jewish schools, however, what is studied is a one-sided picture in which the main weight is Jewish-nationalist and in which the historical perspective is based on learning about the distinctiveness of the Jewish people "with regard to its essence and destiny" (Ministry of Education, 1998: 9).

A series of textbooks for the new history curriculum were published in 1999 (see Bar-Navi and Naveh, 1999; Center for Educational Technology, 1999; Naveh, 1999). A careful analysis of these books, published elsewhere (Al-Haj, forthcoming) shows that these books endeavor to represent change in that they treat the Israel-Palestinian conflict from a more open and complex perspective than did the previous curricula. This change is manifested in the emphasis on the Zionist-Palestinian conflict as between two national movements. Also, they present a complex picture regarding the creation of the problem of the Palestinian refugees and to some extent try to present a more balanced picture regarding some events in the Israel-Palestine conflict. However, the narrative presented in these books remains the typical Zionist narrative in which the Jewish side has just national aspirations that it realizes by immigrating to the Holy Land, making the desert bloom, pioneering and developing the country, establishing economic, educational, and cultural institutions, and successfully organizing for self-defense against Arab assaults. With regard to the 1948 war (the War of Independence, as they refer to it), the Zionist narrative is the unifying thread in the tale of bravery and triumph of quality over quantity (Al-Haj, forthcoming).

At the same time, Palestinian society appears as a collection of individuals with no institutions and organizations, without its own social and cultural life, and with a tribal and religious leadership. The Palestinian population seems to be hostile to the Jewish Yishuv in order to prevent its development and the realization of its national aspirations, by means of terrorism and pillage carried out chiefly by disorganized gangs.

It seems that the statement in most of the books that the conflict was between two national movements is declarative only and derives from the current conciliatory atmosphere in the wake of the Oslo Accords. It is not reflected in the survey of developments and key events in the Zionist-Palestinian conflict over about a century, because the books present the Palestinian national movement as a direct result and reflex action to the Zionist movement rather than as existing in its own right and as based on a historical, ideological, social, and cultural infrastructure. What is more, according to these books, continuing the line that prevailed previously, there is ideological pluralism only on the Jewish side; the Arab-Palestinian side is monolithic, with no culture of political debate and with a single position concerning the Jewish Yishuv and the Zionist-Palestinian conflict.

Conspicuous in all these books is the passive role they assign to the students. None of them evince any tendency to give students an active role in critical thinking, confronting existing myths and narratives, and taking an active role in the development of alternative narratives (see Weinberg and Porath, 1999). Even in the treatment of the issue of peace in the Middle East the material is conveyed in a "banking" fashion (Freire, 1971) of depositing information rather than in a way that could lead in the direction of education about peace in which the students are partners in thinking and potential partners in action (Al-Haj, forthcoming).

Arabic and Hebrew Languages

The asymmetric goals and contents of the history curriculum in Arab and Hebrew schools are also to be found in the Hebrew- and Arabic-language curricula. In Arab schools, Hebrew is a mandatory subject from third grade till the end of high school. Both the linguistic and cultural aspects are taught—to some extent in even more depth than Arabic is taught. The aims of teaching Hebrew in Arab schools emphasize the exposure of Arab students to the culture and heritage of the Jewish people: "To open the gate for the pupil to become acquainted with the basis of the cultural and literary heritage of the several Jewish generations and to value the Hebrew culture" (Ministry of Education and Culture, 1977: 4).

Arabic in Hebrew schools has a completely different status. Until 1985 it was optional; students could choose between French and Arabic. In 1985, Arabic became mandatory in the intermediate level (seventh through ninth grades). A comparison between the aims of teaching Hebrew in Arab schools and Arabic in Hebrew schools again reveals a great asymmetry.

While the teaching of Hebrew in Arab schools is oriented mainly to deepen bicultural and bilingual education, the aim of teaching Arabic in Hebrew schools is mainly utilitarian—to provide students with a basic knowledge of the Arabic language in order to satisfy instrumental needs (Al-Haj, 1998). The aims of teaching the Arabic language in the Hebrew schools are stated as follows:

1. Learning Arabic as a living language
2. Acquiring an instrument for communicating with Arabic speakers
3. Basic familiarity with Arabic newspapers and literature
4. Acquiring basic ideas about the life of Arabs and their culture. (Ministry of Education, 1975: 2)

The comparison between how Hebrew is taught to Arab students and how Arabic is taught to Jewish students is even more striking when it comes to the methods used in Arab and Jewish schools. In Arab schools, pupils learn Hebrew through Jewish religious or traditional sources, such as the Bible, the Mishna, and Aggada, and by systematic study of classical and modern Hebrew literature. All this is clearly oriented to reinforce the positive image of the Hebrew language and culture and to inculcate in Arab pupils the Jewish right to "Eretz Israel" (The Land of Israel). In contrast, Jewish pupils learn Arabic mainly through the media and "street language" (Al-Haj, 1996). Intentionally or unintentionally, this may reinforce the negative image that most Jewish pupils already have of Arabs (Hofman, 1988).

In addition to the asymmetric goals and contents of the curricula for Arab and Hebrew schools, the Hebrew educational system is also infused by contents that reinforce stereotypes about Arabs. In a large-scale study, Adir Cohen examined the reflection of the Arab-Israeli conflict in Hebrew children's literature. He analyzed about 1,700 books and textbooks published after the 1967 war. Among these books, 520 presented an image of the Arab. He found that some 80 percent of the 520 Hebrew children's books presented a negative image of the Arab, as ugly, inferior, and hostile to Jews (Cohen, 1985).

A similar study by Bar-Tal and Zultick on the Hebrew language and literature textbooks for schools in the Jewish sector came to the conclusion that they convey a negative message about Arabs and reinforce Jewish students' prejudice about Arabs as inferior, backward, and hostile (Bar-Tal and Zultick, 1989). They reported that subjects related to Arabs occupy only a marginal place. What is found, however, presents Jewish-Arab relations mainly at the collective level, rather than the individual aspect. Most relations appear in the context of war, conflict, and estrangement.

In the wake of the Israeli-Palestinian peace agreement, Bar-Tal conducted a follow-up study in order to examine whether this historic transition from conflict to reconciliation is reflected in the textbooks (Bar-Tal, 1996). He examined 124 Education Ministry-approved textbooks on Hebrew language and literature, history, geography, and social studies, used at the different levels of schools in the Jewish sector. While he found a variegated picture, there was more continuity than change with regard to Jewish-Arab relations. Societal beliefs emphasizing "security" and Jewish heroism, positive self-image, and victimization appeared frequently. Most of the books presented a negative stereotype of Arabs (Bar-Tal, 1996).

Civics

In Israel, the state and its authorities occupy a position of central importance, symbolically as well as in practice. National-political symbols such as the flag, national anthem, and army became a focus of national identification (Ichilov and Naveh, 1981). Various factors associated with the sociopolitical structure work for the creation of a "subjective" rather than "participatory" orientation toward citizenship. The most important of these factors are the fact that a large part of the Israeli population lack a democratic-civic tradition, the strong dependence of citizens on the authorities, and the close linkage of nationality and citizenship (Ichilov and Naveh, 1981).

Discussions of the orientation of the political culture in Israel have tended to be restricted to the Jewish population, excluding the Arab minority. For a long time, even Jews who originated in Arab and Islamic countries were excluded from the Israeli core culture. The "melting pot" strategy that prevailed until the mid-1970s was usually based on melting the Oriental Jews into the Ashkenazi pot. Thus the Eurocentric character of the curriculum was conspicuous (Stahl, 1979: 361–365).

Various factors led to a change in the curriculum in the direction of recognizing the cultural uniqueness of Oriental Jews and legitimizing their cultural and ethnic identity. The main emphasis, however, remained on the shared national similarities (370).

Studies of citizen orientation among urban Jewish youth in Israel found that they tend to describe the citizen's roles as limited and specific, rather than diffuse and inclusive (Ichilov and Naveh, 1981). Accordingly, civics education in Israel directs youngsters mainly to a narrow definition of the role of citizens.

The political orientation of Arab youth in Israel reflects their alienation from the state and its institutions. This is the result of the alienation of Israeli Arabs from the major ideology and symbols of Israel as a Jewish-Zionist state, in addition to the Arabs' limited autonomy of Arabs and restricted socioeconomic mobility (Ichilov 1988).

After reviewing studies on democratic and citizenship values among students, teachers, and school curriculum in Israel, Ichilov concluded that the concept of citizenship is narrow and somewhat vague. A large part of the younger generation finds it difficult to apply universal values of democracy, in particular toward the Arab citizens of the country. As far as curricula are concerned, Ichilov found a tendency to avoid discussion of controversial issues. The civics curriculum deals mainly with the formal aspects of law and order. In addition, the materials taught to different groups of students ignore diversity and pluralism.

In a later study (1993), Ichilov emphasizes that civics education is marked by an overemphasis on the passive dimension. Students are educated to obey the law and act in conventional ways. In addition, citizenship is associated with the procedural-formal arena, and the universal-international aspect is overlooked.

As in Hebrew schools, in Arab schools, too, the civics curriculum leaves a minimal role for students. It focuses on basic information about the political structure and about the various levels of government. Despite the changes that were introduced over time into the curriculum for Arab schools, it is still far from giving students a genuine opportunity to deal with the complex issues that face them as a national minority in a Jewish-Zionist state and the possible contradiction between this character and the democratic principle on which Israel is founded (Al-Haj, 1996).

CONCLUSION

This chapter has dealt with the state of multiculturalism in Israel. After presenting a theoretical framework, we have focused on the Israeli case, as reflected in the Jewish-Arab encounter. Our analysis has shown that despite the multicultural social structure in Israel, there has been no tangible effort, official or public, to deal with the internal divisions by nurturing a multicultural concept. As a result, there is a wide gap between the social structure and the official culture. While the social structure is increasingly multicultural and pluralistic, the official culture is based strictly on an ethnocratic Jewish-Zionist character.

The Israeli educational system reflects the power system and the dominant culture that prevail in the wider society. It mirrors to a large extent the ethnonational character of the state of Israel and the asymmetry of Jewish-Arab relations. In addition, the school system is a "mirror" that functions to maintain the status quo rather than act as a catalyst for social change.

From the theoretical aspect, the curriculum for Jewish schools remains very far from multicultural education, even from the positivist-establishment perspective. This curriculum has failed to instill the idea of multiculturalism, whether in the Jewish-Arab or the internal Jewish-Jewish sphere. The scanty material that is supposed to expose students to Arab history and culture reflects the state's ideology and in some respects reinforces negative stereotypes about Arabs. Even the civics curriculum adopts a traditional-conservative approach, leaving both students and teachers with a minor role. As such, it hardly leads toward multicultural education.

The curriculum in Arab schools, by contrast, does reflect a multicultural perspective. But this multiculturalism is not compatible with the positivist-establishment approach and certainly not with the critical model. It is not compatible with the former approach, which accents the cultural and national distinctiveness of the minority group and highlights its partnership in the state and society. Nor is it compatible with the critical model, because it does not lead to questioning the status quo and presents the topic of citizenship in a conservative and passive fashion devoid of political messages.

We may conclude that the education system among the indigenous Arab minority reflects a state that may be phrased as "controlled multiculturalism." The Arab minority has a limited say as far as its education is concerned, at the administrative level and contentwise. The cultural content of Arab education, which is supposed to reflect the uniqueness of the national Arab minority, and also the intercultural contents meant to expose Arabs to the majority culture, have both been determined by the majority. Thus the minority is required to internalize the values of coexistence, multiculturalism, and pluralism, while acquiescing in the superiority of the majority group and its definition of the nature of the state and society.

NOTE

1. The Peled Committee was appointed by the Ministry of Education in 1975 in order to draw up the goals of education in Israel for the 1980s. This committee was chaired by Matty Peled with the participation of Arab and Jewish scholars. The committee stated, for the first time, specific goals to Arab schools, along with the goals to Jewish and Druze schools.

REFERENCES

Al-Haj, M. (1995). *Education, Empowerment and Control: The Case of Arabs in Israel.* Albany: State University of New York Press.

Al-Haj, M. (1996). *Arab Education in Israel: Control and Social Change.* Jerusalem: Magnes Press. (Hebrew)

Al-Haj, M. (1997). Identity and Political Orientation among the Arabs in Israel. *Medina, Mimshal ve-Yahasim Benle'umiyyim* 41–42: 103–122. (Hebrew)

Al-Haj, M. (1998). Multicultural Education in Israel in Light of the Peace Process. In M. Mautner, A. Sagi, and R. Shamir (Eds.), *Multiculturalism in a Democratic and Jewish State* (pp. 703–713). Tel Aviv: Ramot. (Hebrew)

Al-Haj, M. (forthcoming). *The History Curriculum for Arab and Jewish Schools in Israel: Policy, Content, and Goals.* Haifa: Center for Multiculturalism and Educational Research.

Amara, M., and Mari, A. (1999). *Issues in Linguistic Education Policy in Arab Schools in Israel.* Givat Haviva: Institute for Peace Studies. (Hebrew)

Banks, J. (1981). *Multiethnic Education: Theory and Practice.* Boston: Allyn and Bacon.

Banks, J. (1997). Multicultural Education: Characteristics and Goals. In J. Banks and C.A. Banks (Eds.), *Multicultural Education: Issues and Perspectives* (pp. 2–26). Boston: Allyn and Bacon.

Bar-Navi, E., and Naveh, E. (1999). *Modern Times. Part 1, 1870–1920; Part 2, 1920–2000.* Tel Aviv: Tel Aviv Books. (Hebrew)

Bar-Tal, D. (1996). *The Rocky Road toward Peace. Societal Beliefs in Times of Intractable Conflict: The Israeli Case.* Jerusalem: Institute for Research and Development in Education, The Hebrew University of Jerusalem. (Hebrew)

Bar-Tal, D., and Zultick, S. (1989). The Reflection of the Image of Arab and Jewish-Arab Relations in Textbooks. *Megamot* 3: 301–317. (Hebrew)

Belay, G. (1992). Conceptual Strategies for Operationalizing Multicultural Curricula. *Journal of Education for Liberty and Information Science* (Fall): 295–306.

Ben-Eliezer, U. (1999). *The Militaristic and Civil Society in Israel: Forms of Neo-militarism and Anti-Militarism in a Post-hegemonic Era*. Paper presented at the conference Civil and Militaristic Society in Israel: Towards an Era of Peace, University of Haifa, Center for Multiculturalism and Educational Research.

Center for Educational Technology, Unit for Adapted Pedagogy (Ketzia Tabibian, team leader). (1999). *Journey to the Past: The Twentieth Century, by Virtue of Freedom*. Tel Aviv: Center for Educational Technology. (Hebrew)

Clark, S. (1993). The Schooling of Cultural and Ethnic Subordinate Groups. *Comparative Education Review* 37(1): 62–68.

Cohen, A. (1985). *An Ugly Face in the Mirror: The Reflection of the Jewish-Arab Conflict in Hebrew Children's Literature*. Tel Aviv: Reshafim. (Hebrew)

Estrada, K., and McLaren, P. (1993). A Dialogue on Multiculturalism and Democratic Culture. *Educational Researcher* 22(3): 27–33.

Farah, N. (1991). Teaching of History: Curriculum and Textbooks. In M. Habib-Allah and A. Kupty (Eds.), *Education for the Arab Minority in Israel. Issues, Problems and Demands* (pp. 109–113). Haifa: Al-Karmah. (Arabic)

Fisher, H. (1999). Foreign Workers: Actual Situation, Formal Network and Government Policy. In R. Nathanson and L. Achdut (Eds.), *The New Workers: Wage Earners from Foreign Countries in Israel* (pp. 13–40). Tel Aviv: Hakibbutz Hameuchad. (Hebrew)

Freire, P. (1971). *Pedagogy of the Oppressed*. New York: Herder and Herder.

Giroux, H.A. (1992). *Border Crossing: Cultural Workers and the Politics of Education*. New York: Routledge.

Giroux, H.A. (1997). *Pedagogy and the Politics of Hope: Theory, Culture and Schooling*. Boulder, CO: Westview Press.

Goodstein, L. (1994). Achieving Multicultural Curriculum: Conceptual, Pedagogical and Structural Issues. *Journal of General Education* 43(2): 102–116.

Hofman, J. (1988). To Be Jews and Arabs in Israel. In J. Hofman (Ed.), *Arab-Jewish Relations in Israel: A Quest in Human Understanding* (pp. 175–216). Bristol: Wyndham Hall Press.

Ichilov, O. (1988). Citizenship Orientation of Two Israel Minority Groups: Israeli Arab and Eastern-Jewish Youth. *Ethnic Groups* 7: 113–136.

Ichilov, O. (1993). *Citizenship Education in Israel. Current and Pre-State Trends of Development*. Tel Aviv: Sifriyat Poalim. (Hebrew)

Ichilov, O., and Naveh, N. (1981). The Good Citizen as Viewed by Israeli Adolescents. *Comparative Politics* (April): 361–376.

Kimmerling, B. (1998). The New Israelis: Multiple Cultures with No Multiculturalism. *Alpayim* 16: 264–308. (Hebrew)

Kymlicka, W. (1995). *Multicultural Citizenship*. Oxford: Clarendon Press.

Lynch, J. (1986). *Multicultural Education. Principles and Practice*. London: Routledge and Kegan Paul.

Mari, S. (1978). *Arab Education in Israel*. Syracuse, NY: Syracuse University Press.

Mazawi, A. (1994). Palestinian Arabs in Israel: Educational Expansion, Social Mobility and Political Control. *Compare* 24(3): 277–284.

McLaren, P. (1995). White Terror and Oppositional Agency: Toward a Critical Multiculturalism. In C. Sleeter and P. McLaren (Eds.), *Multicultural Edu-*

cation, Critical Pedagogy, and the Politics of Difference (pp. 33–70). Albany: State University of New York Press.

Ministry of Education and Culture. (1975). *Arabic Curriculum for Hebrew Schools.* Jerusalem: Ministry of Education and Culture. (Hebrew) (Mimeographed)

Ministry of Education and Culture. (1977). *The Hebrew Language and Literature for the High Grades of the Arab Secondary School.* Jerusalem: Ministry of Education and Culture. (Hebrew) (Mimeographed)

Ministry of Education and Culture. (1998). *History Curriculum for Grades Seven to Nine in the State Stream* (2nd rev. ed.). Jerusalem: Ministry of Education and Culture, Pedagogic Secretariat. (Hebrew)

Ministry of Education and Culture. (1999). *The History Curriculum for Arab High Schools.* Jerusalem: Ministry of Education and Culture, Pedagogic Secretariat. (Hebrew)

Nakhleh, K. (1977). The Goals of Education for Arabs in Israel. *New Outlook* (April–May): 29–35.

Nathanson, R., and Achdut, L. (Eds.). (1999). *The New Workers: Wage Earners from Foreign Countries in Israel.* Tel Aviv: Hakibbutz Hameuchad. (Hebrew)

Naveh, E. (1999). *The Twentieth Century: On the Threshold of Tomorrow.* Tel Aviv: Tel Aviv Books. (Hebrew)

Peres, Y., Ehrlich, A., and Yuval-Davis, N. (1968). National Education for Arab Youth in Israel: A Comparative Analysis of Curricula. *Megamot* 17(1): 26–36. (Hebrew). Also in the 1970 *Jewish Journal of Sociology* 12(2): 147–164.

Roads, R. (1995). Critical Multiculturalism, Border Knowledge and the Canon: Implications for General Education and the Academy. *Journal of General Education* 44(4): 256–273.

Rouhana, N., and Ghanem, A. (1998). The Crisis of Minorities in Ethnic States: The Case of the Palestinian Citizens in Israel. *International Journal of Middle East Studies* 30: 321–346.

Sarsour, S. (1981). Arab Education in a Jewish State: Major Dilemmas. In A. Hareven (Ed.), *One of Every Six Israelis* (pp. 113–131). Jerusalem: Van Leer Jerusalem Institute. (Hebrew)

Schwartz, E. (1995). Crossing Borders/Shifting Paradigms: Multiculturalism and Children's Literature. *Harvard Education Review* 65(4): 634–650.

Sleeter, C.E. (1996). *Multicultural Education as Social Activism.* Albany: State University of New York Press.

Stahl, A. (1979). Adapting the Curriculum to the Needs of a Multiethnic Society: The Case of Israel. *Curriculum Inquiry* 9: 361–371.

Statistical Abstract of Israel. (2000). No. 51. Jerusalem: Central Bureau of Statistics.

Weinberg, S., and Porath, D. (1999). Students Out of Controversy. *Haaretz,* December 19. (Hebrew)

Wieviorka, M. (1998). Is Multiculturalism the Solution? *Ethnic and Racial Studies* 21(5): 881–910.

Yiftachel, O. (1999). Between Nation and State: "Fractured" Regionalism among Palestinian Arabs in Israel. *Political Geography* 18: 285–307.

CHAPTER 13

Is Silencing Conflicts a Peace Education Strategy? The Case of the "Jewish State" Topic in Israeli Civics Textbooks

HILLEL WAHRMAN

THE CHOICE OF PEACE EDUCATION STRATEGIES

Mature citizenship has many attributes, among them both (1) the ability to participate in the public sphere, defending private interests and conceptions of the public good, and (2) the ability to deal peacefully with a reality of conflict, without resorting to violence. It is often declared that public education should advance both traits, energizing democracy with civilly competent and responsible citizens.

But when politics is involved, there is a long tradition of fear of the "public." The republican strain of democratic thought has openly warned against mass political participation, fearing the shortsighted, easily led, and highly flammable mobs. Democracy is understood in its representative form, depending on the few who are chosen and able. The task of educating the general public on civic matters is therefore quite delicate: How do you constrain participation and involvement of the majority through responsible nonviolent behavior? This sensitivity particularly pertains to societies with a turbulent public sphere like Israel, where rigorous public debates on core matters raise high tensions and threaten stability. "Unmanageable conflicts can ultimately destroy a democracy" (Merelman, 1990: 47). In countries like these, effective peace education policies are particularly high in priority.

It is of importance therefore to understand the image of politics that public education in countries like Israel advances among youth. If the educational goal of enhancing civic competence would be considered alone, the curriculum would no doubt contain an in-depth treatment of conflicts and debates currently troubling the polity. Political literacy is understood to aid political involvement and participation. "Politics" would then be grasped, essentially, as an arena of conflict and debate. This image may be problematic since exposure to the full extent of conflict in society can encourage future patterns of controversy, perpetuating the conflicts and facilitating future friction. To address this danger, an educational strategy can be devised to minimize the internalization of society's divisions and fractions. This logic promotes a curriculum that downplays controversies and highlights agreed-upon policies (such as formal democratic practices) and shared values (such as being a democracy). It promotes a policy of tension avoidance, in the hope of cultivating a peaceful future generation.

Silencing conflict is at the heart of this possible peace education strategy. Those who know not of a debate cannot participate in it, they will not take sides, and they will not attempt to use force upon each other. The political disenfranchisement of the youth is balanced by the learning of the theory of government and the working of the system. If in need, the young citizen will turn to the formal existing system—for example, the courts—to settle his case. "Politics" would then be grasped as the arena of agreed-upon formal procedural mechanisms.

It can be argued that ignorance of counterpositions may facilitate their delegitimization and raise tensions instead of eliminating them. If so, peace education should not avoid conflicts but seek to expose a balanced view, encouraging deliberative attitudes. This is extremely difficult. How is a "balanced" sketch of politics achieved? Can teachers be trusted to do this? Are all opinions to be presented in this "balanced" overview of politics? Perhaps it is safer to ignore in schools the more bitter political conflicts, avoiding the strong emotions that may be difficult to treat in the classroom.

There are, therefore, two opposing peace education strategies. The first stresses consensual procedural mechanisms; the second emphasizes a balanced view of debates. The first seems safer for constraining the "masses," while the second is empowering. The scope of the first is limited and technical in nature but is a matter of consensus. The second demands a larger knowledge base and more refined teaching skills. Which of the two prevails in Israel's public education?

FOCUSING ON THE "JEWISH-DEMOCRATIC DEBATE" IN ISRAELI CIVICS TEXTBOOKS

One prominent controversy in Israel can be generalized as "the Jewish-democratic debate." This debate centers on the "Jewish state" concept, which conflicts to a certain degree with the sanctity of the individual in liberal democracy. Jews who envision "a state for the Jews," which posits a political entity that frees individual Jews of anti-Semitism, oppose others who strive for "a Jewish state," which promotes a Jewish collective culture. Secular Jews and various Jewish religious sects disagree on the nature of this "public Jewish culture." Arab residents and citizens protest, as well, not only against Jewish national symbols like the flag and anthem but also against the allocation of funds and land, city planning, lack of planning for Israeli-Arab population growth, and political power. It is therefore clear that the "Jewish state" idea is central to an understanding of daily confrontations in Israel. Often, heated public debates are reduced to a comparison of definitions of "democratic" and "Jewish." It is the treatment of this debate that has been chosen for an analysis of the image of politics and of peace education strategy.

Civics is the subject in the official Israeli curriculum that deals explicitly with the relationship of student to state. It is an obligatory course in all nonvocational high schools whose students take matriculation exams. As such, the civics curriculum is studied by a significant number of Israeli students. This chapter's purpose is to determine the choice of political education strategy in Israeli civics textbooks. What image of politics do the civics textbooks introduce when addressing the Jewish-democratic debate?

The formal Israeli civics guidelines seem to lead to a conflicting image of politics. They declare that "equal weight is given to the subjects of Israel as a democratic state and Israel as a Jewish state . . . and a thorough examination should be undertaken regarding the Jewish and democratic values on which the state of Israel and its regime are based" (Ministry of Education, 1994: 5–6). Although the end goal is to reach a position that bridges the two terms, it seems to promote a policy of exposing students to a spectrum of definitions and interpretations of both "Jewish" and "democratic." The declared position of the Israeli Education Ministry seems to exclude only "extreme" views that promulgate the idea of only a Jewish state. Extrapolating from these guidelines, we would expect the Israeli civics textbooks to contain complex and multivision content regarding the Jewish-democratic debate.

This expectation, however, does not coincide with the actual content of civics textbooks in other Western democracies, as has been widely documented. Researchers worldwide point out that social science and civics textbooks tend to ignore severe societal conflicts. Bridges (1986), in articulating the particular sensitivities of civics curricula, notes that although most topics taught in school contain controversies, those in civics can influence the power structure and are therefore carefully censored. Kozol (1984) questions the ability of teachers and educators to portray a balanced perspective of competing political agendas. Parents and other interested parties exert pressure to silence ideologies they oppose. Ornstein (1992) shows how the economic motivation to reach larger audiences brings civics textbook publishers to censor themselves, omitting controversial content. Kane (1984) claims that American interest groups are actively engaged in censoring civics textbooks. Carroll (1987) shows how the tendency to avoid conflicts causes civics textbooks to be dry, "lifeless" descriptions of government. Extrapolation from these trends to the Israeli context would encourage us to expect Israeli textbooks to ignore "conflict politics" and address only shared visions of democracy and procedures.

This discrepancy between the formal guidelines ("discuss the debate") and the literature ("don't discuss the debate") raises the question as to what strategy will we find implemented in Israeli civics textbooks. Israeli civics textbooks are probably constrained as in other countries—leading them to omit controversies. But can they ignore the official guidelines? It is this chapter's hypothesis that Israeli civics textbooks follow the guidelines, but on a superficial level, avoiding an in-depth exploration of controversial concepts.

METHODOLOGY

Four independent categories are suggested as an analytical framework for expressing the presentation choices of the Jewish state concept in civics textbooks:

1. *Centrality*. The level of attention the "Jewish state" topic receives.
2. *Meaning*. The degree of effort exerted to define and clarify the term.
3. *Relevancy*. The degree to which the textbooks portray the topic as necessary for complete understanding of regime and democracy in Israel.
4. *Value judgment*. The degree to which the texts encourage students' personal involvement with the concept, so that they wish to formulate a personal opinion.

Quantitative and qualitative methods were used in the process of content analysis, in order to establish the choices made in Israeli civics textbooks regarding these four categories. Quantitative methods deal with data that can be counted, such as the frequency of appearances of a word or the number of pages that contain specific content. This "hard" evidence is supplemented by "softer" qualitative methods, such as:

• *Reconceptualism*. Examines the ways the text repeats and portrays predefined ideologies and theories that exist in society (Apple, 1979). Here we shall search the text's portrayal of ideologies regarding the character of the state, the essence of democracy and the value of education.

- *Sociolinguistic analysis.* Examines the specific usage of words as clues to the speakers' social status, cultural tendencies, and ideological inclinations (Pattee, 1998). Here we shall focus on the choice of words describing Israel as Jewish.

- *Discourse analysis.* Examines the larger text context (blocks, paragraphs, chapters, whole book) for extra meanings to specific words or sentences. Here we shall evaluate the centrality of the term "Jewish state" in the text as a whole.

- *Null curriculum.* Examines the absence of information or analysis, which are considered to be part of the theoretical knowledge field. Here, missing definitions for the "Jewish state" concept will be explored.

These methods will be applied to establish a profile of all four categories in the civics textbooks chosen for content analysis. Textbook research in Israel tends to base its corpus on the list of authorized textbooks published yearly by the Ministry of Education. Thus, textbooks that pass official inspection tend to be researched most. But noninspected books are increasingly finding their way into the Israeli education system, and some—particularly at the high school level—achieve quite a high exposure. Taking this into consideration, this research based its corpus on books with a high degree of student exposure. During the chosen school year of 1998–1999, three Israeli civics textbooks were found to be circulated the most in Israeli schools:

1. David Shachar—*Israel's State Regime* (Mishtar medinat yisrael), 1993
2. Rachel Groman—*Israeli Democracy* (Democratia yisraelit), 1997
3. Yoram Peri—*The Democracy in Israel* (Hademocratia beyisrael), 1996

These civics textbooks will be addressed in the following discussion as *Shachar, Groman,* and *Peri.* Circulation level was determined by a survey of the public nonvocational high schools and confirmed by interviews with educational civics inspectors. None of these books has received formal authorization from the Education Ministry. They were written and published in the private sector and marketed to student and teacher clientele. Only later, in the 2000–2001 school year, did the Education Ministry issue its own textbook, which is not included in this study.

This inquiry is then limited to civics textbooks mentioned as circulated in the school year 1998–1999 and to the "Jewish-democratic state" debate. It is intended to expose a peace education strategy choice prevalent in Israel's textbooks during most of the 1990s, influencing a generation of students. Options for further research may include other educational agents, other textbooks from other years (such as the new civics textbook issued in 2001 by the Ministry of Education), and other debate topics.

THE TREATMENT OF THE CONCEPT "JEWISH STATE" IN ISRAELI CIVIC TEXTBOOKS

Centrality

This category indicates the level of attention the "Jewish state" topic receives in the texts. This may indicate higher educational aims; those who wish to integrate the young into the existing system will stress the system's particularities, explaining and familiarizing them to the students. Bahmueller (1992) asserts that in America "[c]ivic education should consist of the intensive study and understanding of the nation's system of self government, its values, commitments, and assumptions, and its relevant history; in short . . . democratic society as it developed in America."

Following this view, Israel's civics education should then consist of "an intensive study" of *its* system of government, values, and assumptions. If the textbooks were to implement this policy, much attention would focus on the "Jewish state" topic.

On the other side, those who wish to promote social change in Israel might prefer to attend less to the current "Jewish state" features. Instead, they would focus on abstract universal concepts, such as rights or checks and balances, which are the foundation of any democracy and can support transcending the current Jewish political reality in Israel. Patrick's (1995) notion of civic education expresses a similar view:

Regardless of their difference in history, culture and resources, all people interested in teaching constitutional democracy authentically and effectively must address general educational elements pertaining to civic knowledge, civic skills, and civic virtues. These general and basic categories of civic education may be treated variously by educators of different countries. But there are certain themes within each generic category that are international and trans-cultural.

This strain of civic education is critical to the particular manifestations of the existing state and might wish to downsize the "Jewish state" discussion. To determine the degree of the topic's centrality, five measures are suggested.

Content of Headings, Titles, and Summaries

The title of a book, as well as its abstract or back-cover summary, is meant to highlight the text's essence. It organizes the structure and determines what is central, serving as a map that aids the reader. The titles and summaries of the civics textbooks examined contain many references to democracy and democratic values and practices but no reference to the term *Jewish state*. It is absent in all three books. By this measure, the texts don't consider the concept "Jewish state" even as a minor topic worth mentioning.

Existence of a Chapter Dedicated to the Topic

While *Shachar* mentions the term *Jewish state* in internal subtitles, the two other textbooks contain a chapter titled "Israel as a Jewish State." Titleship and a dedicated chapter can indicate a topic's centrality. But when examined, it is apparent that only *Groman* focused a chapter on the concept. *Peri* sidetracks his chapter in various directions, opening discussion threads on topics such as the Oslo Accords, the Palestinian Authority, and the autonomy plan. The connection to the title "Jewish State" remains unclear. The reader may sense that the term *Jewish state* is rhetorical and quite peripheral.

Frequency of Concept Appearances

When counting the pages that include at least one direct reference to the concept "Jewish state," only 8 percent (*Groman*), 13 percent (*Peri*), and 15 percent (*Shachar*) of the pages are found to contain such a reference. When considering the official policy that "equal weight is given to the subjects of Israel as a democratic state and Israel as a Jewish state," then this quantity factor indicates the topic's marginalization.

Sources in the Presentation of Topics

The civics textbooks contain the *official narrative*, understood to be the "book's truth." They also offer *external sources* that expose the reader to extra opinions and examples, for enrichment, drills, and homework. The narrative is the bulk of most chapters, while external sources are scarce, highlighted in colored boxes, quoting various authors, newspapers, books, or articles. It is well understood that external sources do not necessarily portray the ideas of the civics books themselves. Preparing for an exam will naturally be based on the book's narrative, considered to be the official version of the knowledge field.

Two of the analyzed textbooks, *Groman* and *Peri*, separate the external sources from the main text and locate them in the appendixes. *Shachar*, however, inserts them in the narrative. Interestingly, while discussing ideas and concepts in the realm of democracy, *Shachar* seasons the narrative with external sources, always summing them up with his own conclusion, producing the textbook's official statement. When the topic is the Jewish state, the text includes "only" external sources, giving the impression that while many positions exist, none of them is central enough to deserve an official narrative. There is almost no narrative text in *Shachar* that deals conclusively with the Jewish state concept.

Historical Background

One measure of a topic's centrality is the presentation of the span of time it was dealt with during human history. When discussing the origins of Israel's democracy, both *Shachar* and *Groman* go back to the sixth century B.C.E. (classical Greece), describing the development of statehood and democratic practices over the centuries, by countries and cultures. So central is democracy to those textbooks that it is described as the main theme of human thought and progress.

The origins of Israel as a Jewish state, however, are shown to have a short history, beginning in 1948, with a mere handful of references to the Zionist movement at the end of the nineteenth century. None of the three textbooks stretches the historical timetable relevant to the construction of a Jewish state to include the development of ethnic nation–states or the history of the Jewish people and their various regimes and social orders. Jewish fate with or without a state, Jewish traditions and experiences in terms of the public sphere, diaspora versus a political Jewish center, and other political aspects of Jewish existence throughout history are not part of the picture. The prolonged processes that eventually led to today's Jewish state remain enveloped in shadow.

It seems all five measures expose a peripheral position of the Jewish state concept in Israeli civics textbooks. It is not mentioned in the textbook titles, summaries, and back-cover abstracts. The chapters addressing the topic are, for the most part, not dedicated to it and remain unclear. Only 15 percent of the books (by page count) refer to the concept. Looking back, it might seem that the state emerged out of thin air, with no ancient historical roots. In at least one of the books (*Shachar*), external sources seem to dominate the concept descriptions, without a textual narrative. The texts do not indicate that the Jewish state is a central topic, and it receives little attention.

Meaning

De Tocqueville mourned the lost of precision of language in his classic *Democracy in America* ([1835] 1953). In his eyes, instead of searching ancient languages for words, or creating new ones to express subtleties, it is characteristic of a democratic culture to use terms in a flexible way. A word, particularly if frequently used and widely dispersed, acquires many meanings for different users, and communication can become vague. Such is the fate of many central terms in Israel, such as *democracy*, *Judaism*, or Zionism. When these words are used, a clarification is needed to the particular meaning intended.

Such is also the case with the vague term *Jewish state*, which can suggest various meanings:

1. *The positive ethnic meaning.* This is a state that is meant to preserve a unique Jewish way of life. This state is dedicated to the language, heritage, culture, and destiny of anything Jewish. The state will aim to create a Jewish public system and a Jewish public calendar, enforce Jewish law, and offer Jewish education and Jewish cultural institutes (Liebman and Don-Yehiya, 1983).

2. *The negative ethnic meaning.* External pressures, mainly anti-Semitism, define the Jews as a group that needs a refuge state. If there were no external pressures, there would not be any need for this state. The Law of Return, by which any Jew may find a home in this political refuge, and a Jewish majority are the Jewish features of this state.

3. *Imagined community.* Anderson (1991) coined this term, which has since been used to signify that a "Jewish state" is an oxymoron. A state can only consider its residents (citizens) and cannot encompass an ethnic group dispersed all over the world. The latter can only imagine themselves as a community. Therefore, the term *Jewish state* is a political fiction used to empower sectors of the population in local political struggles. One should refer to an Israeli nation instead and an Israeli state (Evron, 1995).

What meanings of the term *Jewish state* are presented in Israeli civics textbooks? If all of the meanings above are explained, one can assume the books intend to expose the students to the heart of the controversy. If, however, one meaning is preferred, which would it be and what ideological sector in Israel would benefit from it? It is important not only to list meanings that exist in the text but also to establish an order among them and identify those that are absent.

Prominent Meanings

Three definitions of "Jewish state" are clearly visible to the average reader of the three texts: (1) a state that facilitates and encourages *aliya* (i.e., immigration of Jews); (2) a state with a Jewish majority; (3) a state that implements Jewish religious law.

The first—encouraging Jewish immigration—is included in all books but is central in *Groman*'s and *Peri*'s. *Groman* writes: "Israel was instituted . . . as a homeland to all Jewish people of the Diaspora" (12) and "one of the main goals of the new state of Israel is to bring together Jews from all over the world" (15). "The state aims to secure the possibility for any Jew who so wishes to live in an independent state that has a Jewish majority, and build a safe shelter for all Diaspora Jews" (19). *Shachar* proclaims that "the goal of Zionism was, and should remain, building a state that would shelter Jews" (359). "The Law of Return represents one of Israel's most venerable aims, the ingathering of the Diaspora. This law expresses the belief that the state of Israel is one with the Jewish people, and with any Jew wherever he is located" (125).

The second definition—Jewish majority—is mentioned in all the text-books examined but is central in *Shachar* and *Peri*. *Shachar* quotes E. Schweid, a prominent Israeli scholar: "For me a Jewish state is a state in the Zionist sense, that is—a state that has—first of all—a Jewish majority and Jewish sovereignty" (ch. 3). *Groman* asks, "Is Israel a state of the Jews, in other words, does it have a Jewish majority?" (15) and says, "To ensure that every Jew who so wishes can live in a state that has a Jewish majority" (19). *Peri* places "Jewish majority" at the head of his short definition list of the term *Jewish state*.

The third definition describes a Jewish state as implementing Jewish religious values. It is mentioned in all three books, but *Shachar* and *Groman* portray it as central. Most sources cited in *Shachar* relate (pro and con) to the religious features of a Jewish state (ch. 3). The first source is A. Shaki, who is quoted as saying: "The state of Israel has both national and religious foundations that cannot be separated." The second and third sources cited (Supreme Court Judge Berenson and I. Leibowitz, respectively) claim that Israel is not and should not be a religious state, thus highlighting this definition as central to discussion. *Groman* pro-claims "a state of Halacha" (Jewish religious law) as the sole alternative to technical definitions of a Jewish state. She asks: "Is Israel a state of the Jews, in other words, a state with a Jewish majority but not necessarily a Jewish character, or is the State of Israel a Jewish state whose role is to promote the values of Jewish religion and institute a society of a religious character?" (15). In many other cases the Jewish religion is associated with the essence of being a Jew: "The Jewish religion is of central importance in characterizing the Jewish people. . . . The concept 'Jew' has a double meaning: national and religious. That is why when 'Jewish' is written in the Israeli identity card it means belonging to the Jewish nationality and Jewish religion" (21). This equation between "Jewish" and "religious" intimates that a Jewish state is a religious entity. In *Peri*, the Law of Return is portrayed as a religious law (37).

Hidden Meanings

Other meanings that exist in the texts receive a lower profile in larger contexts and topics. Not only is there no in-depth discussion of these definitions, but it is probable that only active and particularly intelligent readers will encounter them at all. These meanings include Jewish sovereignty, a center to the Jewish world, a Hebrew-speaking state, a state that supports and is supported by Jews anywhere, a state whose laws have a Jewish character, a state that is inspired by Jewish tradition and culture, a state that portends the messianic period of Jewish redemption.

Jewish sovereignty is mentioned once in *Shachar* and once in *Peri*. In both cases the term is not explained. Only *Groman* emphasizes Israel as a center for the Jewish people. She says: "Israel should be a secular state that functions as the center for the Jewish people as a whole. The state should encourage connections with Diaspora Jews, fight anti-Semitism" (16). "The state of Israel has an active role in helping Jews in need. Israel heads the struggle to realize Jews' fundamental rights, and Israel conceives itself as the representative of any Jew in need" (19). "The effort to aid Israel is central to Jewish life in the Diaspora" (20). These statements place Jews in Israel not as any other Jewish community but as a center. The other civics textbooks do not discuss this function of a Jewish state.

Only *Groman* provides a short description of the Jewish rationale behind some of Israel's laws. She describes the Jewish agenda in the State Education Law, Israel Lands Law, the Status Law of the Jewish Agency, the law establishing the origins of Israel's judicial system, the Law of Return, law of the flag and the national anthem, the law of national broadcasting, and more. Only *Groman*'s readers will be able to provide examples of the legal implications of a Jewish state.

Most hidden are the meanings that touch directly on secular Jewish culture, such as developing a Hebrew-speaking Israeli-Jewish culture (one note in *Peri*) and "Judaism as a culture" (implied in *Shachar* and *Peri*). Israel as a sign of the messianic period is mentioned briefly in *Shachar* as an opinion expressed in some religious circles but is not expanded on.

Absent Meanings

As shown, civics textbooks supply a theoretical basis meant to enhance readers' ability to understand the connotations of the term *Jewish state*. The average student will probably internalize the emphasized meanings. Sophisticated students might examine peripheral meanings as well or "read between the lines" to expose what is implied. But even observant readers cannot relate to nonexistent meanings such as the following:

"Jewish state" as a case of "nation–state." None of the textbooks devotes any analysis to the concept of a "nation–state," although they expand on other major political concepts. *Shachar* discusses the differences between a "state" and "voluntary organizations" (8), "liberal," "totalitarian," "welfare" and "monarchic" states (10), and "republic" and "democracy" (10). *Groman* defines "state" and distinguishes between "unitary" and "federative" states, "liberal" and "totalitarian" states, "liberal" and "welfare" states, a "one man regime" versus a "group regime," and more (ch. 1). This apparent effort to enhance students' comprehension of political order does not include a theoretical analysis of the nation–state concept.

No comparison, then, can exist between ideas such as "state of all its citizens" or "political nation–states" (United States or Australia); an "ethnic nation–state" (Iceland, Germany, Japan, Israel); states devoted to two or more ethnic groups (Belgium, Switzerland); cases of ethnic groups with no state (Kurds, Armenians). This theoretical flaw impairs an understanding of discussions that appear later in the textbooks. *Shachar*'s textbook notes that it is typical for a state to have "a double base of power and values that justify obedience to the rulers" (8), that "every political regime cannot rely on force alone and wishes to strengthen its positive image in the eyes of the people, basing itself morally and striving to convince the population . . . that its demands and actions should be implemented justly, not out of fear alone" (9). Since there is no theoretical concept of a nation–state, a student would not be able to distinguish between value systems used to justify various states, particularly ethnic states.

In another case, *Shachar* poses the following question: Since every state has its citizens' happiness as the main goal, "how can we distinguish between states?" (10). *Shachar* explains that the difference lies in the "means taken to achieve this goal" (10). Since there is no theoretical analysis of the nation–state, the students cannot deal with cases such as the Vatican or Israel, whose constituency is much greater than the citizens registered within its boundaries.

Groman explains that "any democratic regime legitimizes differences and deliberation, but only within the 'the rules of the game,' and based on loyalty to common core values, of which the most important is democracy" (56). The absence of the nation–state analysis hinders examination of other alternative core values in existing societies. In another place, she says: "In the 20th century, basic human and citizens' rights became the leading principle of democracy, by which a democratic regime stands or falls" (62). The absence of a theoretical analysis of nation–states impedes discussion on democratic rights of *groups* such as ethnic or ideological groups.

In chapter 18, *Groman* maps Israeli political parties, and in a blunt misconception she writes: "The parties on the left support state intervention in social and economic affairs, loosening religious ties and opposing any kind of nationalism. Socialist and communist parties are on the left. In Israel 'Hadash,' 'Mapam' and the 'Labor' party are left-wing parties." In reality, these parties can be considered in Israel to support (to a certain extent) state intervention in social and economic affairs and loosening of religious ties. But not all are against nationalism. Since there is no theoretical concept of nation–state, the possibility that students will be able to comprehend the complex reality of Zionist left-wing parties— such as the Israeli Labor Party—is precluded.

Although Israel is a nation–state, the abstract concept is never dealt with, creating a theoretical void that affects political understanding. The textbooks seem to circumvent the need for an abstract understanding of the concept and skip to the more particular notion of "a Jewish nation–state." Israel is therefore not understood as a particular case of a general nation–state phenomenon.

Comparing alternatives. A concept can be clarified by comparing it to similar or opposite ones. For Israelis who have never experienced a reality other than a Jewish state, it can be useful to consider alternatives. But such a strategy is not employed in the textbooks. The texts do not discuss alternative options to the nonexistence of a Jewish state. There is no reference to the possibility of reducing Jewish nationalism to small-scale Jewish community life. No reference is made to the probability of Jews as a minority in the land of Israel. A vision of an eclectic society of individuals that replaces set communities is also not mentioned.

The idea that the "nation creates a state" supposition can be questioned by the theory that a state creates the nation is also absent from the texts. The first position wishes to see Israel as a state that reflects the Jewish people. The second position wishes to turn Israel into a state that is creating a new society (see Evron, 1995).

Jewish state as a continuation of Jewish political history. Jewish historians such as Graetz (1891–1898) and Dubnow (1914–1916) retold the story of the evolution of Jewish spirituality over the ages, neglecting political aspects. A civics textbook dealing with the notion of a Jewish state might be expected to portray it as part of a long political thread in Jewish history. None of the books portrays Israel as a continuation of Jewish political forms of sovereignty that existed in the Jewish past.

It was Israel's first prime minister—David Ben-Gurion (1976: 24-25)—who said, "After our long journey of four thousand years upon the stage of the world and across countries of the world, we returned to our place of origin to found the third Kingdom of Israel. . . . This is not the first time the Jews are returning to their land and renewing Jewish nationality." This view perceives Israel as a continuation of other Jewish political orders in the past: anarchy (described in the Book of Judges), a royal kingdom overseen and described by the prophets (Books of Samuel or Book of Kings), autonomy (Books of Ezra and Nechemia), a Hasmonite Jewish state and then kingdom (Book of Maccabim), and later on Jewish communities in the Diaspora with internal legislative powers.

Meanings Implied by the Discussion of "Who's a Jew"

All books raise the topic of Israeli citizenship and in that context discuss the question of "Who is a Jew?" The more inquisitive students can draw conclusions from this as to what is meant by the term *Jewish state*. *Shachar* and *Groman* propound a dichotomy for becoming a citizen: (1) blood ties (by being a child of a citizen) and (2) country of birth. The question is then asked: "Which of the two is used in Israel? (*Shachar*, 131), and the answer is: "In Israel it is the blood ties that are preferred" (*Groman*, 28). This dichotomy ignores the complexity of Jewish identity; being a Jew is reduced to blood relation alone and leaves out its philosophical and cultural aspects. This technical definition of who is a Jew implies that a Jewish state also has a technical meaning and is not understood as pertaining to any specific culture or way of life.

The texts do not exhibit much effort in defining the Jewish state concept. The average reader can comprehend mostly technical definitions that deal with the identity of the population (Jewish majority and Jewish *aliya*—immigration). Other more essential definitions that deal with the state's culture and way of life either are religious or are accessible to particularly inquisitive students who read between the lines—or are absent altogether from the texts. The term *Jewish state* therefore remains a "thin" concept with little complexity and diversity.

Relevancy

This category indicates the degree to which the "Jewish state" concept is presented as necessary to the logic of the book as a whole. This is independent of the level of attention the concept receives or the particular meanings that are attributed to it. Civics textbooks are meant to deal with issues of regime, government, and democracy. Intuitively, we know that the texts should deal with democratic procedures and clarify democratic values. What is not necessarily intuitive is the relevancy of the Jewish state topic. For some, this can be an artificially inserted topic, lacking in continuity with the text as a whole. Is the Jewish state topic presented as relevant to the discussion on Israel's democratic regime, or is it portrayed as a misplaced topic, a topic that if ignored does not impair the books' logic or wholeness?

The degree of relevancy presented for the Jewish state concept in the context of discussing Israeli democracy and regime may be influenced by the prevalent opinion on the essence of "democracy." For many, this term connotes protection of basic individual rights such as life, dignity, and freedom. It is also believed that groups have the right to construct their particular way of living in their own public spheres. These two aspects of democracy—individual rights and group rights—often clash. When they do, does "democracy" protect the individual or the wishes of the majority?

Those who understand democracy as a system that honors group rights and majority decisions will most likely feel comfortable with the Jewish state idea or, for that matter, any state that is dedicated to a particular culture. As long as the entity is supported by a clear majority, and is in itself democratic, it will be conceived as a democratic right of the Jews. Others, who feel that in a democracy individual rights should come first, might consider the Jewish state topic as nonrelevant while discussing democracy. Even if the concept is important, it will be considered misplaced. Patrick (1996) argues that the inquiry into the tension between these two aspects of democracy, individuality and community, is central to civics education:

The interactions of individuality and community in a democratic republic have remained the great object of civic inquiries, the perplexing civic problem throughout the more than 200 years of U.S constitutional history. This paper argues that this inquiry should be at the center of civic education today.

In the Israeli context, this seems to mean a strong case for discussing the majority's "Jewish state" idea side by side with the protection of basic individual rights. Six measurements for presenting the relevancy of the Jewish state concept in Israeli civics textbooks are suggested:

Attitude of Groups with a Jewish Agenda to Democracy

The attitude toward democracy of those who hold the "Jewish state" as an item on the political agenda can be a statement about the ability of these two value systems—democracy and Jewish nationalism—to overlap. If those who believe in a Jewish state have strong democratic convictions, then it is relevant to analyze the connection between the two. If, however, they are neutral or opposed to democratic values and procedures, it may signify a dissonance between the two value systems. The civics textbooks tend to identify Jewish state agenda groups with the religious political parties, which are portrayed as nondemocratic. Being religious and democratic or ideologically Jewish and democratic are not discussed as options.

Shachar, for instance, talks about "the religious parties" without distinguishing between them, stating that "they" are against a constitution. He quotes a religious political leader as saying:

Can it be that religious schools will study a secular constitution, should it unfortunately be accepted? The conclusion pupils might arrive at is that the *Tora* [the holy scripture] is irrelevant and is nothing but an historical document of no current use. Any objective thinker will realize that a secular constitution should be boycotted in religious schools, and by any Jew who believes in God's Pentateuch. (111)

The text also states that it was the religious who in 1988 and 1989 objected passionately to the acceptance of the basic law on "Human dignity and freedom," but no solid reason is given for this position. But more bluntly, *Shachar* adds:

The religious have clear-cut answers to all the problems that Jewish Israeli individuals or Jewish Israeli society as a whole must struggle with. Jewish holy
law encompasses all of life's arenas. This general coverage gives the believer a
sense of security and certainty, and a cure for another modern "ailment"—deliberation, skepticism, uncertainty and ambiguity in questions of norms, values
and morality. (183)

This undifferentiated description of "the religious" situates all of the
religious outside the realm of democratic values and practices. *Shachar*
clearly states that

religious circles do not know how to treat the state that declares itself to be
secular and modern, since Jewish religious law [the Halacha] cannot come to
terms with the secular point of view that is reflected in the state. In their perception, the laws of the Halacha are absolute values that transcend human val-
idation, and obligate all Jews wherever they may be. (183)

Shachar also presents the extreme right-wing party "Kach," long since
banished from Israeli politics, as having a Jewish agenda. He quotes a
Kach member: "There is an internal contradiction in the law, since the
negation of the democratic character will originate from the wish to constitute the state as a state for the Jewish people" (163). The overall impression is therefore that those who care for the Jewish state agenda are
against virtually all democratic values and practices.

Groman draws a distinction between "the first faction which believes
the state of Israel is the state of the Jewish people, which should guard
the traditional character, cultivate Jewish consciousness, and merge the
ancient Jewish tradition with modern needs" and the "faction that argues
that the [state] should keep its liberal-democratic contents, with no relation to religious tradition, like developed countries in the world" (ch.
3). This dichotomy ranks those who want a Jewish state with those opposed to a democratic state, who thus do not support the model of developed countries.

Only *Peri* implies the possibility that religious parties are actually
working in the framework of democracy. He says that religious laws
expose "the fact that despite the growing dispute between the religious
and the secular on the place of religious laws in Israel, the goal is to find
a way for co-existence, peace and understanding" (37). *Peri's* presentation portrays religious laws in Israel as the result of compromise.

Relationship of "Religion and State" Issues to Democracy

The texts under examination mention the religious characteristics of
certain state laws, characterizing them as religious coercion imposed
nondemocratically by religious parties against the will of a secular ma-

jority. *Shachar* asks bluntly: "To what degree do you agree with those who oppose religious regulation on the assumption that it is a nondemocratic coercive act?" (340). *Groman* explains that a democracy depends on an accepted consensus within the population and that in Israel there is a deep schism on religious and state issues (59). These issues are therefore a threat to the existence of democracy. She adds: "All religions, including Judaism, can act against the rules of the democratic game. This is because religious people owe their immediate allegiance to the word of God" (94). She then presents a long list of cases in which the Israeli Supreme Court overruled decisions on religious issues (such as allowing women on religious councils). *Peri*'s is the only text that does not portray religious-state issues as nondemocratic.

Missing is a context in which religious laws in Israel were accepted, like all other laws, within the democratic framework (for more on this following position, see Katz, 1978). A change in the political constellation, which is dependent on the will of the population, can change laws. If a secular majority was intent on changing these laws, it could easily replace them. The fact that these laws persist is a testimony to the strong bargaining power of the religious parties, who are democratically striving to influence the character of their state, and of the low priority this issue represents in the secular majority's agenda.

Relationship of the "Jewish State" Idea to Democracy

The main criticism voiced today against the idea of a Jewish state derives from the reasoning that it is, in principle, a nondemocratic entity, since it discriminates against non-Jews. Although it is quite probable that students will encounter this criticism out of school, while reading newspapers or listening to news broadcasts, the civics textbooks do not relate to it, remaining silent on the true difficulties that arise with this political concept. Discussion of this criticism is conspicuously absent, especially given the numerous opportunities to raise it, such as when mention is made of political parties that make this claim (*Groman*, 85; *Shachar*, 121, 154).

Relationship of Jewish Thought to Issues of Democratic Politics

The image of Jewish "political and democratic theory" can imply the degree of relevancy of the Jewish state topic in Israeli civics textbooks. If Jewish political and democratic theory is considered original and noteworthy, then it is relevant for Israeli civics textbooks to expand on one of its manifestations, the Jewish state. In this view, discussing the Jewish state illuminates particular and unique Jewish democratic ideas.

When democracy and political thought are discussed, the texts quote many Western thinkers but not the Bible or any Jewish thinkers. Such is the case when, for example, the principle of "rule of law" is discussed. *Shachar* (20), *Groman* (103), and *Peri* (70) all quote the classical platonic passage about Socrates preferring death to disobeying the city's laws. *Shachar* asks: "Why should a citizen obey a law or a judgment that he does not morally agree with?" (20). It seems that a serious discussion on this could have benefited from the absent Jewish political perspective; the Bible mentions many cases of immoral laws that *are* questioned, including those given by God himself (see Hazoni, 1998). This point of view is absent and therefore cannot contribute to the books' analysis of democratic theory.

In fact, Jewish resources are not used at all for political information. We are not informed about the various regimes Jews encountered during centuries of changing fortunes: slavery (in Egypt), anarchy (the period of the Judges), autonomy (during the return from the first exile, from the Persian empire), and statehood (during the Hasmonite period). We are not told what Jewish thought says about the social management, political leadership, or the system of law. The books do not clarify if Jewish tradition has anything of value to contribute to the ruling of today's Israel. All these could have produced a richer analysis of democracy and democratic thought in the Israeli context.

Relationship of Jewish History to the Development of Current Democratic Practices

Another dimension of the relevancy of the Jewish state topic to Israeli civics textbooks lies in its power to explain the current characteristics of Israel's society and the democratic culture it developed. Abstract political thought is not the only factor that shaped the state that Israel has become. Jewish historical circumstances drummed practices of a democratic nature into Jewish society, molding Israel's political traits. Neuberger states:

Judaism has many democratic features. Jews are equal before the religious law. . . . Judaism does not recognize a permanent elite group, and does not put into power a leader that can do no wrong. . . . There are many references to majority influence on policy, and Jews in the Diaspora have a long tradition of self-governance, with some democratic features. The community was voluntary, and was based on popular acceptance. . . . [T]here were elections, majority decisions, and time-limited public positions. . . . Jews did not have one recognized center . . . and had a federative system of community relations. (in Levin, 1992: 38–39)

In a book published in 1928 titled *The Democratic Impulse in Jewish History*, Abba Hillel Silver, rabbi and political leader of American Jewish community, said:

No revolutionary literature of mankind breathes a profounder distrust of royalty and indicts in harsher terms the ways of kings, their despoliation and corruption, than the eighth chapter of the first book of Samuel. . . . The ritual of the synagogue was itself a triumph of democratic thought. It depended upon no priest or rabbi or other indispensable functionary. . . . It is no accident of history that Israel was the first nation of the world to develop a universal system of popular education for both young and old, rich and poor. Among no other people was so much stress laid upon the education of children, of *all* children. (Silver, 1928: 4–16).

The textbooks do not portray the various trends of Jewish political practice during the centuries that could have influenced Israel's current democratic culture. There is no note regarding the Jewish focus on public education, on the culture of legitimate conflict, or on the dispersion of the Jewish people that caused a noncentralist political organization. *Groman* mentions only the fact that Jews lived for so long under oppressive foreign rule that they developed disrespectful attitudes toward laws of states (104). It is also only *Groman* who states that the democratic structure of the Zionist movement in the nineteenth century influenced the development of democracy in the State of Israel.

Relationship of Israel's Political Symbols to Judaism and Jewish Identity

The relevancy of the Jewish state topic is perhaps mostly apparent in the rich Jewish symbolism imbedded in the structure of Israeli politics. The textbooks do not expose the readers to any of this symbolism. Students are not exposed to fundamental information as to why the state is named "Israel"; why the parliament is the "Knesset" (the ancient sovereign Jewish institution during the Temple periods); why the number of Knesset members is 120 (the same as in the historical institution); or that the Knesset's hall is shaped like the Jewish menorah. Its opening date is the Jewish holiday of the fifteenth of Shvat, the Jewish "New Year" of the trees, symbolizing the Zionist implanting of trees in the old-new land of Israel. A large portrait of Herzl, the visionary of the Jewish state and founder of the Zionist congress, hangs on the Knesset wall. Also absent are discussions of Jewish meanings imbedded in the Israeli flag or national emblem (the Star of David or the menorah). Since the symbolism remains untouched, it can't be a factor in presenting the relevancy of the Jewish state in the Israeli civics textbooks.

Regardless of its level of attention and clarity, the Jewish state topic seems somewhat misplaced in civics textbook discussions of Israel's democratic regime. The concept "Jewish state" seems in dissonance to democratic values since those who hold it as a priority to be addressed

are presented as nondemocratic. This relationship is never clearly discussed. The very issue of religion and state is presented as hazardous to
democracy. Jewish political thought is not presented as having contributed to democratic theory, and Jewish historical circumstances are not
considered as having influenced Israel's current political conditions.
Even basic information on Jewish symbolism imbedded in Israel's political system is ignored. The "Jewish state" discussions, as few and unclear
as they are, remain therefore irrelevant and do not seem to be necessary
for a full understanding of the textbooks' knowledge field.

Value Judgment

This category indicates the degree to which the textbooks encourage
readers' personal involvement with the Jewish state concept. More than
explaining or analyzing the concept, the texts can influence readers' judgment and feelings toward it in terms of agreement or disapproval. Fear
of indoctrination in a conflict-laden society can produce considerable
sensitivity to this category.

Three positions can be identified in Israel regarding value education
(Firer, 1980): (1) against value education—schools have no right to influence the young to any particular set of values; (2) for value education—
the essence of education is to advance values; (3) for minimum value
education—only accepted core values should be promoted in public
schools. The textbooks examined seem to prefer the second position
when teaching "democracy" and the first when teaching the "Jewish
state." To support this contention, the following measures are suggested:

Absence of a Clear Statement for or against a "Jewish State"

None of the textbooks comes out with a clear outspoken statement
that evaluates the Jewish state concept. There is no official judgment that
can be quoted.

Absence of Value Discussion on Political Phenomena

A position toward a Jewish state might be influenced by value statements on wider, more diverse political phenomena, but these are absent
as well. Also absent is a *value analysis of political ideologies.* The Israeli
civics textbooks examined do not include any discussion of political ideologies, such as "right" or "left," "conservative," "liberal," or "radical."
The textbooks do not empower the students in any way to evaluate the
ideological differences and similarities among leaders of different countries or among diverse political thinkers.

Also nonexistent is the *value analysis of nation–states.* None of the textbooks deems it necessary to rationalize the existence of nation–states. The books do not discuss how nation–states function for the physical or cultural survival of nations, or the enrichment and diversification of political models of statehood. Criticism of nation–states is absent as well. No mention is made of the fact that while there are approximately 5,000 ethnic groups in the world, there are also only about 200 states, which means that most ethnic groups will not have a state. India alone, for example, has about 400 ethnic groups struggling and competing internally. The readers are not exposed to justifications or oppositions to this entity and lack the opportunity to develop their own opinion toward it.

Ignoring the Morality Debate on the "Jewish State"

Peri is the only one to state a reason why a Jewish state can be important: "a state where the Jewish people can renew their spiritual and cultural life and economic life" (26). He goes on to say that "for long periods of time Zionism fought assimilation of Jews, and saw it as a potential disaster for the Jewish nation" (27). "The land of Israel, Zion, was always and is now a Jewish territory, and the Jewish nation has always aspired to reach the land of Israel" (27). These statements value the Zionist movement and its Jewish state goal. Neither *Shachar* nor *Groman* articulate any justifications or arguments of their own for or against the existence of the Jewish state.

Positive Language in Descriptions of the "Jewish State"

A form of value judgment that does exist in the textbooks is a terminology with positive connotations that is used when the "Jewish state" is mentioned. *Shachar*, for instance, chooses to call the Law of Return "one of Israel's most *honored* goals" (125). *Peri* notes that "it was always the Jewish people's wish to reach the land of Israel, and Zionism made this *honored* goal happen" (27). The texts have many of these positive connotations in relation to the Jewish state concept.

Emphasizing Religious Aspects of the "Jewish State"

The textbooks often stress religious aspects of the term *Jewish state*. For instance: "The Jewish religion is critically important in setting the national character of the Jewish people. . . . This is reflected not only among orthodox Jews or national-religious Jews, but also in rulings of the Israeli Supreme Court, that stated more than once that Jewish nationality should not be separated from religion" (*Groman*, 21). "On the one hand the state aspires to be Jewish, on the other, it knows it cannot realize this aspiration without harming its secular essence" (*Shahar*, 340). For a secular audience, who constitute the majority of students in the public schools, these statements are not comfortably associated with. Secular students may find these aspects of religion disturbing to their own core identity and perceive the term negatively. It is interesting to note that *Groman*'s quote ignores the fact that the Israeli courts usually rule against the religious establishment, While *Shahar*'s statement is not followed by any ideas on how the state can be Jewish and remain secular. It stands to reason that secular readers are missing a possible secular interpretation of the term *Jewish state* that has a better chance of being evaluated positively.

Absence of the Notion of Consensus

Students' value judgments might very well be affected by what they conceive to be the "majority opinion." When it comes to "democracy," students are exposed to a large variety of outstanding figures that express a positive attitude toward the concept, thus implying that those who oppose it are extreme and few. This course of action inspires students to be the same and to support democracy. But when it comes to the "Jewish state," only a few figures are quoted, providing a low profile and nonconsensus image for the concept. It is not shown as an accepted idea, held by many in the Israeli and Jewish world. None of the texts even mentions, let alone explains, Zionist leaders and thinkers such as Hess, Pinsker, Herzl, Zangwill, Borochov, Jabotinsky, Begin, and Ben-Gurion, who were among the many who envisioned a Jewish state. Current-day leaders who support the Jewish state are absent as well, such as Amnon Rubinstein, Uzi Baram, Yithchak Rabin, Yossi Beilin, Yair Zaban, Abraham Burg, and many more who are known in the internal Israeli public sphere. This weakens not only a position supportive of the "Jewish state" agenda but also the understanding that this position received enough serious support to make it worthwhile considering.

Only minimum effort is expended to involve readers personally in the Jewish state concept. Positive language is used in discussing it, but an audience of mainly secular students is exposed to a dominantly religious interpretation of the Jewish state concept, an interpretation they find hard to identify with. No official statement (positive or negative) is issued; arguments for all sides are not portrayed, not even for related issues such as the value of nation–states or political ideologies. The many prominent leading figures involved in the issue are not mentioned. It seems that the texts choose not to encourage students to approach the issues and develop their own stand.

CONCLUSION

The examination of the three most circulated Israeli civics textbooks for the school year 1998–1999 revealed a common pattern of downgrading the "Jewish state" topic: (1) It remains peripheral; (2) the term receives only a minimum defining effort; (3) it is not associated with issues of Israeli democracy and regime; (4) judgments or overviews of judgments of the Jewish state are low profile, with little encouragement for students' personal involvement.

This pattern seems to concur with the initial hypothesis that Israeli civics textbooks, by necessity, reflect the official guidelines requiring discussion of Jewish and democratic characteristics of the state but also reflect the consistent tendency in Western civics textbooks to avoid controversial issues. Thus, the textbooks do mention the heavily debated Jewish state concept but drastically minimize its analysis. The concept is dealt with, but barely enough to give a sufficient overview of positions and opinions.

This is a choice regarding the image of politics. As far as the Jewish state topic is concerned, conflict is omitted from the examined Israeli civics books. The reader receives hardly any clues as to the magnitude and importance of the controversy. What does remain is all that is not controversial; one will read about voting processes, formation of political parties, the idea of "checks and balances," the rule of law, free press, and so on. These are all in the arena of coexistence procedural mechanisms. This approach has its benefits since schools do not appear to have the ability to deal fairly with controversial subjects. It might even be preferable to steer the young away from negative emotions, "taking sides," anger, and perhaps violence that might accompany conflict in the classroom. Peace education may be influencing a generation to care little for divisive "issues."

Five arguments discussing the contrary will conclude this chapter:

First, omitting conflict from civics textbooks may affect the level of political understanding the students achieve. The less the students are able to comprehend the chaos they feel exists in the political world around them, the less they feel in control, and the more frustrated they will be. These are not healthy ingredients for a peaceful society. Peaceful attitudes are most easily cultivated in those who feel control over their destiny.

Second, ignorance of visions and ideologies helps to promote stereotypes, misunderstandings, and eventually, delegitimatization of others' ideas or vision. Exposing the young to a balanced overview may enhance their comprehension of opposing logics.

Third, if conflict is learned outside the school system, one is likely to be most influenced by the parties who are louder at voicing their opinions. The political arena is presented to the unsophisticated audience as more polarized than it really is. If the education system does not endeavor to expose the young to the full spectrum of opinions and agendas, then this error is not corrected, and it might help spreading simplistic polarized positions among youth.

Fourth, democratic procedures of coexistence remain unconvincing if the reason for their existence—controversy—is excluded from the analysis. Crick (1975) describes such a situation:

Hence the political part of education is primarily, as in any possible moral education, an education of what differing view points are held, who holds them, why, in what context and with what restraints. This may seem platitudinous. But how often is political education, if approached at all explicitly, approached primarily through a study of constitutional rules and institutional forms? The cart is put before the horse. Those rules and institutions, which exist because there are disputes and issues, are thought to be prior to those disputes and issues. The British constitution is only meaningful as a summary of the way we contain pre-existing, actual problems. (12–17)

Fifth, omitting conflict can, at the most, develop tolerance in the weak sense. Crick (1978) describes the conditions for a preferable, strong sense of tolerance:

The most important attitude is probably tolerance, not in the weak sense of indifference which can be developed in schools, or permissiveness, but in the more traditional strong sense of having a definite point of view, indeed a definite and expressed disapproval of other points of view, but limiting one's disapproval—limiting it, for instance, to argument, rather than blows, reasoning rather than abuse, ballots rather than bullets. To be able to be tolerant amid a strong clash of opinions, demands, one needs psychologically, considerable empathy, and cognitively, considerable knowledge of the other people's viewpoints. So here tolerance and empathy link directly with knowledge, and with a specific kind of knowledge: the knowledge of the main political viewpoints. (32)

For these reasons, it is argued that the choice of strategy for peace education in the examined Israeli civics textbooks is questionable. The wish to generate peace education through consensus and a focus on procedures can very well backfire and encourage stereotypes, delegitimization, and intolerance. It would be beneficial to invest more effort and resources in promoting an in-depth balanced overview of Israeli public debate in the education system. This is not only an agenda for encouraging political involvement; it is also the agenda of encouraging responsibility and peacekeeping. Although it is risky to leave sensitive and conflict-laden issues to the power of the public education system, the alternative is shown here to be worse.

REFERENCES

Anderson, B. (1991). *Imagined Communities: Reflections on the Origin and Spread of Nationalism*. London: Verso.

Apple, M. (1979). *Ideology and Curriculum*. London: Routledge and Kegan Paul.

Bahmueller, C. (1992). The Core Ideas of CIVITAS: A Framework for Civic Education. *Eric Digest, ED 346016*. Available online at http://www.ed.gov/databases/Eric_digests/ed346016.html.

Ben-Gurion, D. (1976). *Bible Studies* (Iyonim batanach) (pp. 7–40). Tel Aviv: Am-Oved.

Bridges, D. (1986). *Controversial Issues in the Curriculum*. Oxford: Blackwell.

Carroll, J.D. (1987). *We the People: A Review of U.S. Government and Civics Textbooks*. Available online at http://ericir.syr.edu/Eric/adv_search.shtmlED288761.

Crick, B. (1975). Political Education Today. *Trends in Education* 1: 12–17.

Crick, B. (1978). *Political Education and Political Literacy*. London: Longman.

De Tocqueville, A. ([1835] 1953). *Democracy in America*. Reprint. Oxford: Oxford University Press.

Dubnow, S.M. (1914–1916). *History of the Jews in Poland and Russia*. 3 vols. Philadelphia: Jewish Publication Society of America.

Evron, B. (1995). *Jewish State or Israeli Nation?* Bloomington: Indiana University Press.

Firer, R. (1980). *Between Conciseness and Knowing* (Bein todaa leyedia). Ph.D. dissertation, Hebrew University, Jerusalem.

Graetz, H. (1891–1898). *History of the Jews*. 6 vols. Philadelphia: Jewish Publication Society of America.

Groman, R. (1997). *Israeli Democracy* (Democratia yisraelit). Jerusalem: Carmel.

Hazoni, Y. (1998). The Jewish Origins of the Western Disobedience Tradition. *Azure* 4: 17–74.

Kane, F. (1984). The Controversy over Civics Education. *Social Studies Review* 22 (3): 4–8.

Katz, Y. (1978). The Religious Character of Israel's Society (Ofya hayehudi shel hachevra haysraelit). Jerusalem: Hebrew University.

Kozol, J. (1984). *The Night Is Dark and I Am Far From Home*. Boston: Houghton Mifflin.

Levin, S. (1992). *Political Education in Schools* (Hinuch politi bebeit-hasefer). Tel Aviv: Israeli Teachers Union.

Liebman, C., and Don-Yehiya, E. (1983). *Civil Religion in Israel*. Berkeley: University of California Press.

Merelman, R.M. (1990). The Role of Conflict in Children's Political Learning. In Orit Ichilov (Ed.), *Political Socialization, Citizenship Education, and Democracy*. New York: Teachers College Press.

Ministry of Education. (1994). *The New Civics Guidelines* (Tochnit halimodim hachadasha). Jerusalem: Ministry of Education.

Ornstein, A. (1992). The Censored Curriculum: The Problem with Textbooks Today. *NAACP Bulletin* 76(547): 1–9.

Patrick, J. (1995). Civic Education for Constitutional Democracy: An International Perspective. *Eric Digest, ED390781*. Available online at http://www.ed.gov/databases/Eric_digests/ed39078/.

Patrick, J. (1996). *Community and Individuality in Civic Education for Democracy*. Paper presented at the International Conference on Individualism and Community in a Democratic Society, Washington, DC, October 6–11. *Eric*

Digest, ED ED403205. Available online at http://www.ed.gov/databases/ Eric_digests/ed403205.

Pattee, C. (1998). *Sociolinguistics.* University of Oregon. Available online at http:// logos.uoregon.edu/explore/socioling/.

Peri, Y. (1996). *The Democracy in Israel* (Hademocratia beyisrael). Petach-Tikva: Lilach.

Shachar, D. (1993). *Israel's State Regime* (Mishtar medinat yisrael). Tel Aviv: Yesod.

Silver, A.H. (1928). *The Democratic Impulse in Jewish History,* New York: Bloch.

CHAPTER 14

Jewish Education Worldwide:
A Minority Educates Itself

WALTER ACKERMAN

A well-known Midrash[1] teaches that the Israelites merited deliverance from the bondage of Egypt primarily because they did not "change their names, their language or their clothes." (There are various versions, but all express the same idea. See Midrash Rabbah Exodus, 1; Midrash Rabbah, Numbers, 13; Midrash Rabbah, Song of Songs, 4.) A complementary observation attributes the ability to withstand the considerable attractions of Egyptian culture to the schools that the "sons of Jacob established" all over the Israelite settlement in the land of their people's formative trials. While the rabbinic commentators may not have been acquainted with the idea of identity as it is used today, their exegetical remarks disclose a telling insight into the dynamics of the relationship between minority and majority cultures—and particularly so when one is the oppressor and the other the oppressed—and the visible indices of assimilation.

Because one of the functions of Midrash is to deal with the cultural and religious tensions in Jewish society at the time of its composition, it seems reasonable to argue that the texts cited above are less an explanation of the foundational myth of Jewish peoplehood and more a comment about the behavior of contemporary Jews. Several centuries after the destruction of the Second Temple and the end of an independent Jewish state, rabbinical teachers thought it necessary to remind their people that the abandonment of a distinctive pattern of behavior violated the mandate to live as a "nation of priests and a holy people" (Exodus, 19:6).

The first letter of the Hebrew words for *name*, *language*, and *dress* form an acrostic (*Shaleim*) that may be translated as "true" or "faithful." Indeed, ultra Orthodox Jews of our time and earlier use the Midrash as the justification for their adherence to names, language (Yiddish), and dress that set them apart from the society around them. The mission of guaranteeing the beneficence of the Divine Presence on earth can be fulfilled only by those who choose to live "as a people apart"(Numbers, 23: 9). Like other groups, largely religious, they have chosen segregation and separation as the line of first defense against the encroachments of the majority and the baneful influence of its culture.

There is little that separates between the guiding idea of the Midrash and exhortations of more recent times. Jewish schools in Poland in the years between the two world wars and the catastrophe of the Holocaust called upon Jewish families to enroll their children in Jewish schools—as opposed to government-sponsored public schools—and thus to say "no to assimilation" and "yes to a national life and to national creativity"(Frost, 1998). The more benign climate of a democratic American society elicits similar concerns—"intermarriage is increasing at an alarming rate . . . ever fewer Jewish children receive a Jewish education, affiliation with Jewish religious and communal/philanthropic organizations is dropping and . . . the sense of identification with Jewish history, tradition, religion and community diminishes with each generation" (Report of the Commission on the Jewish Future of Los Angeles, 1992).

Jews have always been a minority, if not numerically then certainly culturally. Even when living in their own country—in the early days of their history as a people and more recently in the newly established state of Israel—their own culture has had to compete with the pervasive influence of lifestyles and worldviews that range, over time, from Hellenism to Americanism. Even in the days of the closed, contractual society of the Middle Ages, Christian influence affected Jewish practice (Karnafogel, 1992; Marcus, 1996). The pointed didacticism of the Torah and the panoply of educational activities of modern times are joined by a common intent of maintaining a distinctive Jewish presence. The idea of "Jewish Continuity," the mantra of communal discourse among Diaspora Jewries in recent years, echoes, even if not intentionally, the biblical injunction "not to copy the practices of the land of Egypt . . . or of the land of Canaan" (Leviticus, 18:3).

It is also important to note that during the long years of exile, before the establishment of the State of Israel, Jews differed from other minority groups. They had no state or land of their own; the uniting force of a common religion was often strained by the centrifugal influences of the different cultures in which they lived their daily lives; they owed formal allegiance to innumerable states, sometimes at war with one another; the languages of the countries in which they lived were at least as influential in molding consciousness as was the common language of their faith, even when it was used for nonreligious purposes.

For many Jews, education was—and remains—a form of religious practice; indeed, study of the canonical texts is an act of worship, and the meeting of student and teacher is a *replication* of the theophany at Sinai. The frameworks of formal schooling, together with familial practice and communal norms, signal the belief that "right knowledge leads to right behavior." The intellectual history of the Jewish people, and in some measure even its social history, cannot be understood apart from the belief that the people privileged to receive the words of God were also enjoined to "teach them diligently to its children" (Deuteronomy, 5: 6–9).

The idea of religion as the sole expression of the experience and aspirations of the Jewish people was irrevocably modified, if not altogether rejected, by the forces of modernism. Jewish education today—the entire process by which Jews attempt to transmit their culture across the generations (Bailyn, 1960: 14)—reflects this almost unparalleled shift in consciousness. Over the last 200 hundred years, Jewish education has taken place in an expanding number of frameworks in every place around the world where there are enough Jews to warrant an educational effort. For some, religion still remains the essence of Judaism; others conceive of it as a cultural or ethnic heritage. And still others find their place between these two poles. All of them, except those who live in Israel, are numerically a minority in the countries of their residence; all of those engaged in Jewish education, no matter its form, are concerned "with creating meaningful encounters for children (and adults as well) with a diverse body of ideas, values and practices. [They] seek at once to transmit an intellectual tradition and a set of attitudes and emotional dispositions" (Holtz, Dorph, and Goldring, 1997: 147–166). Jewish education today, in contrast to the schools of the worker's movement in eastern Europe and even the United States between the two world wars and also the current efforts of other minority groups in many places, is not concerned with issues that seek a redistribution of economic and political resources in ways that reverse institutionalized forms of exclusion.

Schools—still the most widespread agency of education among Jews, the growth and spread of youth organizations, summer camps, trips to Israel, and other informal settings notwithstanding—are generally of two kinds. They differ from one another not only structurally but also in their relationship to the society around them. The day school—in some places *Yeshiva K'tanah*—offers its pupils a curriculum of both general and Jewish studies. These schools are independent institutions—even when they receive government support—and function apart from public schools. Once almost completely identified with the Jewish Orthodox population, day schools have also been established by Jews who understand their Jewishness in other ways. Private initiatives, aided by the Department of Education and Culture of the Jewish Agency and the World Zionist

Organization, led to the establishment of a nonreligious day school in Paris by parents who wanted to provide their children with a nonreligious, Zionist, Hebrew education (Kessary, 1995: 1–15). In the United States and Canada the Jewish Conservative and Reform movements as well as communal agencies of education have come to support day schools because they are considered the most effective educational antidote to intermarriage and assimilation.

In the United States the overwhelming majority of the children in Jewish schools attend "part-time" institutions that meet in the afternoon hours or on Saturdays or Sundays. In other countries schools of this sort function on the day of the week when public schools are not in session. In the United States these schools are largely part of a synagogue; in France they are a major aspect of the activities of the Consistoire (Jewish organized community) and its rabbis. Attendance at a part-time school is an expression of the desire to live in the two worlds of Judaism and the society of the majority.

The distribution of pupils between day schools and part-time settings is an important example of the way in which the educational efforts of a minority are affected by conditions in the larger society and its own sense of self. While not a major factor, the fact that in some countries day schools receive government support must surely influence the decision to open such a school. Studies in the United States, France, and Argentina report that increases in day school enrollment paralleled a perceived deterioration in the quality of public schools. Day schools in Argentina became a favored option when the extension of the school day in the public schools made it impossible to maintain the intensive 10- to 15-hours-per-week part-time school. Jewish day schools in South Africa came into being as a counterpart to the private schools that served the white population and also as a response to the pervasive influence of "Christian national education in government schools" (Steinberg, 1989: 365).

The spread of day schools in many countries is also, without question, a reflection of the degree to which Jews have come to feel "safe" and at home. The United States is a case in point. The builders of Jewish education in that country in the early decades of the twentieth century rejected the separatist model of the Catholic parochial school. Neither the genteel Protestantism of the public schools nor the sometimes crude and vulgar programs of Americanization that were calculated to make immigrants "realize that in forsaking the land of their birth they were also forsaking the customs and traditions of that land; and they must be made to realize an obligation, in adopting a new country and to adopt the language and customs of that country" (Richman, as quoted in Ackerman, 1989: 74) were sufficient to uproot the deep-seated belief of the Jews that the public school was the avenue to success and status. That intuitive folk feeling received philosophical backing in the view that stated that the parochial school because "it segregated children along lines of creed was a contradiction of the dictates of democracy which require that . . . during the formative years of childhood" children should "associate with their neighbors with whom they are destined to live together as American citizens" (74). Few Jews of that time argued with the idea that Jewish schools should not interfere "with America's cherished plan of a system of common schools for all the children of all the people" (74).

Moreover, in contrast to other religions and ethnic minority groups in the United States, Jews have never looked to the public school for the transmission of their culture. There is no parallel, for instance, in the history of American Jewry to the demand of German immigrants who, in their desire to maintain the traditions and customs of their homeland, insisted that German be the language of instruction in the public schools their children attended. Neither the introduction of Hebrew language instruction in secondary schools, "released time" instruction permitted by law, nor the more recent inclusion of the study of the Holocaust all over the country challenge the deeply held conviction of most Jews that instruction in Judaism is the concern of the Jewish community and that the interests of Jews and all other Americans are best served by holding fast to the line that separates church and state.

World War II, the Holocaust, which, among other things, left American Jewry the major repository of resources for the Jewish future, and the unimagined place in American life occupied by Jews led to a reassessment of the wisdom received from an earlier time, namely, that though

the Jewish community is larger, better organized, more influential, actually and potentially than it was fifty years ago . . . [i]n the years ahead it will be increasingly obligatory for Jewish educators to promote the establishment of day schools as the intensive core of the American Jewish school system . . . to include 20% of our children. (Ackerman, 1989: 87)

The curriculum of a school, no matter of what kind, is its identity card. It is a story that the school's sponsors—state, church, ethnic organizations, or private individuals—tell about themselves. It reflects what they think is important and worth knowing. A Mishnah in Avot (The Ethics of the Fathers) provides a paradigmatic curriculum statement: "At five years of age one is ready for the study of Scripture, at ten for the study of Mishnah . . . and at fifteen for Talmud" (Avot, 5:21). Until modern times the ability to "swim in the sea of the Talmud" (the Jewish Oral law) was the necessary, if not always sufficient, condition for admission to the ranks of educated Jews. The meeting with the world inevitably led to modifications and even the abandonment of that core curriculum.

David Friedlander, who at the end of the eighteenth century was a leader in the struggle of German Jews for equal rights and whose views were a harbinger of Reform Judaism, founded the Beit Sefer Hinnuch Ne'arim in Berlin with the avowed intention of providing its pupils with a secular education. In response to an inquiry about his school, so radically different in conception from traditional Jewish schools, Friedlander wrote:

My friend you must choose one of two things: either you must educate your son to take his place among the "chosen"—that is you must educate him to believe that we are a chosen people and that the study of Torah is superior to all the wisdom of the West and that it is forbidden to take a German book in hand, or you will educate him for the world in which we live and leave him without any knowledge of Gemara [an alternative name for the Jewish oral law] . . . this is the spirit of our times; we Jews no longer live in a separate quarter. . . . Our traditional ways are no longer compatible with the world. If, however, you wish to educate him to be a citizen of the world, if you are not afraid of free thought and believe . . . that all that is important is that he may grow to be good and honest, then in the name of God send him to us. (Friedlander, 1792: 266–267)

The curricula of Jewish schools today reflect the range of attachments to Judaism and the Jewish people that can be found in Jewish communities everywhere. They also reflect the educational thought and practice of the society in which Jews find themselves. The proliferation of curricula units on the war in Vietnam and its relation to Jewish "values" was an expression of American educational progressivism. I have found no parallel for Jewish schools in France during the time of the Algerian crisis. Those educators who attempt to respond to the problems and needs of students as the basis of curriculum design may similarly be placed within a theoretical framework peculiar to a specific time and place.

The way in which young Jews are taught to understand their place in the society around them is another important element of curricular orientation. The comprehensive curriculum for afternoon schools published by the United Synagogue Commission on Jewish Education (1978), the educational agency of Conservative Judaism in the United States, informed schools and their parents that "the whole point of studying in the religious school is to learn what makes the Jew different . . . and to make a decision as to why . . . to be different" (505). An earlier generation of Jewish educators had stressed the *similarities* between Judaism and the norms of American democracy. That position was, of course, shaped by the immigrant experience. A curriculum that consciously teaches the importance of difference is clearly addressing itself to a changed America and more important, another sort of Jew.

Those Orthodox Jews who remain within the "four ells of the Law" reject the non-Jewish world in its entirety, even though they make use of modern technology to further their ends. Their schools do not depart from the core curriculum brought in the Mishnah. Institutions of this kind can be found all over the world. The more removed the school and the population it serves from tradition, the more idiosyncratic its curriculum. The emphasis on identity, particularly in the United States but increasingly so in other places as well, may be a way of saying that what one knows about Judaism is not as important as wanting to be a Jew, or feeling Jewish, something that can possibly be attained without the effort required for real learning.

The separatism of those who live in a self-created ghetto is matched at the other extreme by those who reject Judaism and identification with the Jewish people in order to find a place, if not always an identity, in other places. This is relatively easy to do in a modern society that requires no overt or official act in order to leave the group of one's origin nor demands membership or affiliation in a recognized corporate entity.

The majority of the Jewish schools around the world today are established and maintained by Jews whose Jewishness has some meaning for them and who want to shape patterns of accommodation between their lives as Jews and their commitments to the society in which they live. Among these Jews the degree of Jewishness, however defined, varies from those whose day-to-day lives are guided by the dictates of being Jewish to those who prefer that their religion or ethnic origin interfere as little as possible with their lives as citizens of their countries. The various forms of educational institutions currently extant in the mainstream of Jewish communities everywhere reflect, in one way or another and with varying degrees of attention and intensity, developments in the history of the Jewish people during the last 100 years. Among these the establishment of the State of Israel and the Holocaust are the most prominent; the latter has become more and more central. The following with its emphasis on peoplehood seems to state quite clearly what concerns most Jewish schools of our time:

[T]eaching the beliefs, content, and spirit of Jewish civilization in a manner that reflects the diversity of that civilization today ... to heighten the Jewish consciousness of Jewish youth at all levels of education, to deepen their roots in our nation's past and its religious and historical heritage, and to strengthen their attachment to world Jewry out of the recognition of the common fate and historical continuity which unites Jews everywhere in their lands and across the generations. It is education which recognizes the vital importance of the Land and State of Israel and the national and spiritual character of the Jewish People. (Elazar, 1998)

Schools that subscribe to the broad statement will, in one degree or another and with varying emphasis,

1. Instruct pupils in the fundamentals of Hebrew as a language and as a means of expressing Jewish ideas.
2. Acknowledge and celebrate the State of Israel and its holiday.
3. Teach classic Jewish texts such as the Bible, the Talmud, and the Siddur (Prayer Book).
4. Enable students to spend time in Israel.
5. Teach Jewish tradition, both religious and national.
6. Teach Jewish civics and commitment to the unity and solidarity of the Jewish people.

No one, of course, knows which of these items, separately or in combination, is most effective in moving students, young and old alike, toward desired ends.

The centrality of the collective, if not the dominant, motif in the education of a minority as one of its more important commonplaces is periodically challenged by other conceptions of Jewishness. The recent emphasis of identity, as an example, creates a climate that requires that Jewish schools, particularly in the United States, contend with the consequences of "privatized" Judaism—that which is not meaningful is not worth doing. The emphasis on self and its realization often means the rejection of commitments and obligations to the group. Those who think that a "personalized lifestyle," no matter what, is an authentic expression of Judaism will look for their education in places other than those schools that have traditionally taught that personal fulfillment is possible only through identification with the experience and aspirations of the Jewish people.

Jewish schools, like all others everywhere, teach more than is implied in the detail of the course of study. The work of Jewish educators in the last 100 years has created, for example, pockets of resistance to oppressive regimes and centers of a counterculture. There is a straight line that connects between volunteer teachers in Vilna in 1893 who taught Hebrew in private homes all over the city in order to avoid detection and the more recent underground Hebrew study groups in the former Soviet Union—particularly those in the prison camps that served, among other things, as vehicles for preserving personal identity in a situation calculated to obliterate all individuality. The Jewish concept of *Tikun Olam* (Making the World a Better Place), for some schools a motif that integrates all that they do, resonates with the utopianism that characterizes revolutionary movements; today's youngsters can achieve the same spirit that moved their peers of an earlier time who attended socialist Yiddish schools that stressed the development of class consciousness as the route to an egalitarian society. The larger message of cultural pluralism remains implied in the idea that Judaism and democracy are not only compatible but also positively influence one another. Pupils in Jewish schools of all kinds who do their lessons well will sense that identification with the Jewish people promises a feeling of community that is difficult to find in society at large.

Few subjects in the curriculum of minority schools—ethnic or religious—are as important to the maintenance of a distinctive culture as the language and literature of the group. Even though Hebrew does not fit completely into the category of a "mother tongue"—the language spoken by immigrants in the countries of their origin or in the countries to which displaced people owe their allegiance—as that term is understood by students of ethnicity and ethnic language maintenance, its enthusiasts assign it a role in the process of fostering identification with Jews and Judaism and promoting the continuity of Jewish life that is identical to that marked out for other ethnic languages in attempts to guarantee loyalty to the group and its traditions. The task was more difficult in the case of Hebrew because until very recently there were no grandmothers who spoke the language.

Hebrew, perhaps outside of Israel best understood as a "heritage" language, was and remains the hallmark of the Zionist-national education; schools of this orientation, together with Zionist religious schools, set a standard unmatched in other settings. Their spirit is wonderfully captured in the following description:

Most of our teachers were then newly arrived young immigrant scholars, who had come from post–World War I Europe to seek a secular education in Boston's universities; they taught Hebrew in the evenings to earn their living. They despised Yiddish, a language I knew from home, for to despise Yiddish was their form of snobbery; and as a matter of principle they would speak no English in class, for their cardinal political principle was Zionism. They were about to revive the Hebrew language and make it a living tongue; after a little pampering with English in the first and second year, as we learned the ancient alphabet and pronunciation, we were into the Bible in Hebrew—it was explained to us in Hebrew, pounded into us in Hebrew, and we were forced to explain it to one another in Hebrew.

   . . . What I learned . . . from age ten to age fourteen, when I went on to evening courses at the Hebrew College of Boston, was the Bible. We learned the Bible from Genesis to the Book of Chronicles, from the Book of Kings through all the Prophets, major and minor. We learned it, absorbed it, thought in it, until the ancient Hebrew language became a working rhythm in the mind, until it became a second language. Its balanced cadences, its hard declarative sentences and its lacelike images structured the sentences we wrote in public-school classes. (White, 1978: 21–22)

Hebrew in Diaspora schools today is in retreat, even in such bastions of the language as Buenos Aires. It has suffered the same fate as other ethnic languages whose speakers have integrated into a society that uses another language. The process seems irreversible; the use of the ethnic language is most widespread among those who remain removed from the norms of practices of the core society. Over time only an elite segment of the ethnic population maintains its loyalty to the language. As ethnic traditions and competence in the ethnic language become less and less important in the lives of adults and children, language instruction is either curtailed or abandoned.

The revival of Hebrew, and its unquestioned primacy, in modern Israel is one of the many extraordinary achievements of Zionism. Paradoxically, that very success may have contributed to the decline of interest in Hebrew; dedication to the language was an expression of identification with the movement of national rebirth. Learning the language, a process that required serious investments of time and effort, was a sort of vicarious participation in the struggle for the State of Israel. The gain of sovereignty and the concomitant guarantee of the status of Hebrew may have made its use in the Diaspora less compelling.

The promotion of the use of Hebrew in Jewish schools and other settings around the world remain one of the major activities of Israeli educational agencies, government and otherwise. Indeed, Jewish education today cannot be defined without reference to the role played by the State of Israel. On one level the complex of activities sponsored by innumerable agencies—emissaries to schools all over the world, trips for teenagers and families, study years in Israeli universities, instructional materials, conferences, in-service training, and the like—may be likened to the work of the British Council or the French Cultural Centers. The conceptual underpinnings of all these efforts posit that Israel is central to the continued existence of the Jewish people; the state stakes a claim in the consciousness of Jews everywhere because the "territory" is a national homeland for Jews everywhere. A less prosaic explanation teaches, "There is a mystery about Jewish life. . . . [T]he Land of Israel is . . . somewhere near the center of the mystery, and the mystery cannot be truly understood without being 'on the inside' of what the state of Israel is about" (Eisen and Rosenak, 1997: 39).

The manner in which Israel is treated, in both formal and informal settings of Jewish education, has undergone noticeable change over the years. In the years immediately following the establishment of the state, the dominant tendency was to picture a utopia inhabited by fearless pioneers concerned only with the future of their people. The attraction of the "homeland"—sometimes more imaginary than real—was tied to a new image of the Jew. The passage of time, the constant flow of information from Israel, events that do not always create a positive picture, greater methodological sophistication, and the deepening of roots in the countries in which Jews live have all combined to force instruction to move closer to the reality of life in the Jewish state. A striving for cogent analysis and balanced criticism has generally replaced the romanticism of an earlier time. In that process, *aliyah* (settling in Israel)—the ultimate goal of pristine Zionism—remains a complicated and somewhat unique issue in minority education.

Teaching about the Shoah, along with the establishment of the State of Israel, the most critical event of modern Jewish history, is faced with even more vexing problems. Methods and materials cannot be separated from the central issue: What purpose does teaching about the Holocaust serve?

One approach contends that

the *Shoah* must be treated within the framework of an essential theological concept, the nature of Jewish existence, and a critical approach to Western civilization. . . . [O]nly after the student is exposed to the major issues in Jewish history and thought . . . can he be ready to grasp some of the awesome and mystical implications of the *Shoah*. (Ury, 1964: 169–172)

Teaching the Shoah requires attention to man's capacity for cruelty, a real matter in the history of many minorities.

[S]tudy of the Holocaust must not be wrapped in the gauze of abstractions. If the child is not to be pampered, he cannot be spared learning . . . that Jews are especially vulnerable to the worst excesses of history. He cannot be spared reading about the agony of the boy who dies slowly on the gallows in Elie Wiesel's *Night*. He cannot be spared the photographs in albums on the Holocaust; the frightened little boy who has his hands up in the air . . . the pious-looking, elderly Jew whose beard is being snipped off by an amused German lout. Though such photographs are hardly things of beauty and joy forever . . . they can be an occasion for underscoring the truth that to be human is to be open to the suffering of others; that to be human is to look on the other as a brother and not as a stranger. . . . [A] hard light needs to be kept on the atrocities and suffering. (168–172)

The patent intractability of this view is countered by those who maintain that a "hard line" is neither good history nor good education. "To see only man's *yetzer hara* (evil), or view history's evil acts alone, is to distort both men and history, both our past and more significantly our future" (Shulweis, 1976). The idea that a relentless recounting of Jewish suffering will somehow result in a heightened identification with Jews and Judaism is a vain and unfounded hope; the denial of the human capacity for compassion as exemplified by the selfless acts of those many Gentiles who risked their lives to save countless numbers of Jews produces an imbalance that enthrones death over life. The wholesale condemnation of the non-Jewish world blurs all real distinction, blots out the memory of saintliness, records only the acts of infamy, and reduces us all to a paralyzing despair (Shulweis, 1976).

Along with everything else, the centrality of the Holocaust in the collective Jewish identity creates a tension between that which is specifically Jewish and the increasingly widespread use of the term for all manner of instances of man's cruelty to man. Having made the world conscious of the enormity of the catastrophe has achieved the unintended end of diminishing the uniquely Jewish.

Minority cultures find it difficult to maintain themselves not only because they are foreign and even "strange" but also because they sometimes adhere to core values that contradict the ethos of the majority. An example is the concept of "chosenness," a central tenet of traditional Jewish belief. Jews who know little about Judaism, along with those who though knowledgeable no longer accept its imperatives, have not altogether divested themselves of the notion that there is something special in being Jewish. Philip Roth speaks for many Jews when he writes that in growing up a Jewish child of his time he received

a psychology, not a culture and not a history in its totality. What one received whole . . . what one feels whole is a kind of psychology: and the psychology can be translated into three words—"Jews are better." That is what I knew from the beginning: somehow Jews were better. I'm saying this as a point of psychology, I'm not pronouncing it as a fact. (Roth, 1963: 21)

That sense of superiority, doctrinal or psychological, is offensive to democratic sensibilities. Civility forbids the trumpeting of ideas such as "the one true church," "only Jesus saves," "the chosen people." The retreat from the idea of "specialness" has resulted in an anomaly:

[T]he American experience asked and continues to ask something previously unknown and almost unthinkable in the religions: that they become split personalities . . . each sect is to remain the one true and revealed faith for itself and in private, but each must behave in the public arena as if its truth were as tentative as an aesthetic opinion or a scientific theory. (Hertzberg, Marty, and Moody, 1963: 137)

The way in which the Conservative movement, the largest of the Jewish religious groupings in the United States, has dealt with the dilemma created by an article of faith—"chosenness"—that clashes with a deeply held belief of the larger society is an instructive example of accommodation. An examination of curricular documents and statements by key figures in the Conservative movement (Ackerman, 1983) leads us to conclude that the movement favors its retention accompanied by interpretation; the various interpretations stress the idea of service and deny any connotation of superiority; the entire process—from recognition of the problem to proffered solutions—is driven by the mores of a modern, democratic state.

Jewish education in all the countries of its practice except Israel is a voluntary effort. There is no law anywhere in the free world that compels Jews to establish, maintain, or attend Jewish schools. Attendance rates vary from country to country. At any given moment it appears that only a minority of Jewish children are in some kind of Jewish school. A larger percentage will have received some form of Jewish education during their elementary school years. The highest rates of attendance are in the United States—nearly three-quarters of all Jewish youth today will receive some Jewish education by the time they reach adulthood (Woocher, 1997: xi). The differences from place to place may be explained by a number of factors—the history of the Jewish community, the openness of the society to the "other," socioeconomic status of the Jews, practice among other religious and other ethnic groups. I doubt that the quality of the schools has any appreciable effect on enrollment.

The voluntary nature of the enterprise requires justification; that is to say, that Jews for whom the religious imperative has no meaning must be convinced that Jewish education serves a purpose not attainable in other settings. The idea of peoplehood is probably the most widespread alternative to the religious mandate for educating children Jewishly. Jews everywhere send their children to Jewish schools because they genuinely want to identify themselves and their children as Jews. However inchoate the sentiment and without letting their "Jewishness" conflict with their lives as citizens of the countries in which they live, they feel "connected" to the Jewish people and committed to its continued existence. Despite the simply symbolic nature of their attachment, many Jews feel that they cannot and should not leave the fold.

A more sophisticated pattern of rhetoric suggests that loyalty to one's people is enriching, not the least because it provides a definition of self that rescues the individual from the marginality that characterizes members of minority groups, both those who have and those who have not found a place in the society of the majority. It is not, however, only the individual who benefits from the promotion of a culture different from that of the majority. The idea of cultural pluralism (Berkson, 1920),[2] the forerunner of today's multiculturalism, posits that a society can only be enriched by the diversity that results from the presence of minorities, each of which has its own distinctive lifestyle. In addition, a society that attempts to blot out cultural differences suffers an irreparable loss. It deprives itself of the valuable contribution to the strength of the polity that derives from citizens whose ethnic experience retracts the pieties of the majority and subjects them to critical examination. Dual loyalties are the ground in which is rooted the sensibility to the needs of others that is the condition of heightened humanity. Such a duality provides a sense of perspective and serves as protection against mindless indoctrination. Although most powerfully developed in America, these ideas hold everywhere. Jews, and other minorities as well, attempt to introduce successive generations of young people to insights and sensitivities that even though they are peculiarly their own open the way to meaningful engagement with all of humanity.

NOTES

1. Midrash is a process of interpreting the Bible and, sometimes, other sacred texts; the word also refers to collections of the interpretations.

2. This remains an essential work for the understanding of cultural pluralism and its application to the education of minorities

REFERENCES

Ackerman, W. (1983). Choseness: Variation on a Theme. In B. Chazan (Ed.), *Studies in Jewish Education in the Diaspora* (pp. 195–209). Jerusalem: Melton Center for Jewish Education in the Diaspora, Hebrew University.

Ackerman, W. (1989). Strangers to the Tradition: Idea and Constraint in American Jewish Education. In H. Himmelfarb and S. Della Pergola (Eds.), *Jewish Education Worldwide: Cross-Cultural Perspectives* (pp. 71–133). Lanham, MD: University Press of America.

Bailyn, B. (1960). *Education in the Forming of American Society*. New York: Random House.

Berkson, I. (1920). *Theories of Americanism*. New York: Columbia University Press.

Eisen, A., and Rosenak, M. (1997). *Teaching Israel: Basic Issues and Philosophical Guidelines*. Jerusalem: CRB Foundation, Joint Authority for Jewish Zionist Education, and Charles R. Bronfman Center for the Israel Experience.

Elazar, D. (1998). *Jewish-Zionist Education*. Jerusalem: Jerusalem Institute for Public Affairs.

Friedlander, D. (1792). A Letter to Maier Agar. *Zetschrift für die Geschichte der Juden in Deutschland* 5: 266–267.

Frost, S. (1998). *Schooling as a Socio-Political Expression*. Jerusalem: Magnes Press.

Hertzberg, A., Marty, M., and Moody, J. (1963). *The Outbursts That Await Us*. New York: Macmillan.

Holtz, B., Dorph, G., and Goldring, E. (1997). Educational Leaders as Teacher Educators; A Case from Jewish Education. *Peabody Journal of Education* 72 (2): 147–166.

Karnafogel, E. (1992). *Jewish Education and Society in the High Middle Ages*. Detroit, MI: Wayne University Press.

Kessary, Y. (1995). A Jewish Day School in France. In W. Ackerman (Ed.), *Origins: The Beginning of Jewish Educational Institutions* (pp. 1–15). Jerusalem: Magnes Press. (Hebrew)

Marcus, I. (1996). *Rituals of Childhood*. New Haven, CT: Yale University Press.

Report of the Commission on the Jewish Future of Los Angeles. (1992). *If We Don't Act Now*. Los Angeles: Jewish Federation Council of Greater Los Angeles.

Roth, P. (1963). Second Dialogue in Israel—The Jewish Intellectual and Jewish Identity. *Congress Bi-Weekly* 30(2): 21.

Shulweis, H. (1976). The Holocaust Dybbuk. *Moment* 1(7): 36–41. See also subsequent 1976 correspondence in *Moment* 1(10): 77–80.

Steinberg, B. (1989). South Africa: Jewish Education in a Divided Society. In H. Himmelfarb and S. Della Pergola (Eds.), *Jewish Education Worldwide: Cross-Cultural Perspectives* (p. 365). Lanham, MD: University Press of America.

United Synagogue Commission on Jewish Education. (1978). *A Curriculum for the Afternoon Jewish School*. New York: Author.

Ury, Z. (1964). The Shoah and the Jewish School. *Jewish Education* 34(3): 168–172.

White, T. (1978). *In Search of History*. New York: Harper and Row.

Woocher, J. (1997). Foreword. In J. Reimer, *Succeeding at Jewish Education* (pp. xi–xviii). Philadelphia: Jewish Publication Society.

Author Index

Subject Index

About the Contributors

WALTER ACKERMAN is Shane Family Professor (Emeritus) of Education, Ben Gurion University of the Negev. He has written extensively on education. His publications include *The Way It Was: A Source Book for the Study of Jewish History* (1977), *Erziehung in Israel*, 2 vols. (1982) (with Arie Carmon and D. Zucker), *Profiles of High Schools: A Naturalistic Study* (1992) (with M. Avisar, D. Gordon, and M. Katz) (in Hebrew), and *Origins: Studies in Jewish Education*, vol. 7 (1995).

CHADWICK F. ALGER is Mershon Professor of Political Science and Public Policy Emeritus, Ohio State University. He has served as Secretary General of the International Peace Research Association (IPRA), President of the International Studies Association (ISA), and Chair of the Consortium on Peace Research, Education, and Development (COPRED). His research and teaching have three foci: peace research, the UN system, and the world linkages of all human settlements, that is, the world relations of all people in their daily lives. He is editor of *The Future of the UN System: Potential for the Twenty-first Century* (1998).

MAJID AL-HAJ, the head of the Center for Multiculturalism and Educational Research at the University of Haifa, lectures in the Department of Sociology at the University of Haifa. He received his doctorate from the Hebrew University of Jerusalem and pursued postdoctoral studies at Brown University. His most recent work focuses on education and multiculturalism in Israel and the impact of Russian immigrants on Israeli culture and ethnic politics. He has published extensively on the social and political structure of the Palestinians in Israel, Palestinian refugees,

Russian immigrants in Israel, and freedom of expression. His books include *Social Change and Family Processes* (1987), *Arab Local Government in Israel* (1990) (coauthored with Henry Rosenfeld), *Education, Empowerment and Control: The Case of the Arabs in Israel* (1995), and *Sociology of War and Peace in Israel in a Changing Era* (forthcoming) (coeditor with Uri Ben Eliezer).

MARTIN CARNOY is Professor of Education and Economics at Stanford University, where he has taught for the past 30 years. He was a research associate at the Brookings Institution in Washington, D.C. He is the author of *Schooling and Work in the Democratic State* (1985) (with Henry Levin), *Education and Social Transition in the Third World* (1990) (with Joel Samoff), *The New Global Economy in the Information Age* (1993) (with Manuel Castells, Stephen Cohen, and Fernando Henrique Cardoso), and most recently, *Sustaining the New Economy: Work, Family, and Community in the Information Age* (2002). He has had a long association with the International Institute of Educational Planning and the United Nations Educational, Scientific, and Cultural Organization (UNESCO), as well as a number of other international institutions, including the United Nations Children's Fund (UNICEF), the World Bank, the Organization for Economic Cooperation and Development (OECD), the Inter-American Development Bank, and the International Labor Office.

LESLIE FRANCIS is Director of the Welsh National Centre for Religious Education and Professor of Practical Theology at the University of Wales, Bangor, United Kingdom. His research interests in education, psychology, and theology have been recognized by the degrees of Sc.D. from the University of Cambridge and D.D. from the University of Oxford. He has coedited, with Yaacov J. Katz, *Joining and Leaving Religion: Research Perspectives* (2000).

RIVKA GLAUBMAN is a Senior Lecturer in the School of Education, Bar-Ilan University, and was previously the Head of the Teachers Training Department and undergraduate and graduate programs in the School of Education. She served as a counsel for the Ministry of Education in Israel on various topics. Her expertise and areas of research are early education programs, child play, and development; quantitative and qualitative research methods in education, particularly observation and ethological methods; teaching methods and curriculum studies; and evaluation, self-directed learning, and children self-questioning. She has published five books and dozens of articles on education and teaching.

AZIZ HAIDAR is a Professor of Sociology and currently teaching at Al-Quds University's Area Studies Center and David-Yallien College, Jerusalem. He is a Research Fellow at the Harry S. Truman Research Institute for the Advancement of Peace, the Hebrew University of Jerusalem.

YAACOV IRAM is a Professor of Comparative and International Education at Bar-Ilan University, Israel. He has served as President of the World Association for Educational Research, the Israel Educational Research Association, the Israeli Comparative Education Society, and the Israeli History of Education Association. He is Israel's representative of the Peace Education Commission of the International Peace Research Association (IPRA). Iram is currently the Chair holder of the Dr. Josef Burg Chair in Education for Human Values Tolerance and Peace—UNESCO Chair. His research interests, teaching, and publications are in comparative education, the social history of education affecting educational policy, and multiculturalism. Iram was granted the Fulbright–Yitzchak Rabin award for 2000–2001 to advance research and promote peace and tolerance education. He has published numerous articles in American and European scholarly journals, chapters in books, and encyclopedia entries.

YAACOV KATZ serves as the Chairperson of the Pedagogic Secretariat of the Israeli Ministry of Education and as Director of the Institute of Community Education and Research at the School of Education, Bar-Ilan University. Katz specializes in the research of attitudes in the school system, with special emphasis on interethnic, religious, and affective variables. He has edited a number of books and published scholarly papers on these topics.

LESLIE LIMAGE is an educational policy research program specialist in the Division of Educational Policy and Strategies, UNESCO, Paris. She has taught at secondary, adult, and university levels in France, the United Kingdom, and the United States. Her research interests are in basic education, literacy, language, gender issues, as well as European education, democracy and civic responsibility, and currently, education in crisis, conflict, and reconstruction. She has published widely as editor or contributor to collective scholarly volumes, international journals, and volumes edited or written through UNESCO, OECD, and other international organizations. She holds graduate degrees in Comparative Education, Sociology of Education, and Economics of Education, from the University of Paris and the University of London Institute of Education.

GITA STEINER-KHAMSI is Associate Professor of Comparative and International Education, Teachers College, Columbia University, New York. She is author of *Multicultural Education Policy in Postmodernity*

(1992) (in German) and coeditor of *New Paradigms and Recurring Paradoxes in Education for Citizenship* (2002) (with J. Torney-Purta and J. Schwille). She has numerous publications on multicultural education policies, transnational borrowing and lending of school reforms, qualitative cross-national analyses, and political education.

LENNART VRIENS is Associate Professor in the Department of Educational Sciences of the Faculty of Social Sciences of Utrecht University, The Netherlands. He has been involved in peace education since the 1970s and was Professor at the Special Chair of Peace Education at Utrecht University from 1990 to 2000. He has published articles on several aspects about peace education in different languages. He is an associated member of the School of Human Rights Research at Utrecht University.

HILLEL WAHRMAN is a recipient of the doctoral "Scholarship of Excellence" at the School of Education, Bar-Ilan University. His research focuses on political literacy and understanding, values education, and the role of the state education system in enhancing responsible civic involvement. Other areas of interest include current Jewish and Zionist identities and peace education.

YAACOV YABLON is a Ph.D. candidate in the School of Education at Bar-Ilan University and serves as a research assistant at the Institute for Community Education and Research at the School of Education. He specializes in the research of affective education with special emphasis on intergroup relations, conflict, and violence. At present he is completing his doctoral research on violence in the school system and has published a number of scholarly papers on topics pertaining to his research specializations.